I0819485

VAMPIR

FROM TEENAGE FLAK AUXILIARY TO NIGHT-FIGHTING MACHINE GUNNER IN WWII

A RARE ACCOUNT OF TRAINING AND COMBAT WITH THE "VAMPIR" INFRARED-EQUIPPED SMALL ARMS IN WWII

ROLF FISCHER

Library of Congress Control Number: 2022932585

Designed by Christopher Bower
Cover design by Jack Chappell
Type set in Sauber/Minion Pro

ISBN: 978-0-7643-6506-5
Printed in India

Published by Schiffer Publishing, Ltd.
4880 Lower Valley Road
Atglen, PA 19310
Phone: (610) 593-1777; Fax: (610) 593-2002
Email: Info@schifferbooks.com
Web: www.schifferbooks.com

Dedication

This is for Margaret; it might help her to understand my many peculiarities, or rather their origin, better. A view from the other side will, no doubt, show the difference between the world of a fifteen-year-old German boy and that of a slightly younger English girl during those awful days.

Contents

Introduction

The following are the memoirs of Rudolf Heinz "Rolf" Fischer. Rolf was born in Blumenthal, near Bremen, in April 1927. In August 1942, at the age of fifteen, he and his classmates were called up for service as auxiliaries at the local antiaircraft battery. At seventeen, Rolf was drafted into the Heer, the regular army. He went through basic training with the 65th Regiment, 22nd Infantry Division at Delmenhorst. As Rolf alludes to in the narrative, the 22nd Division began the war as a specialized air-assault (Luftlande) unit and was deployed primarily on the Eastern Front during the latter stages of the war.

After basic training, Rolf was promoted to corporal and sent to a specialized machine gun–training course in Denmark. Here a small group learned to operate MG 42 machine guns equipped with early infrared night vision optics. Little has been written about German operational use of night vision optics during World War II, in particular as applied to the MG 42, but on the basis of Rolf's detailed description of the device, it seems to be a variant of the Zielgerät 1229, better known today by the code name "Vampir." From late 1944 through the end of the war, Rolf fights on the Western Front as part of a four-man MG squad. The squad has their own radio link (transported in a wheeled parachute drop canister) to their CO and is empowered to act independently via a printed divisional order to be carried at all times. They are instructed to fight only at night. Rolf briefly describes his captivity as a prisoner of war and eventual homecoming.

Rolf Fischer found work as a wool trader after the war and resided primarily in the UK, where he married an Englishwoman. He did not begin work on his memoirs until quite some time after the war, when he was already in his early forties. He wanted to explain his wartime experience to his wife, since it occurred during his formative years and shaped him into the man he was.

Rolf wrote his manuscript in the third person, and the publisher saw fit to verify the author's identity before acquiring his work. Fortunately, the author's estate was able to provide his birth certificate and discharge papers from the army, along with a small collection of photographs, showing Rolf in Heer uniform and at the flak battery.

It is likely that many of the locations specified during the latter half of the narrative are recorded incorrectly. This is understandable, simply given the time elapsed between the events described and the writing. Rolf was a teenaged machine gunner, constantly moving across the front to provide fire support as needed, not a staff officer with a clear picture of the greater situation. Exacerbating his disorientation was the lack of good maps. In the eight or so months that Rolf's squad spends at the front, they navigate almost exclusively with two maps: first a guide to the youth hostels of France, picked up at travel agent's office shortly after disembarking, and second a bloodied American map, recovered from a dead officer. The prized American map has to be handled gingerly by the end of the war, tattered from constant use. Also, a great deal of the fighting took place in the border area among France, Germany, and Belgium; many towns, villages, and landmarks in this region have changed names, in some cases several times.

As a sort of fire brigade, Rolf's squad moved from unit to unit across the front. Rolf attempted to specify the units in his book; in some cases these are accurate, in others probably not. The same goes for names of soldiers and officers in these units. In regard to discrepancies in places, units, and names, some basic sleuthing reveals some likely answers. Given the chaotic state of the Wehrmacht during the latter stages of the war, it is possible that remnants of units that Rolf reports coming into contact with may actually have been where Rolf places them, even if the official record indicates otherwise.

The publisher has elected to present this narrative largely as the author wrote it, including his specified places, names, and units. Rolf spoke fluent English and wrote this manuscript in British English. Certain terms have been edited from British to American English (such as "metres" to "meters"), and occasionally, unmistakably German sentence structure has been tweaked for the benefit of native English-speaking readers. Whatever Rolf typed on did not have all German characters, and he did not use any accent marks. Some accent marks have been added for this edition, where they were obviously missing. Along with photos, additional chapter breaks have been added for readability (since Rolf's original was broken into just two chapters).

Rolf Fischer died in Lincolnshire, England, on April 1, 2020. He left his memoirs to his grandson, Anton. This is the first edition of those writings in book form.

CHAPTER 1
The Battery

The "Stundenweg" started life as a street in Vegesack but after two miles had lost its pavement and houses, their place having been taken by gravel and birch trees on either side. It was as straight as a Roman road and seemed to have no end to it, which was probably the reason for its name.

On a hot August morning 1942, a group of fifteen boys cycled through the dust following their orders, which had told them to do so until, at Habichthorst, they would reach an antiaircraft (AA) battery, where they were to report for duty. Their age was fifteen on the average, and they were in an extremely happy mood because, at least to a great extent, they were getting out of the clutches of school and parents.

After about five miles, gun barrels grew in the distance, two on either side of the track, and then wooden huts emerged between bushes and trees. The boys dismounted at the first one, which was presumably the battery office. Already on the way there, Fischer had been chosen to be in charge ("You held the highest rank anyway"), so he knocked and went inside only to be greeted by a bellow; there was no knocking on doors in this place and what did he want, anyway, this was military property! This reception came from the sergeant major, recognizable by the two silver stripes on his left sleeve. Having listened to Fischer's report, he smiled broadly, got off his chair, opened another door and said, "Captain, sir, the new ones are here."

The man who came into the office was not exactly what one would imagine a German captain to look like. He must have been close to sixty, and one could see his braces as he wore no tunic. He came across to Fischer, shook his hand for a long time, and said, "Welcome, my boy, welcome! Are they all big chaps like you?" "About half of us, sir." "Excellent, fall your men in outside, I will talk to you shortly." He had actually said "men."

The "men" put their bikes together in pairs, lined up, and waited. They looked decidedly odd in front of this martial backdrop. They wore shorts, as short as decency allowed following the fashion of those times, all sort of shirts, and socks rolled over boots. There was definitely some apprehension in the air. The captain came out, now wearing his tunic which was covered in World War I decorations, looking more like it. "Tenshun, the eyes left!" To Fischer this was old hat, but it had obviously impressed the CO who was heard saying to the SM, "They will do, Müller, they will do!"

To the boys he carried on: “A warm welcome to you! We have been waiting for you desperately. A number of our men have been transferred recently, which has left us almost depleted of gunners. You are going to take their places, and I am giving you a week to learn the job. I have spoken to your school; you do not have to attend lessons for this week (unrest in the ranks). You will not let us down, and I shall report combat-readiness in eight days. SM, take over!” With this he disappeared.

The SM was a different kettle of fish compared with the CO. He was gruff, as probably expected of his rank; he wore an eye-patch and limped slightly. On his tunic was the Iron Cross First Class and the wounded badge in silver, most unusual for an AA rank. Obviously, he must have come from a frontline unit. “You heard what the captain planned for you, you have one week to turn into useful members of the Army and may God help you if it takes one day longer! You will now go across to the quartermaster’s store and collect your fatigues, boots, and helmets. That’s all you will need for the next week. When you have changed out of these holiday clothes, report to me again and I shall allocate you to your guns. Dismissed!”

The quartermaster’s store was located opposite the Battery office, thus forming the third side of the parade ground, the second being the mess and kitchen. The quartermaster was an elderly corporal; he also had a limp, but this time quite pronounced. Normally in the army, packs of clothes were thrown at you, and one was expected to swap for sizes within the group. Not so here; the corporal ran an obviously experienced eye over the boys (later they found out he was a tailor) and the uniforms fitted perfectly. They changed into them there, and then the only problem lay with Köhler and Hauenschild, the two smallest. There were no helmets to fit them. Although they had an adjustment inside, they still came down over their eyes. The corporal’s advice was to put folded newspaper inside, “but use something patriotic, that will increase your fighting spirit!” A humorous quartermaster, probably something quite rare.

On the way back across the parade ground, Horn said, “Have you noticed that up to now we have not seen one really fit soldier?” The change when the boys fell in was unbelievable. Within ten minutes the uniforms had turned them from a school class into a group of soldiers. Family, girlfriends, school, all that had faded into the background and friendships had changed into something much stronger, providing the security that everyone could rely on his mate no matter what. Everybody had felt this transformation, that came out when they talked about it later. Even the “attention” crashed louder, but that might have been the heavy boots.

The SM was clearly pleased, and he expressed this by remarking that they almost looked like human beings now, but he stressed the "almost." Four NCOs, whom he introduced as the gunnery sergeants, had joined him. One of the biggest four boys was allocated to each gun, and Fischer ended up at Berta. The same happened to the medium-sized ones until only the three smallest were left. "You're for the pom-pom!" said the SM. Horn muttered under his breath, "Like a bloody slave market!" "Ah," said the SM who must have had ears like a watchdog, "we have a comedian amongst us, keep it up, lad, keep it up, you will need every bit of it here!" Horn had turned as red as a tomato.

"Your day will look like this," he continued. "You will go back to the quartermaster's now and collect your bedding. You have about an hour to put your bits and pieces away and make up your beds. Lunch is at 1200 sharp at the mess hall. At 1400 you will report at your guns for your first training session until 1700. At 1800 two of you will come to the kitchen to fetch your evening and morning rations. Go to bed early because there will be night training. It has to be dark for that, so it will be between 2300 and midnight, anyway, the bell will waken you. Off you go, your huts are the first and second on the left down the sleeper-track. Dismissed!" As an afterthought he bellowed, "Fischer, report to me at 1900 with all personal details of your lot, including next of kin!"

The sleeper-track was exactly what the SM called it: a track made up from old railway sleepers. It led to the command center, quite a distance away from the guns. The Radar, a large box able to house four operators inside and the even bigger dish on top, dominated the scene. The range finder hid behind its own earth wall, the plotting-hut had its own enclosure again. The huts for the different crews had meticulous little gardens, and they looked more like an allotment than an AA battery.

Their homes-to-be were two wooden huts, brand new by the look of it. The insides were like an oven, the smell of fresh timber overwhelming. There was a "living room" in the middle, furnished with a large table, eight stools, and a tiled coal-heater, whose stovepipe lead through the dividing wall into the bedroom roof space, heating that as well. Four double wooden bunks and four double narrow wardrobes almost filled the room. The mattresses were standard German army issue: straw in a bed-size Hessian bag. After a few months, the straw would be burned and the bags freshly filled. They were wonderful to sleep on and could not be more hygienic. The other end of the hut held a small washroom with eight aluminum basins, but no tap. The boys split into two groups; eight stayed here, seven went next door. There were very precise rules for storing their belongings in the wardrobes, somebody would no doubt tell them. It was the same with the beds: they had to look "square" all over, but how to achieve that with a bag of straw (pillow ditto), not a clue. They just put the sheet on the mattress, the blanket into the cover, the pillowcase on the pillow, and it looked awful! That left one thing to organize: the daily roster for two important jobs, the room-orderly, and the table-orderly, the former being responsible for the general cleanliness of the quarters and blackout shutters, the latter for washing up after breakfast and the evening meal, who also fetched the daily rations from the kitchen. The two beds on the left made a start and then it went down the line, so everyone had an additional duty every four days. Fischer was going to find out where the bog was, and there were actually two of them, a large one with a three-seat arrangement and, some distance away, a brand new single one. "Auxiliaries only" somebody had chalked over the door.

At twelve the cook said, "Gawd, another fifteen mouths to feed!" Lunch was very good, thick pea soup with a lot of meat, and they could have as much as they wanted. About thirty soldiers were having their lunch as well, mostly middle-aged or even elderly men, and they came over to introduce themselves. They said they were glad the boys had joined because "now the war would go our way and once the bomber crews knew, they would surely refuse to fly this route," all very jolly.

When marching back to the hut, they passed a column of strange-looking men in dark green uniforms with a white stripe down the trouser legs. They clattered along in clogs and grinned at the boys, who, for loss of anything to say, grinned back. Later they found out they were Russians, POWs first, then turned Hiwi. A Hiwi, army slang, was a "Hilfswilliger," someone willing to help, and they performed simple tasks, in this case feeding the shells to the guns. They might have changed sides for dislike of their political system, but more likely it was the guarantee of regular rations. Whatever the reason, they were trusted and not guarded. The subject came up again when Fischer reported to the SM in the evening. Apparently the boys were entitled to one Hiwi for fetching water in the morning and the coal in winter. "I have picked one out for you, his name is Popow, first name Ivan, what else. He's a cook from Kiev and understands quite a bit if you speak slowly and simply. He was the one who filled your mattresses, but he is not here to clean your boots; you do that yourself!"

"Another point is school," he carried on. "For every hour you spend at the guns after 10:00 p.m., you can leave half an hour later in the morning. You will work it out after each alarm, and I'll hold you personally responsible that there is no fiddle! Your school is trying to rearrange the lesson so that important subject will be taught later in the morning. We get about forty-five minute warning of the raids, and I'll ring the school to send you back. It shouldn't take you longer than half an hour to get here. We aim to give you one weekend at home every fourth week, from after school Saturday until school begins Monday. I will work out a roster; obviously you cannot disappear altogether."

"Let me give you a word of advice: the captain is very kindly disposed toward you boys and he will always do for you what he possibly can, but he is a stickler for what he calls military manners. Pass that on and there will be no upsets. Dismissed!"

The guns (4.5") were placed in a square, about 250 meters apart. They were protected by earth walls, seven feet high and very thick. The inside was timber shuttering, the outside sloped like a dyke and grassed over. They would direct any bomb blast upwards. The earth wall was thick enough for a bunker for ten men as shelter during long breaks in winter, in the opposite wall was the entrance, leading zig-zag into the interior. There were also three ammunition bunkers, holding eighty shells each.

The NCO in charge of Berta was Sergeant Hoffmann, an East Prussian, and his dialect was something to behold. He said: "Normally, we teach a lot of theory to new men, but I believe that has to wait in your case until later—we have got to get shooting again first! You will report here every day at 0830 until 1130 and in the afternoon from 2 to 5. Night training will vary and hopefully we can lock on to real targets, without shooting, of course.

"Just a few words about the gun first: you know the caliber is 10.5 centimeters, it is semautomatic, which means the gun pulls its own shells in (they are too heavy to load by hand), the breech closes, and the shot breaks. It is fired by electricity, not by a pin. The big cylinders under the barrel absorb the recoil, they have coil springs inside, the one on top works the other way 'round and brings the barrel back afterwards."

"Now about the crew: I'm in charge here and don't you forget it! It is imperative that my commands are being executed in seconds, in split seconds! You will see later why. I am constantly connected to the command post," he pointed to a single earphone with a strap to hold it in place, and two odd-looking mikes clamped to his throat. "When we are firing, nobody would understand me, these pick up my voice only."

"This seat is for No. 1; he lays the elevation and traverses with the gun. The seat on his right is for the No. 2, who is responsible for the side. No. 3 loads the gun, 4, 5, 7, and 8 bring him the ammo (our Russians do that), and No. 6 sets the fuse. The big bloke," that was Fischer, "will make No. 1

and you," pointing to Horn, "look like a good No. 2. You," that was Kaufmann," will be No. 6 on the other side of the gun."

"Now then, 1 and 2 get on your seats, No. 6 stays here to watch, I'll deal with you later. The gun rotates and the barrel rises by electric power. Grip the 'steering wheel' in front of you, turning it right rises the barrel, turning it left lowers it. No. 2, turning your wheel right turns the gun clockwise; left rotates it the opposite way. Play with it for a few minutes to get the feel of it!"

It was great to be in control of this huge gun which responded to the slightest touch. It almost brought on a feeling of invincibility. Hoffmann shattered that by saying: "Back to business! In front of you is your receiver. It has three concentric rings of small light bulbs, ten in each ring. Above each ring rotates a square pointer, which moves when you adjust the 'steering wheel.' When the outer pointer has traveled once round his ring, the middle one has moved just one lamp on. The same happens with the middle ring: one full revolution means one bulb on the inner ring. When it becomes serious, one bulb in each ring will light up, and you have to cover those with your pointers and then follow the movements of the lighted bulbs. It is really very easy; the only problem for you beginners is that you will overshoot your setting, because you are nervous. Don't be heavy-handed with your wheel, that's half the battle. Right, lets have a go then!" He switched on his mike and said "Berta ready!"

The lights started to wink immediately but the command post kept them stationary for the boys to catch up with them and only very slowly the speed was increased until it resembled that of a moving target. The sergeant had been quite right, chasing the lights was not too difficult, but the gun responded so easily—too easily. The pointers overshot the lights all the time and only practice would glue them to the bulbs. A comforting thought was that they had about thirty hours of daylight-training and probably a similar number in the night ahead of them, that should do the trick. When the pointers were sitting on the lights, the layers called out:, "No. 1 covered!" and so on, and once all three had reported, the sergeant in turn would tell the command post, "Berta covered!" All this should not take longer than thirty seconds. The gun had now locked on to the target and the fire order could follow any time.

Every hour's training improved their confidence, and the nervousness started to drop off. The gun moved less jerkily and Hoffmann was pleased. On Thursday they were treated to another one of his monologues: "Up to now, it has been child's play for you. As you know, we get our power from the National Grid, but what if that breaks down or the lines are down after a raid?

Then we start our own generator. But what if that won't start or we are running short of diesel? Now this would be a situation where you can show if you are really the men you think you are! The wheels with the handle on either side of the receiver are our salvation! One for the left hand, one for the right, and you will bloody well need them both. You spin them and we operate the gun that way. I will say that the No. 2 has the easier job, although you have to turn the whole weight of the gun, which is about four tons, by your muscle power, it sits on roller bearings and that helps a lot. The real hero is the No. 1. That's why I gave you the job, Fischer, being the biggest. All you need to do now is be heroic as well! (laughter in the ranks). There cannot be any ball bearings to help you; you really have to shift the barrel, over transmissions, with your muscles. Strip off, all of you, this is going to be a hot morning!" The next three hours were grueling, and by the end of the session their arms were hanging uselessly by their side. "Pretty good,", said Hoffmann, "I can give you one comforting thought on the way: This situation has never happened to me so I can't see that you should ever have to deal with it!"

CHAPTER 2

First Shots

At the start of the Friday afternoon session this came from the sergeant: "Tomorrow comes the moment of truth, you will shoot. One shell only but everybody will be watching and measuring and criticizing and result will determine whether or not we can report combat-readiness. Need I say more? Now, I'm not worried about your tracking, in fact I'm very pleased with it. But what we have not yet practiced is the Wechselpunkt (change-over). Imagine a plane is heading straight for the battery, there comes a point when the barrel cannot be raised any higher. What we do then is to swing the gun around 180 degrees and follow the target with decreasing elevation. This change is always executed clockwise! Now then, Horn, it is in your hands that this old girl turns like on a dance floor, and don't overshoot once you're there! No. 1, you have little work because you pick up the target at more or less the same angle as you left it 180 degrees back. The same goes for the No. 6. The time allowed for this maneuver is thirty seconds from when I shout 'Wechselpunkt' to the moment when we can continue firing on the other side of the gun, if you know what I mean." They trained all afternoon, backward and forward, the sticking point was indeed stopping the big gun after exactly 180 degrees, but by the end of the session Horn was perfect at it.

"We shall have a real target, a plane towing an airbag at 30,000 feet. We have some red star-shells here and we shall use one of those. The guns will fire singly, so the chief will see if you messed up! Kaufmann asked: "Sarge, how will they be able to tell how good a tracking-job we are doing?" "They can't," answered Hoffmann. "the captain can only judge whether all four barrels are moving exactly together like on a string because all guns have the same laying data. And believe me, he will get a very good idea that way. May the Good Lord help you!" They were all feeling uneasy about the next day, similar to the apprehension on the day before a math test.

Saturday was beautiful, very hot and not a cloud in sight. At 0800 the lamps started to glow and it was "Target in 9," that meant West, the rose being divided like a clockface: 12 was North, 3 East, and 6 South with the remaining hours in between. One run lasted about ten minutes, the imaginary plane weaving, rising and falling. Then a target approached from a different angle, doing more of the same thing. The boys were drenched in sweat, mostly because of the concentration but also fear that they would let their Sergeant down. After an hour came the order "five minutes break" through the wire. By now the No. 3, the loader, was standing on his platform, he had fetched the shell himself.

"Right," said Hoffmann, "this Wechselpunkt-lark will be on us now and as soon as I have 'covered' from all of you, I shall fire. AND OPEN YOUR MOUTH! The captain will stop the time between the Wechselpunkt-command and the shot breaking, remember, thirty seconds or less!"

It finally happened during the next run. The plane was flying a circle and suddenly headed for the battery, direct approach. Everybody knew this was a friendly aircraft and yet a feeling of danger crept in, as if from instinct. Then came "Wechselpunkt," covered, covered, covered "Fire!" and then this terrific bang, the gun shook, cordite fumes belched from the opening breech and the spent cartridge clattered loudly against something. So that was that, then.

After Caesar and Dora fired their shots, the order came "Guncrews to command post!" and perspiration flowed freely again. Little groups of four were converging from the gun-emplacements to the place of verdict. Rapport from the sergeants, "at ease" from the captain. "Well, boys," he said, "that was a first-class performance! Berta and Caesar clocked up twenty-seven seconds; Anton and Dora, twenty-eight. All your shots were well placed and all four damaged the target. I am happy about your enthusiasm and we shall show them now! You will have tomorrow off, you had a tough week, catch up on your sleep. I shall report combat readiness to Division now, so as of now, every alarm is in earnest. Thank you once again, you have not let me down." The boys felt about ten foot tall. "You know," said Behrends on the way back, "when this bloody war is over, I shall write a book 'From Vegesack Grammar to Potential Killer in Seven Days' or something like that."

When they came out from lunch, the SM was coming out of his office and he barked "Fischer!" across the parade ground. "I've heard you've done well this morning. I have spoken to the captain and he has given permission for you to all go swimming tomorrow. A mile from the crossroad toward Lehnhorst is a rifle range; it has a lake on it. Keep your ears open, and when you hear the sirens going, you double back here! Another thing: I have arranged with the farmer across the road that he will deliver some milk to the kitchen every morning. That is only for you and before you leave for school, you'll report to the cook AND YOU WILL BLOODY DRINK IT! It's half a liter. Dismissed!"

They went to the lake on Sunday afternoon. It was a beautiful, peaceful place. The water was not very deep and the ground was muddy, and there were some water lilies and a lot of frogs. But after a week of sweat and grime and the only way to wash in a bowl, it was bliss. They took their time walking back through the woods because Horn said he could smell mushrooms. He was right; there were loads of them and they filled their towels literally within minutes. Drieling fancied himself as a cook, and he would prepare them for supper. "I'll ask the cook for a pan," he said. The cook was not helpful: "Lend you a pan? Are you out of your mind or something?" "But we brought you some mushrooms." He relented immediately, "But I want it back spotless!" he grumbled. "Can you spare a couple of onions, please?" Drieling kept on. He could, muttering under his breath all the time.

In the evening Drieling lit the heater, the weather was still very hot, all windows were wide open but it was still almost unbearable in the room. The mushrooms were first class; he was really good at it. While they were eating, the SM came past the hut. He stopped, sniffed the air, and came in. "What the hell is going on here?" he enquired. Fischer had already jumped up to report, "Eight auxiliaries having supper, sir!" Drieling, who had a very high voice, squeaked, "Permission to ask the sergeant major to try my mushrooms, sir!" "I hope you don't think you can bribe me, but I'll have some, thank you."

"Where did you get the pan, by the way?" "From the cook, sir." "What, from that grumpy old beggar? How did you manage that?" "We bribed him, sir." "Well, lads," he said, looking round the table, "I think you'll be all right here!"

He left with a parting shot: "One day next week after school, you will report to the military hospital in Lesum for your first vaccination, typhoid, I think. There will be five more: dyptheria, cholera, tetanus, dysentery, and yellow fever, you can't say the Army is not looking after you. A word of advice: try to get to the beginning of the line, those butchers have only two needles for 100 men and after fifty they are getting pretty blunt!" In the event, it turned out the needles lasted through perhaps twenty chests (not arms, they might stiffen up), after that it was pretty gruesome. The SM was probably trying to be kind. The thought of having to go back to school on Monday morning had something almost degrading about it, and only the fact that they could parade their new uniform made them feel a little better. And the heavy boots would make a nice clatter in the corridors!

The SM had ordered a passing-out parade for every morning ("I'll be your mother while you're here'"), boots polished, hair cut and combed, no spots on the uniform, hands and nails clean ("and don't ever give me any of this gun-grease bullshit!") Also the bikes had to be washed and polished. One could only hope he would lose interest in the long run.

The headmaster made an appearance during the first lesson and expressed his pride that students of his school, at the tender age of fifteen, were given the opportunity to do their bit toward the war effort and help to protect their town. It was not all that convincing and rather sounded like a government circular, which it probably was. His voice grew warmer for the second part of his little speech, which was dedicated to the fact that they would without doubt lose teaching time and would they please make up for it by increased concentration. And the amount of homework would have to go up (most likely, see how we go). Well, all this made sense really, and they would make an extra effort to reach the targets the school had set. The head seemed well satisfied; he went through the class shaking hands and wishing them that no harm would come to them. He became quite emotional.

It was the second night into the first week as gunners when the bell shrilled at ten. They stumbled along the sleeper-track (not the easiest of surfaces in the dark) toward their guns. Fischer as No. 1 had the additional job of shooting up the outside of the embankment to pull off the muzzle-cap, a heavy leather cover the size of a small bucket. The cap had to be handed to the No. 2, who in turn passed it on to the Sargent, who then stored it away. The idea behind this was that three men would not forget to remove it, it would have meant disaster if left in place on the barrel. Hoffmann had another lecture ready, short this time. "Keep your face close to the leather shields of your receivers and pull your helmets down over your eyes or the flash will blind you. AND KEEP YOUR MOUTHS OPEN!"

The target was a single plane flying North to South but suddenly it changed course and headed straight for the battery, an exact copy of the "Wechselpunkt" exercise last Saturday! Three or four rounds were fired and then the shout "Wechselpunkt" came from the sergeant, but while the gun was still traversing East, there was a tremendous flash above, turning quickly from white to green to red. Immediately, what sounded like a hand-held air-raid warning siren wailed from the command post and Hoffmann shouted: "Take cover, into the bunker, on the double!" The Russians stood the shells they were carrying against the inner wall and scuttled in last. "What was that about, Sarge?" Fischer asked. "Well, we were in luck! We hit and exploded a Pathfinder plane full of air-raid markers. When it's dark you can't make out whether it's right on top of us, so we go into hiding. An exploding bomber sheds a lot of debris, just think of the engines, they would be like small bombs. The captain will be pleased; we were the only battery firing, so we get the full point for the kill, two points in fact because of it having been a Pathfinder. Let's hope the bits and pieces of the markers don't take long coming down. If they are still in the air and the bombers come this way, they will drop their muck on us." However, the markers descended quickly, probably damaged in the explosion, and the night returned to darkness.

The phone bell rang and the sergeant answered it: "Berta!" Nothing for a while, then "Right, sir, I will pass it on." "That was the captain, he said it was probably beginner's luck but very well done by the gun layers!"

CHAPTER 3

The Hiwis

This time they were called out from school, which was great. Two of them had flat tires on the way back; they sat on somebody else's crossbar and led their bikes along the side. All tires and more so the inner tubes were in a terrible condition, dating from pre-war days. Something would have to happen about that. They were just in time for the pre-firing checks, and Hoffmann was already hopping up and down. It was a cloudless sky, and the American formations stood out beautifully, wave after wave. Two planes were hit at more or less the same moment, and the CP said afterwards they had brought a third one down with them.

Suddenly, there wascommotion among the Russians, which wasunusual, as they were always quiet. Only when a break in the firing came, the reason became apparent: Radomov was sitting on the ground, leaning against the wall and still cradling the shell he had been carrying. He had been hit on the head by something; his helmet, dented and bent, was touching his shoulders, completely covering his face. From under the helmet ran blood and something grey onto his chest, which must have been his brain. He was of course dead. It was a gruesome sight, a helmet on a pair of shoulders and no face! Behrends, who was nearest to him, vomited straight over his fuse-setter.

The sergeant broke into Russian, they understood "voda" (water) and "dawai, dawai" (quick). The Ivans picked up their mate and carried him outside; they had not removed the helmet. One of them shot over to the nearest hut to fetch a bucket of water, which was poured over the fuse-setter to wash away the vomit. Behrends was acutely embarrassed, but Hoffmann put his arm around his shoulders: "Don't worry, lad, it did look awful!" Later they found out what had killed Radomov, the bottom of a shell which had not sufficiently broken up. It weighed about three pounds and had fallen something like 30,000 feet. It was too big for their shells, "Probably from Farge, they have 12.8 guns." said Hoffmann. "How come you speak Russian, Sarge?" asked Fischer. "A lot of East-Prussians do, it is not all that far away." "Sarge," said Horn in a shaky voice, "that bloody thing could have hit any of us!" "But it didn't, did it? Put it out of your mind, that was one chance in many millions."

The next day Radomov was buried. A while ago, the captain made arrangements with the local forester who let him use a piece of woodland. Apparently there were two graves already, one Russian had his back broken by a recoiling barrel, the second had died from "natural causes." The battery carpenter had made a nice cross, one of those double orthodox ones, and the Ivans had carved the name into it. Hoffmann said, "It would only be right if our whole crew went to the funeral; he's been with us a long time and he was a good bloke." To everyone's surprise the captain turned up as well, he even saluted the grave. "You might think," Hoffmann mused on the way back, "that was a bit over the top, the CO coming and all that, but the Ivans will die for him now, and for us for that matter. Keep your ears peeled tonight. They will probably gather by the grave and sing, that's something you should not miss."

He had been right:, at dusk sound just like from an organ drifted over from the woods, made even eerier as thick fog had spread and the singing seem to come from everywhere.

Again they were recalled from school, since the Americans started to raid Berlin. This became routine for the next weeks. The battery lay just North of their northerly route and the planes could be engaged during a long fly-past, so to speak. On this particular day, three B-17 Flying Fortresses fell quite quickly and the captain announced that each gun crew would receive a bottle of Korn that night.

All of a sudden a bomber approached from the south, quite low. It had obviously been hit. It was weaving slightly and one wing was down. It was flying too low for the guns to engage but the pom pom started to chatter, that was good old Köhler, the "miniature soldier" as he was called in the battery. It was really a waste of ammunition but who could blame him, he did not get many chances to fire. The tracers disappeared with precision into the large body of the aircraft, but they could take a lot of this kind of punishment. Then the take-cover siren sounded from the CP where they had noticed the bomb doors opening, the Fortress was going to jettison its load. Hats off to the pilot, he must have had good nerves to hang on and wait for a target where his bombs would do at least some good. They all squeezed into the bunker and then the ground heaved and sand fell through the shuttering. The uproar lasted only a couple of minutes and all that could be heard was a cow mooing miserably. It was difficult to believe: the craters marched neatly past the guns, the CP, and the radar. Only the crew quarters for Anton and Dora had disappeared without a trace, but they had of course been empty at the time.

It was ominous that no lights were winking on the receivers, the telephone was dead, as was the power supply for the gun-drives. Hydraulic fluid was spurting from the brake cylinder on top of the gun. "Fischer, off to the CP and report: no power, no signals, no telephone, and a bloody hole in the brake cylinder. Gun is out of action!"

The captain, much to Fischer's surprise, swore violently, "But" Fischer added, "the sergeant said armorers can patch it up." "Good, tell him to get on with it but he must send a runner, all communications are cut. Off you go! Oh, tell him also the Ivans can have a cow, bomb damage, he'll know what I mean. "On the way back to Berta he saw the cook and his helper carrying a large zinc-tub heaped with bloody meat. They tried to run with it, but that was not very easy. Hoffmann knew of course what the chief meant and rattled something off to the Russians, ending again on "Dawai, dawai!" They ran off and returned after twenty minutes with happy faces. "You see," said the sergeant, "the farmer will report these cows as killed, which is fair enough. The abattoir will pick them up (or what's left of them) but nothing must be missing, that would be sabotage, wouldn't it? You don't know anything about any meat, you never saw a thing! Tell your mates too and do it now since we are unemployed." But the mates had been put straight by their sergeants already.

In the meantime another development had taken place. From the CP, being in a slightly elevated position, it had been observed that the plane which had dropped the bombs had crash-landed in a field on the other side of the woods surrounding the battery. The SM had been sent to collect prisoners if any had survived. Apparently he grabbed a couple of rifles (there were only a handful in the battery) and two bikes, and on his way to the crash site, he collected Berta's loader, a big burly man (he was a butcher) and the two of them had ridden off. Half an hour had passed and a little procession emerged from the trees: one American was pushing one bike, a second one the other, but a third one was hanging on it, his trouser leg soaked in blood. The SM and Bartsch were strolling behind with the rifles on a long sling like hunters. Berta's was the first gun position on their way, and they marched the Americans inside. The SM said: "This, Hoffmann, is as good a pen as anything else, keep them here for a couple of hours. I shall ring Division now, I'm sure they will collect them pretty quickly. You keep the rifle, Bartsch, any trouble—don't hesitate, shoot! By the way, the other five are dead, Division will see to them as well. Fischer, you run up to the captain and report this, and ask for the medic to be sent here to attend to this man's leg."

By the time he returned, the two armorers had finished the repair, having welded a patch onto either side of the brake cylinder, refilling it with fresh oil. Berta was actually ready for combat again ("Fischer, up to the CP and report this!"), but it was pointless as no laying-data could be transmitted. The three Americans were sitting quietly in the corner, the wounded one had had his leg bandaged.

Soon afterward, a lorry arrived from division and a helmeted guard took them away. Horn went to the corner where they had waited and picked up three packets of cigarettes they had apparently left. There was a picture of a camel on the packet and one could smell the tobacco through the wrapper. The sergeant put them in his pocket "for safe keeping," he said. "We shall have one each after every alarm. Do any of you smoke?" They didn't and Hoffmann looked happy. "It'll make a nice change not to have to smell the Ivan's bloody Machorka every night!" The lorry which had come for the prisoners had brought a group of specialists who repaired the cables, a long job. The Russians filled in the bomb craters, and the abattoir had collected the bits and pieces. Food improved greatly over the next fortnight, and the cook was subjected to much less abuse.

A couple of weeks after these events, the guns had to be tested for the speed of their shells. Every shell fired from any gun leaves the barrel in a slightly more worn state. This is of course infinitesimal, but after a few hundred shots it becomes measurable. The shell does not fit as tightly as before, part of the gases driving it out escape and the muzzle-speed drops. The AA shot is aimed well ahead of the target to allow for the distance traveled by the plane between firing and, hopefully, impact. If the speed of the shell is lower than entered into the calculation, the shot will fall short of the target.

To correct this, the guns were tested after every 500 shots. This could not be done in the battery; they had to be taken to a special firing range. First the Russians turned up with picks and shovels and removed one side of the enclosure, that took a whole day. In the evening a gun-tractor arrived and towed the gun out and away. It was returned after three days with up-to-date muzzle-speed. The Ivans were back again to rebuild the wall. The captain had ordered that the boys serving at the gun that was away could sleep at home during those days, which was great, particularly as the promised weekend leave had not yet materialized.

It was gun drill with reversed roles today: No. 1 took over the side, No. 2 moved over to the fuse-setter, and No. 6 came across to the elevation position. To imitate an emergency, this was changed every ten minutes, but it was not difficult because the receivers for all position were virtually identical.

"Another thing we shall practice now," said Hoffmann, "is what we do if the gun fails to eject the spent cartridge. The reason is always broken ejector claws, here they are behind the breechblock, see? They crack after a few hundred shots, nothing we can do about it. We have spares here and the loader and I make the repair. See that opening in the wall above the entrance? In there the barrel has to go, or else the Ivans can't reach into it with the cleaning-rod, they push the cartridge out by brute force. If this happens at night, I shall shine my torch on the opening. No. 2, it is your responsibility to get the barrel precisely over the gap so that Fischer can drop it in." After an hour they could do this almost with their eyes closed and Hoffmann was happy.

The evening alarm came late; it was almost eleven. Going through the pre-firing checks, the Sargent bellowed: "No. 6, temperature?" "Oh, shit!" said Behrends, he had forgotten. Each gun had a yellow painted cartridge in the ammo-bunker and it was the job of the No. 6 to unclip the bottom and pull out a thermometer from the charge inside and read off the temperature of the explosive. This was then passed on to fire control at the start of each alarm. A cold explosive burned off more sluggishly than a warm one, making a considerable difference to the shell-speed. "We are not going to fire," announced Hoffmann, "night fighters about." The searchlights in the distance behaved in a strange way; instead of fingering the sky they shone straight upward onto the clouds without moving. The sergeant had, of course, the explanation. "When the clouds are light and low like now, the bombers have to fly above them. The searchlights illuminate the cloud cover and the fighter, flying above the bombers, can see them clearly against the light background, there is no chance of hiding. Usually the fighters are pretty successful on a night like this."

No sooner had he finished explaining when a fireball fell from the clouds. It was some distance away, but the explosion of the bombs on impact was still tremendous. A few minutes later a second plane followed, not on fire but minus one wing; only four parachutes unfolded. The scene was moving past the battery now and searchlights in the east picked up from where the westerly ones had reached their limit. Just before the trees blocked out the view, a third plane fell down covered in flames and exploding in mid-air before hitting the ground. "These boys are good, a great pity we haven't got more of them!" commented the sergeant, then he called out: "Fighter warning! Star shell red, No. 1 50 degrees, No. 2 gun in 9, No. 6 longest fuse!" The loader fetched his own star shell ("can't trust those Ivans"), the fire bell rang, and a huge red square appeared on the sky, softened by the clouds but still clearly visible. If fighters were still lagging behind, they would radio down now and announce their presence, but no response came. The formations continued to come in from the West, but stayed just out of reach of the guns ('They must have heard about you!' said Hoffmann). That meant all the batteries to the East of Bremen had all the fun. All the same, the guns were locked on to the target, but the fuse setter dials remained blank and no shots were fired that night.

The SM had news for them in the morning: "By order from above, you are supposed to have a 'guardian,' an NCO who looks after you specifically and may God help him! You have not met him because he had to have his appendix taken out but we expect him back tomorrow. He is Wachtmeister Schirrmeyer, he is a teacher, so he will, hopefully, be able to show you the way. He will drum general ballistics into you, he will also teach you how to make your beds, which are a disgrace. That goes for your wardrobes too! I hope he will be able to lift you out of this stone age culture you seem to enjoy living in, I don't envy him in this gargantuan task! Dismissed!" In the Army and Air Force, this senior NCO was called a feldwebel; only in artillery formations was he a Wachtmeister.

"Isn't he a funny bastard?" said Jakobsen on the way to school. "Stone age-culture, gargantuan task, what next?" But they all agreed: the SM was a great chap. They learned more about the two men during gun drill in the afternoon. Bartsch, the loader, supplied the information. "You are lucky getting him, he is a very nice man. He looks too young for the job and I bet most of you are taller than him, but don't be deceived by that! He's a grammar school teacher from Cologne and an old mate of the SMs. They were neighbors and both their families were wiped out in the same raid. The SM had just been invalided out of the Artillery, where he had been badly shot up in Russia but he pestered them until they gave him this job here, hoping for revenge, I suppose. You must never upset Schirrmeyer, he has a very serious heart condition. I know a nurse in the hospital and they were not very happy having to operate, I tell you!"

Schirrmeyer had arrived and the boys liked him straight away. He had taught math and physics so his lessons were something to look forward to. He was all Bartsch had told them but with the quiet authority of a good teacher. The plan was to skip every second day's gun drill and replace it with theory. "You will ask yourselves" he introduced his first lesson "the old question which has been asked by countless generations of Latin students: what is it good for? The answer which you know as well is, that it sharpens your logic. It will not help you to shoot down the enemy. If you are good gun-layers, as I'm sure you are, this will not teach you how to become better ones. Why? There is no such thing as a better gun-layer, either you do the job as it should be done, the way you have been trained, or you are sloppy and don't care, in which case you should be taken away and shot. Another point: If you have any dark areas in my subjects, I'm perfectly happy to help out, don't hesitate to ask." That was great, as particularly math with reduced lessons was catastrophic. He made an enormous difference, so much so that after perhaps eight weeks the headmaster came to deliver one of his little speeches, saying that he was very impressed with their increased effort and he always knew they could do it!

The relationship with the Russians was good, what there was of it. The only ones they really got to know were those in their gun crews and of course their very own Ivan who, very soon, did start to clean the boots and nobody ever found out about it. The boys put them in a sack behind the hut, and when it was dark he spirited them away. The daily bread ration was more than enough, so one or two loaves found the way into the sack as well. In autumn bags and bags of apples, pears, and plums ended up in the Russian's hut, the boys all had gardens at home, and the bikes groaned under the weight of fruit when they returned from weekend leave. Consequently, there was always a lot of grinning and waving when they passed each other.

Nearing Christmas, Jakobsen had an idea. "How would it be if we did something special for those poor sods? We could organize some food for them, things they never see here. I know for instance they eat a lot of herring, I think it's part of their national diet. I'm sure I could get a couple of buckets of them from my old man." Jacky's father was a trawler captain with the herring fleet in Vegesack. How they managed to get through their work nobody knew—nobody was supposed to know either. Jakobsen could only tell them that they slipped anchor in the evening and returned early in the morning, the actual fishing was done under cover of darkness. So far it had worked, they lost a couple of boats through mines but they had never been attacked yet.

Gräpel's parents had a pub and restaurant. It was closed (his father had been called up) but he reckoned there was still considerable stock in the cellars. It was strictly forbidden to let Russians have alcohol but two bottles of vodka between thirty of them—who would be any the wiser? Two farmer's sons were among them. They were put down for a sausage each. The rest produced nuts and eggs, apples, a few candles, and a couple of cakes.

A day before Christmas everything was put into a sack, and when Ivan came to bring water and coal, this and the herring buckets were handed over. He was speechless and then he stammered, "I come fetch when dark," which he did, looking over his shoulder all the time. Ten minutes later came a knock at the back window and it was Ivan. "Comrades say spasibo, much much spasibo." He was actually crying, tears rolled down his cheeks. "This for you!" he added, handing over a paperbag as the night swallowed him. The bag was opened on Christmas Eve. They had carved eight little guns with a lot of detail, like the ones outside. Only a Russian could do that!

In a few weeks, Schirrmeyer had become a real friend and they were very comfortable with each other. There was of course no familiarity and "military manners" as the captain called it were strictly observed, and yet it was a very warm relationship. It was obvious that he was used to dealing with young people, but it was more than that. A few months on, it really knocked him when Köhler was killed, so much so that the boys were worried about his health, but the daily slog took care of that in the long run.

He was always there for them. One day Fischer went to him to tell him about the terrible state of their bicycle tires and how flats delayed two or three on their way to or back from school almost every day. Coupons for new ones were absolutely out of the question. A week later the quartermaster brought fifteen new sets back from division; God alone knew what strings he had pulled. All he would say was that division could not ignore the argument that lack of reasonable tires was allowed to interfere with the defense of the country!

Another example was the case of the dancing lessons. "Sir," Fischer confided in him, "we have a problem. In four weeks the next course at the school of dancing in Vegesack will start and our opposite class from the girl's grammar are planning to enroll. It would be one hour a week and straight after school on Wednesday and we were wondering, would there be a chance for us?" Schirrmeyer was genuinely taken aback. "Christ, dancing lessons! Have you no shame? The country is fighting for its survival and what is your main concern? Dancing lessons! Having said all that, I think it's a great idea, grab what you can, lad, it only sounds so incongruous against our background here. I will speak to the CO." They had the answer the next day: "You know what the captain did? He laughed! It's alright you can go, leave the school's number at the office."

The one who did not laugh was Mr. Arff, the owner and instructor of the establishment who had taught the steps plus gentlemanly behavior to countless generations and had reached his seventies over it. "You cannot come on to my floor wearing those boots!" He almost cried. "My beautiful floor!"

He was right, it was a beautiful Parquet floor, polished by many thousands of feet in an old house high above the river. Their boots had thirty-two regulation hob-nails in them and so the course started (and finished) in socks. The girls giggled only during the first lesson. Schirrmeyer found this extremely funny and he must have told the SM about it, who came up with a comment befitting him: "You must have looked a right bunch of fairies!"

CHAPTER 4

Death and Killing

The problem of weekend leave had also been solved. Four men had been drafted into the gun crews, one would stand in at each gun every weekend, and one of the boys could sleep at home every third Saturday and Sunday night, which was not bad. The substitutes were a motley bunch (said Hoffmann), the quartermaster went to Anton, the office clerk to Berta, the second cook to Caesar, and only at Dora they were happy with the assistant armorer, but it worked alright. The time had come around for another shell-speed check, and it was rumored that the battery might be issued with new barrels. If that was the case, the gun crews would have a week "off," as that was how long the changing over took. It had been raining for a fortnight and opening the enclosures was a terrible mess with the poor Ivans looking like earthworms. A week it was then, and the CO did not forget to give the boys leave to sleep at home. "But come back Tuesday, just to be on the safe side!" "Typical." said Horn. No sooner were the boys back from school, the alarm bell went off. As Berta was not quite combat-ready yet, Hoffmann sent the three on a tour, as he called it. "Perhaps you can make yourself useful at other guns." Anton was complete but Behrends was welcomed with open arms at Caesar because the No. 6 had a boil on his behind and could not sit in his seat. "It's all this milk they give you, that must come to a bad end!" Beckmann was the least liked gunnery sergeant; he always thought he was being funny, only he never was. Horn and Fischer had just offered their services at Dora, when the warning came: "Low flying aircraft in 9" and seconds later an engine could be heard and the pom-pom began to rattle. Its caliber was barely an inch but it was the quadruple type with, obviously, four barrels, hence the stopping power and the noise were considerable. The plane fired as well and the pom-pom fell silent. It was all over in seconds, and Fischer and Horn sprinted across the field toward the emplacement, which had been built about 200 yards from the battery in a firebreak running through a low birch forest. They wished they had not come.

Köhler was still sitting in the seat of his gun, his hands and feet firmly on the controls, but his head had disappeared without a trace. Only his empty bloody helmet lay in a corner. Back and front of his uniform were black with his blood down to his feet. It was such an awful sight that it stunned them into a state where nothing mattered anymore. They lifted the body from the seat, put it gently down against the wall, and covered it with the gun tarpaulin. Hauenschild, the second gunner, was groaning on the ground, blood spurting from a hole above the left knee. Horn, who was a first-aid fanatic, ripped out his penknife and slit the trouser leg. He guided Hauenschild's finger to the artery and shouted: "Press all you can!" and the bleeding went down to a trickle. The Hiwi-loader was also dead, half his chest had gone. They pulled the body over next to Köhler, the tarpaulin was big enough for two. Then the plane came back, exactly along the firebreak, guns blazing. Horn and Fischer were safe on the ground against the wall from where the fighter approached, and Hauenschild was in the bunker now. Why was the pilot doing this? He must have seen the gun was not manned anymore? While Horn was attending to Hauenschild, Fischer looked at the gun. The elevation mechanism was in tatters and the barrels were stuck at 45 degrees. "How about training her down the firebreak and if that madman comes back, we let him have it. If we fire when he has to cross that 45 degrees firing line, he won't have time to swerve, if he comes back, that is." Horn thought it might work. It gave them something to do and they did not have time to think about Köhler. They adjusted the direction of the gun and whipped fresh magazines in, Horn the left ones, Fischer the ones for the right barrels. If the plane came back, it would cross the path of the shells about 200 meters in front of them. There were two tall trees at this spot which made a good marker. It was for Horn to peep over the earth wall and give Fischer the command to fire when the plane was near that point. Fischer was on the ground, pressed against the wall, his hand on the foot pedal which fired the gun, he could just reach it. Unbelievably, the plane did return. Horn shouted and dove for cover. Fischer hit the pedal and the four Oerlikons chattered with that wonderful Swiss precision. He kept the pedal down until the magazines were empty. No aircraft had come across, no engine noise either. Peering over the wall, they saw the burning wreckage near the marker trees, Horn shouted: "We got the bastard, Herrmann!" (Herrmann was Köhler's first name). Fischer sat on the ground, realizing that he had just personally and deliberately killed his first enemy. He felt a bit weak for a moment or two, but then the thought came: 'I have to get Köhlers ID disk!' These disks were aluminium, perforated down the middle with the personal details on either half. When the bearer was killed, somebody broke the bottom-half off, the other half stayed with the body. He could not bring himself to take the tarpaulin off, so he groped around under it until he came across the disk. His forearms were covered in blood and he shuddered violently.

It had gone quiet. In the meantime Horn had tied off Hamann's leg with a piece of telephone cable. He was doing fine but was in a lot of pain.

Horn and Fischer were not sure about the chief's reaction having shot without firing-order, well, perhaps they could brazen it out. They went to the command post looking absolutely ghastly: naked to the waist, full of blood and blackened by gun smoke, they still wore their helmets. Fischer saluted: "Permission to report, sir! Senior auxiliary Köhler killed, senior auxiliary Hauenschild wounded, needs urgent attention, one Hiwi killed, gun elevation-transmission shot up, one fighter destroyed, type not recognized, ammunition expended eighty rounds, captain, sir!" The captain saluted back, "You two are unbelievable! Normally, we fire here on order but never mind that now. Have your arms seen to, Fischer." "That's not my blood, sir." "And you, Horn?" "The same, sir." The captain walked up to them, put his hands on their shoulders and squeezed hard, then he shook his head and turned away. They had just about done their "about turn" when he called them back. "One important rule for your future military career: A dead hero is of no use to the high command! Remember that; please!" He had actually added "please." "Get cleaned up and report to me in an hour. I want to hear the details. Off you go!" The medic had already run over to the pom-pom position to attend to Hauenschild.

On the way back to the hut, they met the sergeant major who was going the other way. He stared at them aghast and said: "What have you two crazy buggers been up to now?" When told what happened he became very somber, it was obvious he was genuinely sorry about Köhler. It was known he had a soft spot for him, probably because he was so small. Fischer handed him the ID disc. "There was no need for you to do that, lad!" said the SM. "We were the nearest, sir." He just shook his head. "Permission to go to the lake to wash, sir?" That was a brilliant idea of Horn and the SM nodded.

The captain was completely informal, he wanted to know every detail, in particular who had trained them for that gun. "It wasn't really training, sir, Köhler took us a few times and explained things. But how can a head so completely disappear without a trace?" "It must have been a hit from a shell, not a bullet. The fighters have two or more guns on board, similar in caliber to our pom-pom, but I have an idea they are more powerful. In a dogfight they might get only one or two shots into the target and they have to do as much damage as possible."

Two days later the captain sent a runner. Horn and Fischer had to report there at once. He told them that they had to see a Colonel Benz at division the next morning. "You know the barracks in Lesum? Go to the entrance towards Grohn at 1000. I have spoken to your school that you are not coming or coming later." "Oh, shit!" Fischer thought, "Now we are in for it!" Horn was thinking along the same lines. "Does the captain think it's because of firing without orders?" "You will have to see, won't you?" The colonel was a man of perhaps thirty-five, quite young for his rank, completely gray and his empty left sleeve was tucked into his tunic pocket—another one of those! He started off by saying: "Your CO tells me you two have been playing wild west on Tuesday. Tell me about it in your own words and, for God's sake, relax and sit down." He spoke into an intercom: "Behrmrum, come in and listen to this!" A very young second lieutenant with the lanyard of an adjutant entered. The colonel interrupted their narrative frequently, asking questions. When they had finished, he said: "Well, that was a nice bit of imaginative thinking, well done, and I'm very sorry about your friend. Did you know that your captain recommended you for the EK2? No, of course not. But I had to turn him down. You, not being soldiers, must not be put in dangerous situations or positions. Therefore in theory, you could not possibly have deserved it. Well, you understand what I'm saying. But I want to do something for you. As you know the gun crews of your battery will soon receive the decoration for downing thirty aircraft, what is the tally now?" "Twenty-eight, sir." "I shall give it to you now, here you are, so you still owe me two planes. Don't let it be long or I might get into trouble with my superior officer. Good luck, dismissed!" "Well," said Horn, "that was something! What a nice chap; you can't beat these old frontline soldiers, they never give you any bullshit, do they? I don't want to go to school now, do you?" Of course Fischer did not want to do that either, there was no point. They decided to walk up and down the high street Vegesack, parading their medal. Back at the battery, they reported to the CO that they had been decorated and he seemed genuinely pleased. "I'm sorry it did not work out with the EK, but that is the system's fault, division would have agreed. No doubt you will get other chances, being as reckless as you are. But back to Tuesday's sad events: I shall go to Mrs. Köhler tonight to offer our condolences; can you tell me anything about the family?" "Not much, sir, his father was killed in Norway and there is a sister, but Jakobsen knows them well, they are almost neighbors." "I want to see him now. I will most likely learn the date of the funeral later. You can of course all go, take your bikes."

After dinner came Ivan. The Russians had made a bunch of flowers, sticks of wood shaved down, with an end of the shavings still attached to the stem; they looked like chrysanthemums. They were stunning, a real work of art, and yet so simple. "For dead comrade!" Ivan said. Nobody answered, finally Jakobsen, who was nearest to him, put his arm around his shoulder and said, "Spasibo, much spasibo, we take to grave." When the Russian had left, all of them had to wipe their eyes, nobody felt ashamed.

The funeral was a sad little affair. Köhler's mother wanted to see him for the last time, and the captain had to use a lot of diplomacy to avoid the coffin being opened. Everyone was relieved when their presence was cut short by the wail of sirens in the distance.

Wednesday had been the day of Popoff's funeral. The quartermaster had given a blue-and-white checked blanket cover to the Russians for a shroud, which was made to look even more incongruous by the large bloodstain where his chest had been. The whole battery was there; Popoff had also doubled as the battery-cobbler and would be sorely missed. The captain had come which, one could see, pleased the Russians to no end. Leschenko, the Natschalnik, went to him at the end, saluted, and said, "Thanking the Gospodin captain for coming."

"Listen," said Sergeant Hoffmann, "Easter is coming along and I want to introduce you to, in my opinion, very nice Russian custom. The poor sods are a long way from home and they appreciate every little thing reminding them where they come from. Now then, when two Russians meet on Easter Sunday, one says, 'Christos woskres,' which means 'Christ has risen,' and the other one answers, 'On wistinje woskres,' 'He has truly risen.' Then they kiss each other on the cheek, but we don't have to go that far. So, on Easter Sunday, when you meet one of our Ivans, what do you say?" "Christos woskres." "Right, and watch their faces light up!" "I always thought they were all atheists, sarge?" asked Horn. "Don't you believe it, there might be some among the townspeople and the party hierarchy but for the rural population religion is still very important, perhaps not publicly, but important all the same." Hoffmann had been right,: the Russians were absolutely delighted.

Drieling said afterward that this had been their day of revenge for Köhler—it had been a recall from school, a mist had developed into thick ground-fog and when they approached the battery, only the gun-barrels where sticking out of the pea soup. Shooting had not started well; after the first round, the sergeant bellowed: "Missfire! Out, all of you!" When a shot failed to go off, the shell had to remain in the gun for three minutes and the crew left the enclosure except for the loader and the sergeant. Then, if nothing had happened, the sergeant pulled the breech-block open and the loader caught the shell as it came sliding out from the barrel. He carried it gingerly to the wall and let it roll down on the outside. Next day the armorer would fit a new ignition cap and the shell would be reused.

After five minutes Berta was ready to rejoin, andthere were still plenty of targets. The Americans always flew in groups of five or six in a ring, quite close together, to protect themselves and each other from fighter attacks.

Together they could create enormous firepower. The Fortress had two guns in the tail—one on either side, two on the top, and one or two in the belly, the caliber being between a machine gun and a pom-pom, a most effective screen. Their course led them straight over the battery (Wechsel punkt) toward the East. Once they had left the range of Habichthorst, they had peace for about ten flying minutes, as there was no battery to receive them before Grosse Dunge, thirty miles away, but just before they were safe, something dramatic happened: One shell had obviously hit a Fortress in the bomb-bay and the entire load went up, anything between two and three tons on explosives. The plane disappeared altogether, so to speak, but the explosion brought down four of its neighbors as well, in pieces and not one parachute appeared. One aircraft was losing height rapidly and was also lost, no doubt. "Star shell red!" came the order from the command post. Bartsch ripped the next shell from the loading-tray, pulled the star-shell from the rack ("can't trust those Ivans"), all in a matter of seconds. "Ready!" reported Hoffmann and the fire-bell rang. Four red plumes stood in the clear sky in front of the next formations. and no new fire order came. "I'll tell you what that was about," said the sergeant. "The star-shells were the captain's way of shouting 'Hurray!' to the other planes, the vindictive old bastard! But now he thinks they might have annoyed them so much, they might order one formation to split off, return, and bomb the shit out of us. However, they couldn't see us in the fog, and they would depend on our flashes for aiming. That's why we are keeping mum for a while."

"I wonder," mused Horn, "if we get credited with all that lot?" Hoffmann was quite sure they would not; they would get one point for the initial plane and that was that. However, he had never experienced a chain of events like this, so you never know. In the event, only one point was granted to the battery.

The counting system was quite simple and as fair as it could be. If a plane was brought down and only one battery was shooting in the vicinity, there was no argument and the point went to them. More often than not, more than one was engaged at the same time because the formations were "handed over" from battery to battery as they crossed or flew past. If three batteries fired and a plane was destroyed, each one was given 1/3 point; if four were engaged, 1/4 of a plane went to each of them. When a new point was completed, or given outright, a new ring was painted on the gun barrels. The captain had ordered that the ring for the destroyed fighter was to have a narrow black band in the middle, out of respect to Köhler, and everybody thought this a wonderful idea.

The gun crews had of course not witnessed any of this drama. The information came later from the range finder-team. Theirs was an elevated position and they found themselves just above the fog layer. Their powerful optics showed quite clearly that one engine of the exploding plane was blasted sideways, and it sliced through two Fortresses, cutting them both in half.

When the last planes had gone past, the sergeant major limped from gun to gun, he was quite beside himself, a very strange and unexpected sight. He kept saying, "Oh, well done, lads, well done!" When he had left, Hoffmann reckoned: "He was thinking of his family, you know? Can't blame him!"

At gun drill, the sergeant made an announcement: "I don't know if you heard what happened at Dora last night: the loader had his wrist broken when the loading tray kicked back, so they had to drop out. It is actually specified that you are not allowed to do this job because you are so young and frail, but the captain decided that you be trained all the same. Nobody will know and we have to have emergency cover.

I'm afraid it will only apply to Horn and Fischer. Behrends, you will have to grow a bit first, no offence. It looks easy but you will find it isn't, that's why loaders are usually stevedores or quarrymen." "Or butchers," whispered Horn. "Comedian!" said Hoffmann. "Corporal Bartsch here will train you. He knows more tricks than I do. Have we any exercise shells here, Bartsch?" "Negative," answered the loader, "I think they got some at Caesar. I'll go and borrow one."

It did seem simple enough, one of the ammunition gunners placed the bottom end of the shell into the receiving-tray, and thenthe loader grabbed the top-end and lowered the shell "gently but firmly" into the tray. Its weight depressed a button which released the fuse-setting head to slide down onto the tip of the shell where it adjusted the fuse in a few seconds. At the first sound of the fire bell, the loader jerked the handle of the receiver-tray once, which caused the fuse-setter head to slide upward again, thus freeing the shell so it could be tipped, with a second jerk of the handle, into the loading-tray. The loading-tray in turn swung under the breech, three fast-spinning rubber-rollers clapped down on the shell and whipped it into the barrel. The breechblock fell to and the shot broke automatically.

There was not a lot that could be practiced, these simple procedures came easily enough, but when they had to be done twenty-two times per minute, and it had to be done in a half bent position, the strain on the participants was significant. Bartsch showed them how to stand and where to put their feet, which all helped. The main-pressure the loader was under was that he had to respond to the fire-bell in a fraction of a second. If he was that fraction late, the whole world would know, well, the whole battery anyway, that he was no good and his muzzle-flash and his detonation near the target would appear just that little bit later and give him away. Technically, it did not make the slightest difference, it was just a matter of pride. This perfection came only after a lot of practice, so whether the boys would ever achieve it was doubtful.

"To round off your education," as Schirrmeyer put it, they also had a stretch at the rangefinder, a cleverly designed piece of equipment which could produce amazingly accurate results. The only drawback was that the target had to be visible; on cloudy days or if searchlights could not pick up the plane after dark, it was useless.

In principle, the rangefinder was a tube about 12 feet long with a telescope at either end. These were, over prisms, connected to the operator's ocular in the middle of the tube, his right eye looked out through the lens on the right, the left eye consequently through the opposite one, thus increasing the distance between his eyes to roughly twelve feet, so to speak. The optic for one eye was fixed, the other one could be swiveled until the "beams" of both eyes crossed, the crossing point being the target. The farther the plane was away from the rangefinder, the larger the angle off the adjustable beam, andthe machine could easily convert the angle, on the principle of trigonometry, into distance in meters.

The odd thing was that only one in many thousand men had the ability to "see" the "beams." They had "plastic vision," as it was called, and they were very sought after. However, after the introduction of radar, the traditional rangefinder became obsolete, although on clear days the traditional method was still preferred because it delivered more precise distances. Radar was, after all, still in its infancy. Two more men were assisting the operator, one kept the target in his crosshairs elevation-wise, the second one corrected side movements, so the operator could concentrate entirely on establishing his crossing-point. None of the boys had, by the way, plastic vision.

The bell cut the homework short on a very hot afternoon with not a cloud in the sky. The planes came from southwest, flying northwest, a very unusual behavior. They were well within range and the barrage was terrific because all batteries around Bremen could join in. Five bombers came down in quick succession but then a number of fighters joined in and firing had to stop. They chalked up another five, so altogether not a bad result. But now they started their bomb-run and there was no doubt about it, the stuff came down on Vegesack, Blumenthal or thereabouts, the dust and smoke from the exploding bombs gave the area away. Only woods stood between the battery and those townships, then came the river, on the other side only grazing land, they would hardly bomb that. The fighters were still at work and the gun crews just hung around watching.

"Fischer to the captain!" The CO, thoughtfully, had already contacted division to check the location of the attack, and it was Blumenthal and Vegesack that had caught it. "You will want to know what happened," said the captain. "I suggest you cycle home and check. We can't do any more here because of the fighters. How many of you from Blumenthal?" "Two, sir, and two more in Lüssum and Rönnebeck, next to it." "Can you cover that as well?" "Yes, sir!" "We want someone for Vegesack and Lesum, Who is the quickest?" "Horn, sir." "See to it. How many from the other side of the river?" "Four, sir." "Whom will you send?" "Drieling, sir, he lives central." "Right, set it in motion. As soon as you find anything of importance, ring here and we will send the men in question home. So it's no news, good news. See that you all have the number. Good luck, I hope you will not have to telephone. Off you go!"

Horn and Drieling left together, as the ferry across the Weser was located in Vegesack, so they had the same way. Fischer took the direct road toward Blumenthal. Closer to the town the barrels with artificial fog were still spewing out their smelly contents by the roadside, cycling through it left on with a feeling of sunburn and irritated eyes. The approaches into Blumenthal looked untouched, but when Fischer entered his street, which was quite a long one, the damage started. Five houses on either side had disappeared, fire brigade and neighbors were digging down into the cellars. The houses further on were just damaged to varying degrees, but Fischer's house, the last one on the left, looked unharmed—well, not quite, the windows and the front door were missing. His mother was busy doing what millions of women all over Europe did: sweeping broken glass into buckets. His father was not there, mother reckoned he was overseeing some water main's repair. They had been very lucky indeed. Only a few yards from the house ran an old disused railway cutting and into there three bombs had fallen, but the banks had directed the blast upward. There was time for a quick meal, and then Fischer checked the other three houses in his area. They had all been lucky, Kaufmann's had not been touched, Behrends and Simon had their roof tiles blown off, repairs had already started. Horn and Drieling came back with equally good news, but Drieling, who came from a farm, had seven milking cows killed. He was most incensed about it, but he brought back two large bags of meat (one for the Ivans). Losses had been surprisingly high for a place the size of Blumenthal:

about three hundred killed. More than half were Polish workers in a textile mill, as there had been a direct hit on their shelter. The battery was credited with two planes, and the twenty-ninth and thirtieth rings were painted on the guns. The battery was due for the decoration now, and it was rumored Colonel Benz would do the honors, which was just as well somebody else would have wondered why two of the youngest were wearing it already. "Fischer," said the SM, "you will report your lot separately to the colonel, after the captain. Do I need to remind you of your appearance? Particularly your boots, tell your Russian to put some extra effort into it. You didn't think I knew that, did you?" Fischer did not know what to answer, he blushed instead. The battery stood waiting on the parade ground and a sorry sight it was! Instead of the regulation 120 soldiers and two junior officers, there were thirty-five (and no officers) and they, apart from the gunnery sergeants and the radar crew, did not look so fresh either. The fifteen auxiliaries brought the figure up to fifty, the rest was made up with Russians.

When the colonel passed down the ranks and he came to the SM (who was carrying his stick), he said, "Morning, Müller, the old peg not so good today?" "No, sir, it's lousy, it's the weather."

"I know the feeling!" replied the colonel, waving his empty sleeve at him; they obviously knew each other. Coming to Fischer, he said: "Morning, Fischer, done anything heroic lately? And where is your bloodthirsty mate?" "Senior Auxiliary Horn, here, sir!" "Morning, Senior Auxiliary Horn, behaving yourself?" "Always, colonel, sir!" The captain did not bat an eyelid, andthe sergeant major wore a pained expression.

By way of celebration, Colonel Benz had brought some things in his car: there was a crate of beer and a few bottles of Korn for the soldiers, a tin of chocolate for each of the boys, and a tin of pork for each Russian, plus a large bag of Machorka. The chocolate was called Schoka-Cola, normally issued to airmen to keep them awake, asit contained a high dose of caffeine. God knew where the raw material for chocolate came from, in the fifth year of war!

The wailing of sirens far away caused the colonel to disappear in a cloud of dust. Then came a time when sleep was at a premium. The alarms sounded regularly every night, usually lasting from 9:00 to 11:00 or thereabouts, then a break of one our two hours before the formations returned. Sometimes they took a different route, but more often than not, the pilots flew back the way they knew. Damaged planes, stragglers, mostly attempted to go home on their own, in the knowledge that night-fighters would concentrate on large numbers of planes. Nearly always their hope of being left alone came to nothing; invariably they were downed by AA.

The system under which the boys could leave later for school after a disrupted night collapsed; it was simply overwhelmed and fatigue became a real problem. It was quite common that someone fell asleep in class or over homework, the quality of which had suffered anyway. They started to look the part: hollow-eyed, pale, and tempers began to flare up. They spoke to Schirrmeyer about it, but there was nothing the battery could do, shooting came first, everything else was secondary. "I tell you what," he suggested, "talk to you Headmaster, if he is a reasonable man, he might give you day off here and there; he must have noticed you're walking about like zombies."

Dr. Zimmer was actually a reasonable man, if perhaps a bit pompous. He had been taken off the retirement-shelf, dusted, and put back in the job, as he must have been seventy at least. During the main break, Fischer (who else) went to his office and explained the situation. He and the other masters had of course noticed the decline, "But what do you suggest?" Well, that was easy enough. "Could you see your way to give us a day off every now and again as long as these relentless attacks (Fischer became a bit pompous himself) last? We are certain it would pay. If we carry on like this, your efforts would be mostly wasted more and more." "God," thought Fischer, "is this really me handing out this bullshit? And I am putting pressure on our headmaster!" However, Dr. Zimmer took it very well. He would discuss it with the other masters, and perhaps changes could be made to the timetable so as to create an "unimportant" day. "It would probably be best to have it on Monday, that way the week would not be interrupted." Fischer said. That was of course not the reason, but it would mean an extra day at home for the ones on leave every third weekend, providing the captain played along, but they would leave that to Schirrmeyer. The head was as good as his word, he informed them next morning that, until further notice, Monday would be a school-free day. The captain proved to be understanding, but nobody had expected anything else and Monday was, also until further notice, duty-free, no lectures, no gun-drill, only bed! It was amazing what difference this one day made very quickly.

"Why is it, sir," Schirrmeyer was asked, "that with all the banging away we're doing we're not bringing more of the bastards down? Afterall, every shot is calculated as the target moves along, and calculated by machines and human error does not come into it? And we are pretty careful with the laying!" Schirrmeyr stepped into his schoolmaster-role: "Everything we do on the ground is theoretical, starting with positioning the guns. As you know, they are arranged in a square, so, when all fire with the same settings, the explosions of the shells should show the same square in the sky. The plane is assumed to be in the middle of this area and should be blown to bits. But it doesn't work that way. If you ever have the chance to see your shells explode, you won't see a square! I have seen circles, triangles, straight lines up and down or right to left—anything but a square! It is the wind in higher layers of the atmosphere which changes with every second, we cannot estimate, let alone measure it. Tiris pushes the shells off course. Fortunately all AA units of all armies have the same problem, not only us. You know that no straggler having to fly lower than his normal ceiling has a chance, one or two salvoes and he goes to pieces. The shells don't have to be on their way such along time and hence cannot be blown off course so much. The second factor is what the plane does while the shells are travelling up. Let's say we shoot at 30,000 feet, you can reckon it takes twenty-five seconds for them to get there and in that time the target can easily leave the predicted course and move away from the explosion, far enough to render it harmless. Don't be discouraged, our success rate is not bad at all, we shall just keep on banging away, as Jakobsen so delightfully put it!"

Attacks on individual AA batteries increased. It was not bombers who did the damage, something nobody understood, but fighter-bombers. They were armed with cannons and rockets and often carried a small bombload. They could only operate in northern Germany; even with long distance tanks, they could not move away from their English bases too far. Habichthorst had been spared up to now. As precaution a second pom-pom had been installed on the other side of the battery and the guns had been fitted with shields for the gunner's protection, too late for poor old Köhler.

Another thing that worried the captain very much (and everybody else for that matter) was that the earth walls sheltering the guns were not high enough. Almost all heavy batteries had started life as 88 mm units which were most effective against the old Wellingtons, Hampdens, and Blenheims, but as those were slowly replaced by Lancasters, Fortresses, and Liberators, operating from a much higher ceiling, the 88 could not reach them anymore and they were quickly replaced by 10.5 cm guns, like in Habichthorst. These new guns were put in the old gun-pits but, being much bigger, more of the gun and crew were "out in the open," the earth walls not being high enough to give sufficient cover. Division had one pioneer company responsible for all earthworks in the area, but it would take months to modify all the gun-pits that needed it. It should have been done a long time ago. Now, with the appearance of fighter-bombers, the heat was on.

One evening when levelling the gun with the help of small spirit levels in the gun-supports, Fischer said to Hoffmann: "Sarge, it would not make any difference whether the walls are heightened or the gun is sunk lower into the pit, would it? So, if we were to dig down below the spindles, the gun would come down, wouldn't it? It'll be ages before the engineers arrive!" The guns stood on four heavy steel disks attached to spindles at the end of four arms forming the gun-support in the shape of a cross. Two arms were rigid, the two side ones could be winched up for transport. The spindles had about two feet of play so if they could be made to disappear in the ground that might just provide the additional cover for gun and men. "Reckon it might work," said Hoffmann. "Speak to Schirrmeyer about it, he will work it out." The wachtmeister listened without interrupting, then he said, "Put your cap on, we are going to see the chief." "Fischer here has an idea you might like to hear, sir." No interruptions from the CO either. "Will it work, Schirrmeyer?" "I think it will." "What will you need, Fischer?" "Four Russians, sir, some short bits of heavy timber and Horn. They have a carpentry business and he knows how to handle timber." "Starting when?" "Tomorrow first light, sir, if Horn and I can get off school. We are unlikely to need the gun in the morning and we should be finished by lunchtime, sir." "Schirrmeyer," said the chief, "were you as cocky when you were their age?" "Certainly not, sir, it must be a sign of the times!"

The first thing was to hammer the props under the four arms to take the weight of the gun instead of the spindles. That went smoothly enough, but then the trouble started. The ground below the disks had been so compacted, firstly by the weight of the gun and, more so, by the hundreds of recoil-shocks, that it had the consistency of concrete. The Russians hacked and dug and scraped but it still took them over two hours to excavate the four holes three by three feet and two feet down. The spindles could then be turned down! when they made contact with the bottom of the hole, the gun stood on its own four feet again, only considerably lower. The barrel, at zero elevation, just touched the crown of the earth wall.

Fischer went to the CO's hut, not a little proud of himself. "Permission to report, sir, Berta lowered and combat-ready." "I'm going to have a look at her, walk with me." Fischer stayed the customary half step behind and said after a while: "Permission to make a suggestion, sir?" "Go ahead, I have been waiting for this." Fischer had to grin. "The carpenter could perhaps make some covers for the spindle holes; they would be dangerous in the night. And the port for cleaning the barrel in the wall is now not low enough, but he would make a better job of it." "I will bear it in mind, Fischer, I will bear it in mind. Anything else?" "Yes, sir, we left the holes about two inches shallower in case there is renewed compacting; personally I doubt it, the ground is still like concrete. But we can always scrape out a bit more if necessary." The captain looked at him with an amused expression.

Approaching the gun, it was obvious that Berta showed a much lower profile compared to the others. Hoffmann was fussing over the Hiwis cleaning the gunpit up, it was a right mess. The captain waved his apologies aside, "Have you levelled her out yet, sergeant?" "No, sir, I've been waiting for Fischer to come back as the fourth man; we'll do it right away." The chief poked about for a long time, but he seemed satisfied. "I only hope she doesn't topple over when you start firing! Tell me, Hoffmann, why did we not think of this before?" "I don't know, sir, it has been tormenting me ever since they started digging this morning." The captain ordered Hoffmann to carry on with the other guns, one a day and in the morning. "We cannot possibly interfere with these young men's education anymore!"

A restriction had come in which had a curiously demoralizing effect on everybody. The armament industry apparently ran out of brass for shell-cases, not surprisingly, with the area of German control shrinking by the day. There was no copper mining in Germany to speak of. Consequently, steel shell-cases appeared on the scene. Theoretically, they were fine but as the barrel temperature rose, they were difficult to extract. Whereas brass was more or less inert as far as expanding under heat was concerned, steel was not and the result was catastrophic, the whole battery seized up. A cold gun could take twenty steel-rounds before the situation became critical, so the No. 6 was given a new job: counting the shots. The method was up to them, Behrends used the fingers of his left hand; the brain and right hand were needed to set the fuse. When the five fingers were used up, he made a chalk mark on the undercarriage and when he came to twenty he blew a whistle. The Russians then leaned the steel-rounds they were carrying against the wall and grabbed brass ones from the bunker. The gun usually missed one round but that was accepted. When there came a break in the shooting, the barrels were always returned to 60 degrees elevation. From now on it was 90 degrees, straight up, in the vain hope the chimney effect would cool the barrel down quicker. When firing resumed, the loader felt the temperature of the breech and decided how many steel cartridges he could take. He would then shout to the No. 6, who was at his elbow: "Ten!" or whatever he thought was right and Behrends would blow his whistle after ten rounds. It was absolutely ludicrous, but it worked. "What a way to fight a war, with a bloody whistle!" grumbled Bartsch, the loader.

Jakobsen had been quite badly wounded, it happened during the night. At Berta they did not know anything about Jacky's gun being Dora. Apparently, a large shrapnel had come down on his thumb on the steering-wheel, taking it clean off, and was then deflected to his thigh where it caused a lot of damage, fortunately not severing any arteries. The ambulance had taken him to Vegesack hospital, where they visited him after school next day. "That SM of ours is a right callous bastard," he said, "I was in a lot of pain waiting for the ambulance and you know what he said to me? You're lucky, another two inches and it would have cost you your balls."

"He had a point," said Horn.

It was on a Sunday when disaster struck. For a longtime everybody had been wondering why the battery had never been attacked directly, fearing it would happen one day and hoping it would not. An AA battery could of course not be camouflaged in any manner of speaking, and in particular the four gun pits would be clearly visible to anybody from above.

It was a beautiful day, not a cloud in the sky, when two small planes approached, probably Mosquitos. Alarm was never sounded for them; they usually flew too high to reach and they were not armed, reconnaissance being their business. Furthermore they had a plywood fuselage so they did not show up on radar. However, this time the battery was on stand-by, bomber formations were reported in the west, heading east. The Mosquitos had disappeared when shouts could be heard from the CP and Hoffmann repeated: "Smoke markers over the battery, stand by to take cover!" Now they were in for it, four dark red columns above each corner of the battery, more or less. The Russians crossed themselves (one always thought of them as atheists?). But to everybody's relief, the markers drifted off east quite smartly. This was what Schirrmeyer told them: the winds in different layers are unpredictable. The bombers arrived, not a large formation, perhaps thirty or forty, the bomb-aimers dropped their load dutifully between the markers, but the whole lot fell on to woodland. No firing order was given, as the chief probably thought it best to give the impression the battery had ceased to exist. So far so good.

"Low-flying aircraft in 9!" The guns turned into that direction but then the barrels were lowered as much as possible to make them inconspicuous, which was a lot of wishful thinking! The wail of the siren followed and the crews piled into the bunkers. The fighter-bombers could not be confronted with the heavy guns, as they were too clumsy and slow-moving. Only the poor pom-pom chaps had to face the music and they started firing almost immediately. A new technique had been worked out for them: they aimed the guns in the general direction of the attack in such a way that their fire crossed about 500 meters from the battery, forming a primitive screen. If possible, meaning if they had the time, the elevation was adjusted according to the height of the approach but the side-setting never changed. One of the four planes actually hit the screen and disintegrated, but three got through.

The ground shook four times, followed by a single huge explosion. Stones and bits of wood clattered on the gun and a boot fell into the entrance of the Berta bunker; disturbingly it had a foot in it which did not bode well. The victim was Dora, the gun was turned upside-down, and there were gaps in the emplacement wall. “My God,” said Hoffmann, “that’s where the bunker is supposed to be!” They all ran over to help but could have saved themselves the trouble. Dora’s crew had completely and utterly disappeared. The bomb must have found its way precisely into the shelter entrance and in the confined space the result was staggering. The only evidence that eight soldiers had hidden there were bits of blood soaked cloth, blue-gray from the AA men, dark green from the Russians, and some small bone fragments. The luck Jakobsen and Drieling had was hard to believe: Jacky was still in hospital, and it had been Drieling’s weekend at home.

The situation at Caesar was quite different. The tremendous explosion had been their ammunition bunker and the enclosure wall had all but disappeared. The blast had also toppled the gun over, and it was lying across the entrance of the crew-bunker as if sheltering them. Already Russians and soldiers were digging frantically from the outside to get them out that way. Very quickly a hole opened up and the crew crawled out, dazed and bleeding from noses and ears, but otherwise unharmed. Gräpel was missing! The SM, who was of course present, shouted into the hole: “Can’t you come out, lad?” “No, I’m bloody stuck, sir!” Before anybody could say or do anything, two Russians had dived back into the hole, and after a while Gräpel’s head appeared. The SM, clearly worried about him, asked: “Are you all right, lad?” “Not too bad, sir, but I think I’m going to resign.” “Think again, Gräpel, I would hate to have you shot for desertion, we lost enough men as it is!” Gräpel grinned; he had been pinned down by a beam which had broken his left leg. “When I go to hospital, do you think I can get a bed next to Jakobsen, sir?” The sergeant major promised to arrange it.

The men were lined up on the parade ground, also the Russians. “I want to tell you my plans,” said the captain, “Sergeant Hoffmann (who was standing next to him) will translate for our Russian men. As you know, we have always helped ourselves without relying too much on the Pioneers. Today is no exception. We will fill the crater in the Dora bunker making sure that all that remains of our comrades are taken care of, as this will be the only funeral we can give them. Borosov and his men will do that.” When this had been translated, the Natschalnik stepped forward, saluted, and said, “Da, Gospodin Captain!” “The rest of us will concentrate on Caesar, as we can do some good there. I have asked the farmer to come over with two horses so we can upright the gun. The armorers will go over it and see what the damage is. I think it can all be put right here. The ammunition bunker has to be rebuilt today; fresh shells will be brought out tomorrow. There should be enough timber about, Belumaun (that was the battery carpenter) you are in charge, pick any helpers you need. Next job is the gap in the enclosure. We'll leave Dora alone for the time being; the gun's a write-off and so is the enclosure. It will be easier to re-build from scratch a few metres from the present site. The cook will have a warm evening meal ready because we shall be working through the night, providing the bastards leave us alone! We have full moon and no clouds, that must suffice. Get to it, men!"

The boys crowded around Schirrmeyer to find out what was in store for them. "You are not allowed to work, too young, regulations." There was uproar: "With respect, sir, we are doing something or other against regulations every day! We can't just stand here and watch the others, these are our guns as well!" "I'll see the chief," said Schirrmeyer and he came back immediately: "If you were to volunteer for work, he cannot stop you." "He is a tight little Solomon!" said Jakobsen.

The farmer arrived with a face like thunder, "Just look at that miserable arsehole, will you?" Drieling said. The horses pulled two carts which he unhitched at Dora to be loaded with soil from the old enclosure. When full, they would pull them over to the new site. Next, heavy tackle was attached to Caesar to be pulled upright while men were holding the gun back with ropes so that it could not topple over. All went smoothly. The armorers crawled all over her, but as the captain had predicted, only minor damage had been done, and after an hour Caesar was declared fit for work. The carpenter and his helpers had completed the new ammo bunker already and soil could now be packed around it. They had also replaced the missing shuttering of the wall, having vandalized it from Dora. The Russians had completed their burial duties, swarmed over the side, some shoveling soil up, others on top tamping it down, and after another hour Caesar was protected again. The chief was very pleased and produced two bottles of Korn, one for the gunners, one for the Russians (not for auxiliaries, regulations?). The cook had surpassed himself, the soup was based on rice, noodles, and a lot of meat, only he knew where that originated. Actually, the battery suspected him of snaring in the woods. Some liked to point out that one never saw dogs or cats around the place, which never failed to get him wild. The boys had detached the turf from Dora's wrecked walls and some of the Ivans were taking it across to repair the damaged enclosure for Caesar. The work simply flowed along, no command, no shouting, no talking, but everybody knew exactly what he had to do. The captain and Schirrmeyer had in the meantime pegged out the new position for Dora. The carts were being loaded, one by the boys and one by gunners. Around midnight the captain came over: "I think that's enough now, lads, we must think of your school tomorrow, off you go and good night!" "Good night, sir." There was no protest this time but forty-five minutes later they were back at the guns anyway. "No peace for the bloody wicked!" said Hoffmann.

School was beginning to be a farce. If there were any lessons at all, the boys were so tired and consequently disinterested that the whole exercise became more and more a waste of time. Even the day off (for sleeping) lost its effectiveness. School holidays had been done away with to make up for lessons lost, but that did not make any difference; living at the battery, holidays did not exist anyway.

Returning from Vegesack the next day, the work, as much as the battery could do, was completed. The place was deserted, the men had been given a few extra hours of sleep. All the soil had been shifted but the shuttering had to be left to the pioneers as there was no more timber. Since it would take two or three weeks for the new gun to arrive, that did not matter a lot. Schirrmeyer had been waiting for them: "Don't get changed, there will be a short church service at Dora's graveside in twenty minutes, wear your helmets. The Divisional padre is coming out from Lesum." The Russians were there as well and apparently they had asked for permission to sing, opening the service with a hymn (presumably) which sounded truly wonderful. Afterward it took the padre a few minutes to collect himself, he had tears in his eyes. The former crater was now a round low hill, turfed over, three young birch trees had been planted on top. Somehow the carpenter had found the time to make two crosses, a "nonnal" one and the other "orthodox," with two cross-pieces, for the Russians.

Quite late the same evening a runner came to fetch Fischer to the captain. "Sit down, I wanted a chat with you. You realize I have no crew when the new gun arrives, apart from the Hiwis, plenty of those. For the gun-layers I could use the ones taking your places when you're on weekend leave, which means you won't be able to go at all. I don't want to do that, you need the break. In the short term it looks like this: no sergeant, no loader, no No. 2, no No. 6, Drieling is doing No. l, isn't he? Now, you will be acting sergeant until division finds another NCO, can you do it?" "Thank you, sir, of course I can do it, only"... "Only what?" "I might have men under me three times my age." "Do you have a problem with that?" "I'm sure I will not, but they might." "We can disregard that!" "Jakobsen would make a good loader, he is very strong."

"Question is, how long will his leg take to heal, well, we'll work something out, no doubt you will come up with one of your suggestions!" Fischer had to grin: "I have one right now, sir. It is a bit far fetched, but in the year below us at school are a few big chaps and I know for certain they can't wait to be called up to take our places when we have to leave you. Officially they are too young by one year, but if three or four were to volunteer out of patriotism? I just don't know whom they would have to convince!" "I don't either, but it's worth following up, so give me three names and addresses tomorrow." The next morning Fischer took one of the boys aside and put him in the picture. "You can tell the other two but otherwise keep your mouth shut or it might come to nothing. In the next break, give me your names and addresses." The captain must have done something very effective with the list, as three days later the boy, his name was Bauer, run up to Fischer waving a letter: "We've been called up!" he shouted, "Have to report on Monday." They were put into the care of Sergeant Hoffmann, who had one week to turn them into something useful, as he put it. The pioneers had been and gone, one side of the enclosure was still open from pushing the new gun in, minus the barrel. That was planned, because the old one, being undamaged, was to be changed over. One straight from the factory would have shown a better, higher muzzle-velocity compared with the other three "used" ones, and the reckoner would have been unable to compute the discrepancy.

Jacky Jakobsen came back; he still had to use a crutch and had to be lifted on to the loader's platform. Once up there, he would be all right, or so he reckoned. The carpenter had made him a wooden ledge for the top of the platform-railing, so he could perch on it when not actually shooting. He called it his Miseri Cordia.

In the evening Fischer walked over to Dora for a final check. He thought, "This is really crazy, I'm barely seventeen, I'm in charge of this big gun here, eight men obey my orders, I'm expected to kill as many of the others as possible and I've got the wind up because we write a math paper tomorrow!" The early evening alarm caught him still at the gun and the crew came galloping in. The two new ones were obviously jittery, like they had been two years ago and, just like two years ago, Fischer had to shout "No. 6, temperature!" and just like Behrends had done then, Bauer said "Oh, shit!" Now Jacky arrived, two Russians carried him on crossed arms. However, the bombers must have changed course, and the alarm came to nothing.

When they reported back from school the next day, the SM was waiting for them. "Inspection this afternoon, the general himself is coming. Spruce yourselves up and not one thing out of place in the hut! Behrends, when you've eaten, have your hair cut, you're a disgrace to the battery!" The general arrived with a surprisingly small entourage, only his adjutant and Colonel Benz. From the parade ground the men piled into the mess, the general probably had orders to deliver a heartwarming and encouraging speech and, by God, the situation warranted it! However, the alarm-bell shrilled and everybody, including the general most likely, breathed a sigh of relief. The mess hall emptied in seconds.

From his elevated position Jacky could see over the earth-wall and he said in a low voice: "They're coming our way!" "Helmets on!" Fischer hissed, "and you two new ones, if you screw this up, you'll wish you hadn't been born. Concentrate on your lamps, never mind what's going on! Bauer, chalk, whistle?" He held them up. Did one rapport in a situation like this? Probably better. "Gun Dora, Acting Sergeant Senior Auxiliary Fischer, two senior auxiliaries, two auxiliaries, four Hiwis, awaiting laying datas, general, sir!" The general saluted and turned to the CO. "Really, captain, did you have to go that far?" "I'm afraid so, sir, the general might remember the entire previous crew was killed three weeks ago." Through the wire came: "Guns to 9, CO to CP." "You go, captain, I want to see this." "Hallo, Fischer," Colonel Benz grinned, "we are getting on in the world, aren't we?" "Do you know this boy, Benz?" "I do general, I will tell you about him later."

The lights started to flicker and the gun came alive, "No! covered!" Drieling barked, the new one squeaked "No. 2 covered!" His nerves stopped him from calling out naturally. "No. 6 blank!" The target was too far away. The general was a chain smoker and the Russians looked at the cigarettes with hungry eyes. It spoke for him that he did not throw the ends on the ground but flicked then over the wall "No. 6 signals and covered!" shrieked Bauer, his voice also unsteady. "Dora covered!" Fischer reported to the CP. "Just like in the manual" he thought. They fired about thirty uneventful rounds, complete with whistle blowing. "I will go now," said the general, "Well done, boys, but do tell me, sergeant, why is this man wearing house slippers?" He pointed to Jakobsen. "He has been wounded in the legs three weeks ago and he can't wear anything else yet, general, sir!" "Ah, good man, good man." And he went across to Jacky to shake his oily paw. Then he said something lengthy in Russian and stuffed two packs of cigarettes down the jacket of the nearest Hiwi. They came out in a chorus: "Spasibo, Gospodin General!" "Well trained, sergeant, well trained," and he smiled. Colonel Benz winked at Fischer as they left.

CHAPTER 5

Called Up

Three months passed before a new sergeant could be found to command Dora, and Fischer returned to his former place at Berta. Sergeant Hoffmann had changed; he was much quieter and his monologues were shorter. He was no doubt worrying about his family in East Prussia, with the Russians drawing nearer by the day. The bombing raids had slackened off a bit which meant more sleep, but the low-level attacks increased. They were much more unnerving, the planes came out of the blue and the battery was more or less helpless. The pom-poms, which had been increased to three, took the brunt of it. They were constantly manned and actually quite successful, but also had to take some losses. It cost Hauenschild, who was the next one up in size from Köhler, his left foot.

On the next weekend leave, Fischer's father asked to join him hunting, as there was a certain roe buck he had been after for a long time. Father had his rifle and Fischer took a shotgun, which was actually against the law, as gun licenses could only be issued from twenty-one upward. What a farce in the circumstances! They sat on the high-stand, father produced a bottle of Jägermeister and said: "Now tell me what it's really like. I know you've been keeping the grimmer side from us because of mother and I'm glad you did, but I can take it." It was good to talk openly to him, not having to watch every word for fear of mother starting to cry. He listened for an hour and then pulled a brown envelope from his pocket. "This came for you last week, I suppose you are being called up? I kept it out of sight, when do you have to go?" It was in six weeks, and father said: "We should keep that under wrap until about a fortnight before, don't you think? Where do you have to report?" It was Delmenhorst, the garrison from which Fischer's brother had set out in '39 and never returned to, on the surface probably not a very good omen.

It was then that the buck appeared, with only just enough light left. Father nudged him and handed him his gun, Fischer was stunned, what a gesture! He thought, "If I mess this up I'll never forgive myself!" He did not, though, and the buck fell where it stood. Father put his arms round him and held him for a long time, he was saying goodbye to him, there and then. The bottle was still half full, fortunately.

After Fischer had come back with the news, everybody popped home after school the next day to check if they had one of those ominous letters.

They all did, apart from Gräpel, who was just outside the birthday deadline, in any case, his leg was still in plaster. Jacky would send his letter back, his leg was not doing well at all and he would probably have to go back for another operation. The loading had probably been responsible. The chief was very worried because, if he was hospitalized, the loader position at Dora would be vacant once again. When comparing notes it became apparent that they all had to go different ways. Two were heading for the Navy, three for the Air Force, where immediately the question arose how they would fly without petrol. The shortage had become so severe that one hardly saw a fighter plane anymore. The rest were destined for Infantry units around Bremen and Hamburg.

Horn had an idea: "How about a farewell dinner and we invite the captain, the SM and Schirrmeyer?" That was a great thought, but what was there to offer to them? Drieling came to the rescue: "Leave it with me, perhaps I can work something out with my old man." No questions were asked, because what they were going to do was very, very illegal and, if found out, prison was the only sentence for "black slaughtering." The three men accepted happily, if somewhat surprised. The sergeant major put it in his own words: "Nobody can guess what you will bloody come up with next!" The invitation was for a Sunday at lunchtime. The middle of the day was the safest for air raids, and it gave them time for preparations.

Drieling was in charge. He sent three to pick mushrooms, two were peeling potatoes ("peel them, don't carve them!"), one was seeing to the heater, which also served as a cooker, turning the room into a sauna (it was June). Now Drieling dragged an old suitcase in, which he had picked up at home on Saturday after school. In it was the whole roasted back of a pig! His mother had baked it in an old bread oven, which was still standing on the farm. He had been very worried on the Weser-ferry, where a large dog got interested in the case and would not leave it alone. Obviously, the meat would have to be eaten cold, but he had also brought a big jar of gravy, to be heated up. The cook had to surrender a pan again, plus a carving knife, having been promised a piece of the roast. Gräpel had raided the restaurant cellar once more and produced four bottles of wine (Zeller Schwarze Katz) and glasses.

The captain was the first to arrive and he waved Fischer's "Tenshun" away before he could say it. He had brought a bottle of French brandy and he ordered everyone to have a drink now. "I know it is wrong, we should have it afterwards, but they might disturb us and we have to drink to your health and safe return now." When they had put their cups down (some were coughing), he continued: "I have been debating with myself whether you should drink this at all, but then it came to me that very shortly you will be ordered to kill as many of the others as you can. That, I said to myself, must surely be evidence enough for them being grown-ups. Am I not right, sergeant major?" Fischer thought, "I bet you would like to say 'no, you are bloody not!'" but he meekly answered, "I suppose so, sir, it is only that we have brought them up, and they have grown up and now they come and take them away and send them all over the place and who knows what's going to happen to them?" He was really upset. "Now, Müller," said the chief, "we must not get sentimental, there is nothing we can do but wishing them God's speed. Now what about this food you promised?"

There was quite a long silence after they started to eat; it was absolutely delicious. The captain raised his glass again: "I think we should drink to this pig which has given his life for Greater Germany! May I enquire to whom we owe this great pleasure?" Silence. "I thought not. But will you give the cook my compliments, I have never eaten anything remotely as good as this."

The three men left together, but the SM came back and stuck his head through the open window: "I see there is still some wine left, I don't want you falling about the guns tonight, or go to sleep on your seats, just take it easy!" There were only two good portions of meat left, one was the bribe for the cook, the other was for Ivan. When he came later on to bring the water, Fischer said, "Not enough for comrades, you eat here!" Drieling had left quite a bit of meat on the bones; he would take that and make a soup.

Over dinner, it had come home to them that they had to leave this group of men, who had been their family during the last two years. It was quite right what the sergeant major had said, they had grown up here, in a framework of discipline, strict but never harsh, but when other lives depended on it, it was to be expected. They had always been shown a lot of understanding for their problems and had helped whenever possible. "But," said Horn, "I think we did our damnedest not to let them down, don't you think?" Everyone agreed and they felt a lot better.

The last weeks passed quickly. The raids had picked up again; the Americans came in the daytime, the Airforce at night. For targets in the east like Berlin and Leipzig they were now using a route slightly more to the south, as probably the defenses were less concentrated there and the battery did not actually fire very often, the targets being out of range. Only planes erring from the formation, and that was quite common, were picked up and mostly brought down. This happened usually during the night, when the Lancasters could not enjoy the visual contact with the group like the Yanks. One day Bremen was attacked, two days later Bremerhaven.

Over the last weeks the boys had to find some civilian clothes at home, as the uniforms had, of course, to be left at the quartermasters. It was hard going because a lot of growing had been going on between fifteen and seventeen. Shirts were very tight across the shoulders and the shorts appeared to be even shorter. May and June had brought very hot weather and, as the gun crews always stripped down to the waist, they were all the color of red Indians. The legs, having been covered by trousers, had stayed white, an odd sight. Their relief had arrived, a pathetic looking bunch ("Christ, they have to do some growing up!" said Jacky), but that impression might have been created by their own feeling of superiority.

"Permission to say goodbye to the captain, sir!" He put his tunic on! He did not make a speech but walked down the line shaking hands with each of them, having chatted to them first. It was amazing what individual details he knew about everyone. In the end he said: "I hate to see you go. When all this is over and you happen to come to Verden, I order you now to call on me, I'm a lawyer there. Good luck and take care of yourselves!" Before he disappeared into his hut he saluted. Fischer called out "Tenshun!" and that was that. They marched down to the battery office to say their goodbyes to the sergeant major, who was even less at ease than the chief. How could such a gruff man, soldier through and through, be so emotional? "You were a completely crazy bunch and it'll be quiet here without you, now take care of yourselves and remember what the captain said about dead heroes!" Then he shook hands with them (he had a handshake like a vice). Schirrmeyer had come to their hut the previous evening with a bottle of Korn ("That is now allowed, according to the captain"). They talked for hours, but not a word fell about the war. Ivan had been given his farewell present, a penknife, which left him speechless.

They left the battery to a lot of waves and shouts. When they split up for their homes, Horn said: "You know, not one of them urged us to perform great heroic things to save Germany; all they seem to want us to do was to save our skins. Shall we see what we can do about that? Let's shake on it!"

CHAPTER 6

Delmenhorst

The barracks in Delmenhorst were typical of those built in the 1930s, white three-story blocks housing one company each. The whole complex was big enough for one regiment, the 65th Regiment of the 22nd Division, which had, at the beginning of the war, started out as airborne, but had long since been reduced to a normal foot-slogging infantry division. They had suffered appalling losses in Russia, particularly in the Crimean campaign. Fischer vaguely remembered the scenery; between 1937 and 1939 his brother had done his national service here and he had visited him there a few times. The change in atmosphere between then and now could be strongly felt; it was very grim now! Fischer had hoped he would meet up with some old AA mates but there was not one familiar face in sight. Uniforms and equipment were thrown at them. They were divided into companies, platoons, and squads according to the alphabet; consequently Fischer found himself in A Company, First Battalion. The company CO was a one-armed captain; the sergeant major, unbelievably, wore an eye patch and limped, it was simply uncanny! An elderly feldwebel commanded the platoon, in charge of Fischer's squad was Sergeant Wiegert who had a dreadfully disfigured lower face; burned by the look of it. He had no lips left and a steady dribble of saliva came from the corners of his mouth. However, it took only a couple of days for the boys to realize what a caring and wise person he was and they worshipped him.

Next morning the captain addressed them and informed them that there would be no drill: "With your past you must be able to march in step. It is far more important to teach you survival. We, your instructors, command a lot of experience and we shall do our best to pass that on to you. We have two months to do it in, that must suffice. We shall start with ten kilometers night march today, fifteen tomorrow, until you reach forty. Assault pack and water bottle only, so as to break you in. In a week we shall repeat the whole thing with full equipment." The assault pack was a small backpack, just big enough for ground sheet, spare underwear and socks, field dressings, and personal bits and pieces. It clipped on to a leather harness that, back and front, ended in hooks into which the belt fitted. As a lot was carried on that, pouch for rations, water bottle, sixty rounds, bayonet, gas mask, spade, and hand grenades, the weight was thus transferred to the shoulders.

Next came the shooting range. They had been issued with brand new rifles, which meant the sights had to be calibrated. Two armorers joined the company to adjust them if necessary. Twenty-five rounds (steel cartridges) each was considered sufficient and that took all day. No lunch was served ("you can't rely on getting your meals on time in the frontline!"). With aching shoulders from the recoil they marched then back to the barracks and cleaned the rifles. An inspection, taken by the SM himself, followed and Fischer's rifle was not clean enough! There was indeed a tiny speck of something in the barrel, but the SM, in typical NCO speak, made this out to be a major act of sabotage and Fischer could consider himself lucky not to be court marshalled. This was all part of the game and nobody worried about these outbursts, after all, the rifle had not been entirely clean. When the SM entered Fischer's name in his notebook (the Bible as it was called), for the next round of toilet cleaning or potato peeling, he hesitated and asked: "Did you have a brother called Hans? Killed in '40?" "Yes, sir." "Stay behind at the end of the parade!" It turned out that the captain, the SM, and Fischer's brother had been very close friends. "The CO will be very interested and perhaps we can put something your way, you will of course keep your mouth shut!" As he was talking, he crossed "Fischer" out in the Bible.

Digging foxholes was the next attraction in the program. A piece of waste land had been set aside for that purpose, where hundreds or thousands of them must have been sunk over the years. Machine gun pits were next and, to round the day off, the march at night. The soreness wore off slowly; ill-fitting boots had been exchanged and they actually almost fit. They had been introduced to another time-honored piece of equipment in the German army: Fusslappen, "footrags," a square of thick toweling the size of a large handkerchief. The foot was placed on it diagonally and the four corners were then wrapped around the ankle. Even after long marches they never moved, important as far as blisters were concerned, and they were easily washed and dried.

For the next three weeks it was marching and digging, digging and marching. After that it became somewhat easier, rifle and machinegun practice banned them to the rifle range for days. Next came basic training in explosives, mine laying, and the Panzerfaust, a type of bazooka, very effective and light, a real one-man tank destroyer. They practiced on old safes, brought out from Bremen's bombed offices. Fischer had taken a liking to the machine gun, not as a killing machine, but because it was such a clever piece of weaponry, way ahead of its time and not affected by frost or mud. The basic difference was that, when the shot broke, the bolt was arrested by two small steel rollers flicking out of its side and locking in the breech. In all other repeaters this was achieved by turning the bolt about a quarter quadrant, screwing it down so to speak, and of course "unscrewing" it after the shot. Consequently, the MG 42 as it was called, had a much higher rate of fire, in theory 1,400 rounds a minute, which was the reason for its only drawback: high ammunition consumption. The secret was to loosen short bursts only: firstly, continuous fire would burn out the barrel in no time; secondly, the recoil threw the gun off the target and it had to be re-sighted after every burst. This did not matter as each burst sent twenty or thirty bullets on the way and, as Sergeant Wiegert put it: "Quite sufficient, you can't shoot anybody deader than dead."

Tactical training started next: attack, defense, retreat, counterattack, and the old command was practiced endlessly: "Alles hört auf mein Kommando!" "All obey my orders!" If the one in command had been killed and no natural successor was available, anybody of any rank who felt he was able to take over could shout these words and that put him immediately in charge above all other ranks. There was no arguing and this state lasted until the situation had been resolved. After four weeks of this, about 20 percent of the company was separated from the rest, destined for further officer training. They moved out of their present quarters to another block. Strategic lectures became the main subject.

Fischer had struck up a friendship with Brink, who came from Nienburg where his father had a brick mill. He was the type who, a couple of hundred years ago, would have been a pirate, better still, a buccaneer. He was daring, jolly, and very strong, which became apparent during a training exercise where a machine gun had to be thrown up from a foxhole firing it the second it touched the ground. Doing this two or three times was the limit for anybody but Brink could do it, well, they never found out how often. "Christ, Bert," Fischer said to him, "how come you're so strong, that's not normal?" "You would be just as strong if your father would have made you shift bricks from the day you could walk. He believes in learning the trade right from the bottom upward, bless him." The bricks had cost him his right fore finger, which had been broken several times and was useless. He had to pull the trigger with his middle finger, which looked very odd. They were both hoping they could stay together in the months to come; it would make things a lot easier.

The two months were drawing to a close. One evening a runner came from the captain for Fischer to report to him. He was very casual, and all he wanted to talk about was Fischer's brother, as they must have been very close. But then he said: "You will keep under your hat what I'm telling you now, it will be made official in a couple of days. Your further training will take place in Denmark and your group will be promoted to corporal first. I don't know how long that training period will be, but at the end of it I shall try to get you back here as auxiliary instructor. We shall have to see if that works out; you will either be ordered to return here or you will hear nothing."

Fischer wondered if the reason were his soldierly qualities (doubtful) or if the captain trying to keep him safe and sound in Delmenhorst until the war ended. It was a very kind thought, and Fischer's parents would certainly appreciate it. "Before you go to your quarters, see the Sergeant Major, he has something to say to you. From my heart, I wish you good luck!"

"There is not an awful lot I can do for you," said the SM, "but I will see that you leave here in a decent uniform. Tomorrow you will return from field training with your old togs in tatters, but don't overdo it! Have you a mate for whom you would like me to do the same, someone you can trust? It won't look then as if you get preferential treatment." "Grenadier Brink, sir." "Right, go and see the quartermaster when you come back, I will put him in the picture. He knew Hans as well, you know." Fischer took Brink to one side and told him the whole story. "I always knew you would be good for me," said Brink. They made a nice mess of their uniforms on barbed wire and Sergeant Wiegert said, "God, won't the quartermaster just love you!" Feldwebel Klein (that was the QM, one ear, one eye, strong limp) locked them into the store for an hour, having given them a free hand. The envy of the others was understandable.

The last day in Delmenhorst and the last parade came along. The captain gave a little speech, nothing rousing, the main accent being "on his last order to them to make good use of what they had learned, it would help them stay alive because a dead hero is of no use to the army!"' Now, where had Fischer heard that before? The CO had somehow managed to arrange a week's leave for them and after seven days they were to meet again at Bremen Central station to catch, at 10:00 p.m., a train to Hamburg. There they would change for one to Flensburg which, "as you know. is just south of the Danish border. You destination is Kliplev, some twenty kilometers into Denmark. Report there to the town commander who will send you on to a place called Sjoegaard. I could not find it on any map, it must be very small. Fischer will be in command, pick up the travel order for all of you at the office, the SM has your leave-passes here." "Shit," Fischer thought, "after two years at the battery, haven't I deserved a break?" The captain walked down the line and shook thirty hands; the SM limped behind and did the same. Sergeant Wigert looked close to tears. The last act was to return the bedlinen to the QM store and that was the end of Delmenhorst.

CHAPTER 7

Interlude at the Battery

The two months basic infantry training in Delmenhorst was over. Fifteen percent had been considered suitable for further officer schooling, which was to take place in Denmark. Fischer was among them, which was good news for two reasons: Denmark was still the land of milk and honey, air-raid free, and, secondly, the other 85 percent were shipped off to frontline units at once. Much to their surprise the Denmark group was promoted corporal; they were also allowed to wear a thin red cord across the epaulette to show they were future officers-to-be (perhaps). The arrangements in Denmark were apparently not complete and the regiment had the wonderful idea to send them home for eight days, which was their first and last leave. It was great to be home again for longer than the usual weekend break from the AA, the first time in almost two years. But after two days Fischer became restless and he decided he would go and see how things were shaping up at Habichthorst.

"Corporal Fischer requesting permission to enter the battery, sir." The sergeant major was speechless for a while. "Hell, Fischer," he said then, "you were always good for a surprise but this takes the cake, and being corporal and all! That's a pretty smart uniform you're wearing, one would not think we are in the fifth year of the war. How did you wangle that again?" "I found I had some old family connections in the regiment. But how are things here, sir?" "Well, we are still trying to win the war, what do you think?" "And how are the new ones making out?" The SM hesitated, "It's like this: we can't fault them where their work is concerned, they took a bit longer about it but then they were younger than you. So we have no worries on that score." "But" he blurted out, "they are so bloody boring! You lot you were all crazy, every one of you: Horn with his awful violin, or Drieling with his eternal cooking, or Hahn making up the Latin proverbs all the time and how proud Jakobsen was that he was the only one who had to shave. And Hauenschild with his forever leaking fish tank and having dancing lessons in your socks! As for you, we need not go into that! But we got used to you, I don't mind telling you, what was it, year and a half? That's a hell of a long span in a soldiers life." He suddenly looked embarrassed but at this very moment the alarm bell shrilled. "It's been going night and day lately, no let up. I say, have you some time to spare? Your old Sargent is in a fix, he has no loader, Bartsch is in hospital, could you help out?"

"I hear you need a loader, sarge?" Hoffmann of the long monologues was lost for words, his mouth opened but he could only point to the loader's platform. Then he reported over the micro: "Berta combat ready." They had a loudspeaker now backing up the sergeant's earphone and the captain's voice came back: "Who is loading for you, Hoffmann?" "Fischer, sir." "Which Fischer would that be?" "Our old Fischer, sir." Silence, then the speaker crackled: "I would like to see him in my hut when this is over!"

"Target in 7!" Fischer jumped onto the loader's place, tore off his tunic and threw it to Ivan, who caught it with a huge grin on his moon face. He folded it neatly and put it carefully down on top of the ammunition store. The new ones stared, Fischer did not know any of them. They came from a school in Bremen and, by God, they did look weedy! It turned out to be one of those "fly pasts" to the south, probably bound for Berlin. They flew just within the maximum range and a lot of explosions stood between the planes, four or five batteries were probably shooting. The 12.8 centimeter at Grosse Dunge fired across their heads with very low elevation, their shells screaming across the battery, and at every salvo the new ones pulled their heads in. It always seemed a miracle that any planes got through these barrages at all, but the Fortress was known to be able to absorb a lot of punishment. If no vital parts were hit like the fuel tanks (and they were all self-sealing) or the control lines to the tail or the pilot himself, they flew on and on. All the same, about eight or ten came down, out of perhaps 600, what sort of ratio was that? The feeling of confronting an overwhelming majority was depressing.

The firing lasted well over an hour and Fischer's arms were falling off but Berta did not miss one round. "You better have a wash before you see the chief," said Hoffmann, "you'll find soap and towel in my room. Have you noticed, we have a new explosive? It's more powerful and puts another 20 meters on the muzzle-speed, but it gives off a lot more smoke, you are absolutely black. And thanks for standing in, we are knee deep in the shit at the moment!" Fischer promised to say goodbye on the way back from the captain.

The CO was in his favorite uniform: braces. Fischer saluted but the captain held his hand out. "Good to see you, corporal, and thank you for helping out." There were the "military manners" again, no more "Fischer" or "lad," it was "corporal" now. "You know you should not salute me like that, don't you?" "I'm sorry, sir, matter of habit." Which was a lie and, what's more, the captain knew it was. A few weeks ago, there had been this attempt on Hitler's life and Göring had decreed that the forces must give up their old salute for this ridiculous party salute, which was uniformly despised. Something important had been taken away from the soldiers and they hated it! The idea was that the troops documented their loyalty to Hitler, but it had completely misfired and they tried to avoid saluting altogether. One could do that if one carried something in the right hand, one simply straightened up and looked at the person to be saluted. That was an old procedure and now the whole army walked about carrying something. It was ludicrous but nobody could be faulted.

The captain wanted to know how Fischer made corporal so quickly. "I really can't answer that, sir, they told us we would be trained for a special task in Denmark, and that we would need some authority as we would be operating on our own. That is all I know but it sounded like a right ascension job to us." "I should not worry about that if I was you, it is always better to be alone or in a very small group. You can make your own judgment and decisions and you like that, I know you well enough. One thought I like you to take back with you is that we all enjoyed having you here, it was like breath of fresh air. The rest of the battery, well, half of them should not be in uniform at all and they all worry about their families day and night. They all do their duty well enough but you brought something else in to it. Thank you!"

Fischer took a deep breath: "I would like to thank the captain as well and I am speaking for all of us because we talked so often about it. I can honestly say that none of us missed home a lot, the conveniences perhaps, but that was easily made up for by the knowledge that we were doing something useful and we were treated as soldiers and not the young boys we really were. We always appreciated what you did for us, sir, and the sergeant major and the wachtmeister, we shall never forget the years here, serving under you; Sir!" Fischer was sweating profusely now. The captain just looked at him and said: "Oh, thank you, corporal."

"Permission to ask the captain a difficult question? How will it go on from here? In the west, the Allies are pushing across France and the Russians are getting ever closer. Their resources must be unbelievable, it hit me when I saw these hundreds of planes today and they could not care less if we shoot down twenty or two hundred. I had seen it all before but then they were just a target, somehow today was different." "Fischer," said the CO somberly, "don't you ever speak to anybody about this, you know that would be high treason, don't you? I appreciate your trusting me and I would of course deny that this conversation has ever taken place, for God's sake, you are risking your life! Since when have you had your doubts?" "We all had them, sir, ever since America entered the war, the parallel to the last war was there for everybody to see!" "I have no idea what sort of answer you expect of me, I can only say we are soldiers and we obey orders, in the meantime inflicting as much damage on the enemy as we can." That was that by the sound of it, but what else could the captain say? Fischer felt awful having put him into this position, there was no answer to his question anyway. The rest was well-wishing, cap on, salute? (old but what the hell!), at the end of the path connecting the hut to the sleeper track Fischer stopped, turned, and saluted again, hoping the captain would feel the affection he felt for him.

At Berta, the new ones were still cleaning the barrel, which was quite hard work but Hoffmann said grimly: "I let them do it instead of the Ivans, it might toughen then up a bit! So what have they planned for you now?" Fischer told him about Denmark and the mystery training, and the Sargent reckoned he should hang on there as long as he possibly could, "Every week out of trouble counts now!" They had walked out of the gun position. "Sarge," said Fischer, "I must ask you something, hope you don't mind. Your family in East Prussia, you must be worried about them? The shitty way things are going?" "Good of you to ask, but the wife has a sister in Bavaria and I insisted a while ago that she and the kids go and visit her as long as it takes. I suppose we shall never see the old place again but thanks for asking, much appreciated." He pumped Fischer's hand hard: "Now you take care, never mind any heroics, they won't get us out of this mess!" They said goodbye and when Fischer had walked a few steps, Hoffmann called: "Rolf!" (he actually said Rolf), "Keep your head down!" Fischer grinned and waved.

The SM's advice was along the same lines; he had no illusions either. "I will remember it, sir, and thank you again for all the things you did for us, it was great serving under you." Old salute, also from the SM.

Fischer had cycled quite a distance when he stopped to have a last look at the battery. The barrels were turning again to about 4 or 5, southeast, so the bombers were returning. Judging from the time elapsed, they had been to Berlin. Or Leipzig perhaps. The SM was still standing there, waving his stick. Fischer waved back.

CHAPTER 8
Denmark

Fischer had not been on a train for two years, what a change! Most windows had been replaced with plywood, the inside (and outside) was tatty to the extreme and the lights did not work. The most disturbing thing was the neat row of bullet-holes in the ceiling, evidence of a fighter attack. At least they would be safe from them, traveling at night. The way the carriage smelled, it must have been a troop train, it was this mixture of sweat, leather, dubbing, and gun oil. When they finally rolled, the car was swaying from side to side on clapped-out axles and rails. They passed through a part of Bremen that had been completely flattened, only the odd church spire was left standing. A former AA auxiliary from Grosse Dunge was in the group. "We didn't do our job awfully well, did we?" he said to Fischer, "How many did you bring down?" "38." "That's not bad, we had 41 but, of course, 15 cms guns." "Don't I know it, one of your shell bottoms came down on a Hiwi of my gun." "I'm sorry, was he dead?" "You joker!" "But all their losses did not make the slightest bloody difference, did they?"

There was a break of an hour in Hamburg (looking even worse than Bremen), they used the opportunity to fetch the rations. Food was still plentiful, but the quality had dropped. The bread was good, it never changed, only the flour on the outside had been substituted by sawdust. Connoisseurs claimed they could taste whether it was pine, oak, or beech. The standard sausage was called "rubber-sausage," of vivid pink, no taste, and if dropped it jumped up as if indeed made from rubber. Nobody wanted to know what it contained! The next delicacy was a cheese, packed in portions the size of a small cucumber; it tasted good but the smell was excruciating, hence it was dubbed "body-fingers." A sort of artificial honey was not bad. The worst thing was without doubt the margarine.

They had slept all the way to Flensburg, where the train arrived at first light. Fischer went to the MP presenting the marching order and enquired after the best route out of town. It was an elderly grumpy lieutenant who said, "The country is crying out for soldiers and you're going on a holiday in Denmark!" "An order is an order, sir," and he thought that directing the traffic at a railway station was not so heroic either, you stupid bugger! On the way to the border they passed through a hamlet of farms and split up to forage for eggs or whatever was going. They had money but, more importantly, cigarettes since none of them smoked. It worked beautifully, eggs, some bacon, the odd piece of sausage, and everybody had a water bottle full of milk. Fischer thought an hour for breakfast would go unnoticed, and a fire was lit out of sight from the road.

No wonder Sjoegaard was on no map, being just a compound of barracks, huts rather, compliment the Danish army, beautifully situated by a small lake. It looked deserted but then a lieutenant appeared out of the blue. When Fischer reported he said, "I expected you earlier, corporal!" "We took a wrong tum, sir, we had no map." Clearly he did not believe that but he kept quiet. "Put your things away first in the hut over there and then report to me in that one in thirty minutes. Dismissed!" They had a quick wash, and a few needed to shave.

Lieutenant Wagner looked in his late twenties, highly decorated, all fingers of his left hand were missing, and he had a glass eye. "Men," he said, "you are here on a very special mission. I believe you all had intensive machine gun training and I shall continue this, turning you in to gunners shooting with night-sights. This will be the first unit of its kind in the German army, or any other army for that matter. I said that I would train you, take that literally, there is no one else here apart from a small kitchen staff. This is all hush-hush and you are not to leave the compound. While I think of it: should you later on have the misfortune of becoming prisoner, your equipment must not fall into enemy's hands, so make sure that you'll smash the sights! This afternoon the guns will come from the depot in Kliplev, brand new, so we shall have to calibrate the sights. There is a shooting range at the north end of the compound. Hopefully, the actual night-sight will arrive in the morning, they have been delayed. We must get to know each other because, when we have finished here, I shall go with you and lead this unit. Any questions?" Nothing, one could have heard a pin drop! "Come on," said Wagner, "you don't look that bashful! Here, that big chap, Fischer?" "Yes, sir. Can you tell us why we were picked for this unit?" "I can't. Perhaps because you all have handled guns in the night for a long time, you must find your way in the dark. And you certainly passed some psychological test, which you probably did not realize. Anybody else?" Nothing, they were still shocked. "Right, Fischer you're in command today, next man in the alphabet tomorrow, and so on. Lunch is at twelve, sniff the kitchen out yourself."

Lunch was great, vegetable soup, but it had been cooked in Denmark! The meat in it was unbelievable; they had not seen that for years. And there was as much as they wanted! Wagner was eating with them, as he would for the rest of the time here. "After lunch give your rifles an extra good clean and oil them generously inside and out. You will not need them anymore, the lorry bringing the guns will take them back to the depot. You will carry machine pistols instead. The rest of the day you will spend de-greasing the machineguns, a really nasty job; you'll find plenty of rags in the little hut by the lake. Take your time over it, it is very important that you get all the factory grease off them and, more importantly, out of them, otherwise the gun might jam when it's getting hot." He was leaving and somebody shouted: "Tenshun!" "Look here, lads, we leave that for the moment, I know you know all about drill but let's just concentrate on our job. There is much to learn and I have no idea how long they will give us. One more thing: we will be issued fifteen guns, you know each other well, don't you? Pick a mate you would like to be with and the two will share a gun, more about that later."

"You know," said Schulze, "I would do anything for that man." "You will probably have to!" said Brink.

They found some trestle tables, stripped to the waist, and set to work degreasing the guns. The lieutenant sat with each "pair" to get to know them. He explained how they would work: each gun crew would operate independently, and they would later be joined by a No. 3 and a radioman. "We shall respond to calls for help from frontline units, but only if nighttime action would benefit them. They have their own machine gunners, you and your equipment are far too valuable to be burned up in every day fighting. On the spot, you will follow the wishes of the local commander as to the help he needs, but the final decisions, firing positions and such, are yours only. You will carry a divisional order in writing, stating what I'm telling you, which you can flash at anybody trying to talk you down. It will also protect you from MPs stopping you, funneling you into some alarm-unit or, worse still, thinking you are deserters. There is always that danger as you will be moving behind the front on the way to a new job. You are responsible to me and division only, you are not part of an attacking, defending, or retreating unit, you are only supporting them when it's dark or foggy, get the picture? I'm sure they will appreciate that much more. You will get your orders from me, I shall be at the central transmitter twenty-four hours and you can get me any time. We must not be further apart then, say, 25 kilometers, because of the radio link. Well, Brand, why are you sitting there with your mouth open?" "With permission, sir, each lecture from you is a bigger surprise than the last one." "Good, that'll keep you on your toes!"

The next morning was spent at the shooting range. Considering the guns being new, only four sights had to be adjusted. Everyone had to loosen a few bursts and the results were good enough for Wagner to be pleased.

Machine pistols and pistols did not take up much time either, the latter was for the No. 1, the MP for the No. 2. Both their positions were interchangeable and "I suggest you do that daily, No. 1 today is No. 2 tomorrow. Using the sights a long time is tiring for the eyes and you must have a night 'off' so to speak. As the No. 1 is in command, you can also spread your responsibility. All we want now are the bloody sights!" A big worry for Wagner was the night practice. "After all, we are not in Germany and anybody hearing us might put 2 and 2 together. After dark you dissemble and re-assemble the guns five times, without lights of course!"

"Bert," Fischer said to Brink, "do you remember the pile of hut-parts in the far corner of the compound? Do you think they would be big enough to go across the lanes in the rifle range?" After the weapon inspection, they walked across to measure and found them just wide enough. As before, Wagner sat among them during the meal and Fischer asked, "Permission to make a suggestion, sir. The old hut-walls near the compound-edge would cover three lanes of the rifle range, we could turn them into dark tunnels." "Well, I'll be damned, I never noticed them. We'll try it when we have finished here." It worked, but it took their last ounce of strength to shift the large segments; however, they were rewarded with three pitch dark tunnels and the lieutenant was quite beside himself. "All we need are those damn sights!" he said once more. "By the way, I have some good news for us: I have confirmation that we will definitely operate in the west, not against the Russians. Hooray to that! We have become so precious that train or roads are too dangerous, we shall take to the seas. A mine-sweeping flotilla has been clearing the stretch between Leer and Esbjerg for years to keep Elbe and Weser open. It's done at night, one half steaming from Germany to Denmark and the other half doing the opposite run. That way they can hole up in the ports during the day. They will take us in two groups and we shall meet again in Leer, where my old feldwebel is making further preparations, and close your mouth, Brand!"

The sights had finally arrived. Each group received a well-padded box containing the "generator," which looked like an oversized flashlight and the actual periscope sight. Both clipped on to the gun, power was supplied from a battery and that was the drawback; it was very heavy and lasted only about six hours. There was a spare which could be re-charged in the meantime but whether the two would go round remained to be seen. The radioman would do the charging with a crude apparatus made from bicycle pedals and a generator. "Aren't they just going to love that!" said Wagner.

"We can bang away now, there is plenty of ammo, although steel cartridges, so watch your temperature! You will each carry one box of tracers, always use them sparingly so as not to give your position away. Take every tenth bullet out of the belts and replace it with one of those, and see how you feel about it when you shoot. If you think you need more guidance, make it every ninth or eighth. Important, as few tracers as possible, very important!" The sights responded to body temperature, which could of course not be imitated on the rifle range, but the lieutenant had got hold of a tin of luminous blackout paint for the target and that worked very well.

What did not work very well was the shooting, or rather, the hitting of the target. The figures were clearly visible and yet they were all way off the mark. Wagner ordered the belts to be replaced by100 percent tracers, and the success rate went up immediately. They practiced like that until every shot was on target and then reduced the tracers one by one until down to the ideal tenth. For a break, Wagner had organized a few boxes of hand grenades. "Not that you will use them much, but you never know." The German grenades had a wooden handle which made them look a little antiquated (the other side called them potato mashers), but they were superior because the handle in a way extended the arm and they could be thrown further; secondly they worked through the explosion rather than shrapnel, so they could be thrown and followed up immediately without fear of being hit by one's own shrapnel. If a larger charge was needed, six of them could be tied in a circle around a center one, and when that one was set off, it resulted in a formidable explosion, which could easily cripple a tank for instance. The break was very welcome because, as the lieutenant had warned, nearly everyone experienced trouble with the eyes, seeing spots mostly.

"Always keep your eyes open for abandoned tanks!" was the next lesson. "Ransack them for ammunition, they usually still carry brass cartridges. The belts are hanging in pouches around the inside of the turret." "Sir, why would crews abandon their tanks?" "Because they have run out of petrol, you can recognize it easily, the gun barrel is hanging down, always made me think of a dead elephant. We are running out of three things: brass for ammunition, petrol, and men. But don't let that discourage you! You will nick the ammo from somewhere. We don't need petrol because we march, and consider yourself worth ten normal soldiers!"

After lights-out the day was, as always, chewed over again. Horstmann said, "That was pretty defeatist talk, running out of petrol, brass, and men!" Now, Hostmann was a singularly unpopular chap, nobody knew actually why, but nobody could stand him. His father was rumored to be some bigshot in the party, perhaps that was it? Brink, who slept above Fischer, jumped out of his bed with a crash and turned the lights on. "Who said that?" Bert was a bit of an actor, of course he knew who it was. He walked over to Horstmann's bed: "Can't you realize the man is only preparing us for the shit we're about to be dropped in to, you dumb bugger? The lieutenant has risked his live for five years, he's a cripple, and he did not want to be invalided out, for what? To be lumbered with arseholes like you!" He was shaking with rage now. "I tell you something: if I ever hear one word against Wagner from you again, I'll turn you inside out, that's a promise!" Somebody started to slow clap and the whole room joined in, not loudly, but that made it really sinister. "And" Brink added as an afterthought, "just watch out you don't fall overboard, it's going to be a long night on a little ship, you bastard!" Horstmann was frightened out of his wits, which was not surprising, Brink was frightening!

The following week was uneventful, shooting in the morning only (to save their eyes), dismantling and cleaning the guns in the afternoon. The lads and, more importantly, the lieutenant, felt confident that the results could not be bettered. He even gave them an afternoon off to visit a cafe in Kliplev.

("Stay together, don't get into trouble, carry a pistol or MP.") Only half of them could go, the rest had to wait until the next day. They had been paid in Danish Kroners, which were all blown on cake, an unforgettable experience. Sadly there was no coffee to be had, only some sort of tea.

The same evening Hansen said: "Look, you will take me for a wimp, I've got the wind up. I am not frightened about going out, I'm frightened of not being able to do what is expected of us. We have no bloody experience, have we? What if we make fools of ourselves? Being attached to hard-boiled front-line men, what will they think? They will laugh about us, you just watch!" It turned out that the same thought bothered everybody, but Hansen was the only one who had guts to come out with it. We should talk to Wagner about it, perhaps he can put our mind at rest. Will you tell him, Rolf?" Consequently, after the morning's shooting, Fischer "requested permission to talk to you privately, sir." He listened without interrupting and said: "I was going to give you a talk tomorrow night, but I' II bring it forward. Several things I have to tell you, we'll deal with your problem then. 2000 in the mess."

"Fischer told me about your concern. Now, I cannot provide you with experience, all I could do was to train you to a standard that will see you through any situation. I know for certain that you will be very welcome on your missions. You can give them help which they could not get from anybody else, they'll be glad to have you and sorry to see you go. I want to hear no more about it and order you not to belittle yourselves. You all are experienced artillerymen, is that nothing?" It was amazing how this pep talk turned apprehension into self-confidence; there were no more problems.

"Hanke and Sturm, go across to my quarters, there's a crate of Danish beer, fetch it." When everybody had his bottle, Wagner continued: "Right, men, this is it! We are leaving on Sunday and Monday. We have to split up, as the ships are not big enough. We will drink now to success, good luck, and a long life!" The beer was strong, not like the weak imitation in Germany. He pulled out a tattered notebook. "I have drawn up a list of call signs, Brink/Fischer as the first in the alphabet will be Anton." This brought an immediate reaction from Fischer: "Permission to ask for Berta, sir." "Why is that?" "Berta was my old gun in the AA and I would think it a good omen, sir." "Yes, I can see that, Berta it is then." Two more such wishes for Dora and Frieda were also accommodated. "I spoke last night to Feldwebel Wörner who, as you know, is making preparations the other end. He will await you at the quayside and take you to your quarters. At a depot near Leer they will kit you out with reversible camouflage clothing, white inside for the winter, night glasses, and map cases. This is a sore point: maps have not materialized and you will need them like your daily bread! You will remember from the old days when paras actually jumped from planes, that they were equipped with small two-wheel handcarts for weapons and ammo. The feldwebel has found one for each crew, chiefly for radio and batteries. The signaler is in charge of it. These chaps have not yet arrived, and I hope that doesn't mean another delay. The radio equipment is complete, though."

"One thing I'm not sure about are your daily rations. On a mission, the unit you are assisting is obliged to feed you, but when you are roaming around to find the next one, you might have to live off the land. I just don't know but we'll work something out." Then he gave everyone a celluloid pouch with the divisional order. "This will protect you; you must not be re-directed by MPs or SS either, they are good at it." "May we shoot our way out of it?" Brink asked. "I'll not answer that one. I will come with the second batch. You have a free day tomorrow, get your stuff together and throw away anything not absolutely necessary. Any questions?" There were none, but they would no doubt pop up in the morning.

Only the very thick-skinned ones slept, and it was well into the small hours of the morning that the room fell silent, but as there was no waking-up call in the morning, it did not really matter. The whole group descended on Kliplev again to have a decent haircut, probably the last one for a long while.

The lorry came for them in the middle of the afternoon and, although there were only sixteen of them, it was packed to capacity: the guns, sights, batteries, and ammunition. The driver said: "Christ, are you going to tum the war around? I have never seen so much gear for just a few blokes!" The trip was uneventful, with no danger of air attacks, as they did not happen in Denmark for fear of killing Danes as well.

The ships had not arrived; they were re-fueling in another part of the port. They all had some Kroners left which were pooled; it was enough to buy three Salamis at a butcher's shop near the quay. Later in the afternoon four little ships made fast. "My God," said Fischer, "they look like fishing trawlers!" And so they were. The only thing military was a large white number painted on the bow and a pom-pom behind the wheelhouse. The afterdecks were filled with cable drums and buoys, that would be the sweeping gear. The minute the boat moored, a helmeted guard appeared over the railing. Fischer went over and called out: "Special MG-unit 22nd Division, permission to come on board?" "Permission granted, how many of you?" "Sixteen." "No way, we can only take four, go to the other boats."

The captain was a grizzled NCO; as the Navy had their own ranks, they could not make out what it was. "You can see for yourself," he said, "space on board is limited. Aft is closed for you when we are sweeping. Lines could break and whip back, throwing you overboard or cutting you in half. There is room on the foreship if it stays calm; if not, you could be swept off. That leaves the mess below, but don't you dare and be sick all over it. Take a bucket down with you! Store your gear in the starboard fish tank, also your belts and all that's hanging from it. Like this you wouldn't have a chance in hell if you fell into the drink. In that locker (what was a locker?) are life belts, carry one with you. They were the old-fashioned cork-block kind and one of the ratings showed them how to put them on. "Here!" the captain called out, "Don't eat anything, you'll only bring it up again!" "I had quite different ideas about my first sea voyage!" muttered Brink.

The first half of the night was calm and warm, and they sat on the foredeck planks. Of course nobody thought of sleeping. To the southwest the horizon was alive with flashes,AA guns presumably. All of a sudden the waves had white caps, the boat began to roll, and immediately Brink and Werner were sick—they just made it to the railing. Fischer knew he was immune and also Hanke was spared. When it became too rough to stay on top, they dragged the two sufferers down the companionway, plus a bucket. The stink of diesel below deck did not help, and the rest of the night passed painfully slowly. The pom-pom firing and a number of mighty explosions, which tossed the boat about like a cork, did not improve things. One of the sailors called through the hatch: "Not to worry, that's only mines we are blowing up!"

Feldwebel Wörner stood at the end of the pier. They stumbled toward him and Fischer reported. "God help me," he said, "I have never seen such a bunch of scarecrows in all my life! And you stink!" He marched them to what looked like Naval barracks, half of the buildings were down. "But there are rooms with beds in the cellar, you'll be safer there. I have seen showers too, see if they work, you need it! Catch up with sleep until lunchtime; in the afternoon, we'll go to the depot and you'll meet your No. 3. The radiomen have still not arrived."

The camouflage outfits were great; they certainly put them ahead of everybody. The No. 3 for Berta was a farmer's son from Oldenburg, their age and a man of few words, very likeable, which was so important for a small self-contained group. The signalers (said Wörner) were coming from some training outfit in Bavaria, "but with the state of the transport system these days, bridges down, trains shot up, their arrival is anybody's guess. The lieutenant will be livid!" He certainly was that when he arrived with the second group the next morning.

Another three days passed before the bedraggled-looking sparks (radiomen) arrived; they had had a terrible journey. One more day was needed for them to test, get used to, and set up their equipment. Everybody was getting restless. Leer could not have been the flower of the north at the best of times but now, with half of it down, it was a most depressing place to stay at.

The radioman for Berta, his name was Müller, was middle-aged and it was quite obvious, this was the last place where he wanted to be. He told them of his wife and three children in Frankfurt, where they had three narrow escapes, but as it happened, he turned out first class under fire, unshakable and reliable, and that was important. He was not called upon to do anything heroic.

While exploring Leer, or what was left of it, they saw in a news agent's window a map: "The Youth Hostels of Northwest Germany, Holland, and Belgium." They were not exactly Ordnance Survey standard, but good enough to be a great help, considering no maps would be available at all. The shop had ten left in stock and they bought them all for the others. Transport was organized, a large lorry and trailer, very battered. The lieutenant had confiscated, no doubt with the weight of the division behind him, an armored scout car. They had been very useful at the beginning of the war but had become much too vulnerable for the present kind of warfare. What made them ideal for this purpose was their powerful radio equipment. This was to be Wagner's CP, with him were only Feldwebel Wörner and a driver/radioman.

CHAPTER 9

Paras

The weather was overcast when they set off, very low clouds, which enabled them to travel during the day, as no planes would operate. They arrived in France in the middle of the night, but there was no peace for the wicked. "Berta!" Wagner called out, "your first action is near Avancon, a para battalion needs help. It must be serious, as they are leftovers from Cassino and I would have thought they could handle anything. I made a sketch based on my map for you. You have about thirty kilometers to go, see you catch a lift if you can. You, Sparks, have your receiver on air from 7:00 to 8:00, morning and night, you'll get your orders in those two hours. However, you can reach me round the clock. Off you go, be there as quick as you can, good luck, and don't show me up!" They were on their own now, no lieutenant to give orders or to turn to for advice, not a very good feeling! At least Avancon was still on the map for Youth Hostels.

Hitching a lift proved difficult. The lorries going their way were all loaded up to capacity, with men or ammunition or food, all the same they would have been taken but for the trailer. It was designed to be pulled by one man; behind a truck it would have fallen to pieces at once. So it was marching, but thirty kilometers was not a big deal. They took it in turn pulling the trailer, keeping to side roads if at all possible because of air-attacks. The "youth hostels" were a great help.

For the first time they could hear rifle and machine gun fire and the odd explosion, probably mortars. Brink said, "I think I have to crap." No sooner had he disappeared, Fischer and the No. 3 followed him in the woods. Was it fear? Fischer didn't think so, it was this colossal wave of excitement, not knowing how it would be and of course the thought that they might fail, what a mixture! A motorbike approached on the track, stopped, and a voice shouted: "Military police, what are you doing in there?" Blink called back: "Having a shit!" They were two sergeants: "Where are you heading? Marching orders?" Fischer, who was "in charge" on that day, said: "Look, sarge, there is no need to shout, we are looking for 2nd Battalion, 2nd Para Regiment, can you direct us?" The MP looked at the camouflage uniforms with obvious suspicion: "Why should I?" "Because of this, sergeant!" Fischer pulled the divisional order out from under his tunic and held it out for the MP to read. It brought him down immediately. "Are you all together?" By way of answer, the other three produced their pouches as well. They worked like magic, the MP became very helpful. He told them to continue on that road for another three kilometers, where they would find a small hamlet, in ruins, he didn't know the name of. To the west was a low hill and the paras were on the other side of it. It was close to 7:00 now, and Fischer decided to stay put until the radio hour had passed in case there were new directives. They could also use the break to eat, as there probably wouldn't be time later. Müller tested the radio link, but no further news came through.

They arrived at the village and searched for a good and safe cellar for the radio; it would not be stationed nearer the frontline. Fischer left Brink and the gun there as well and went out on his own to make contact. He got just across the hill when he was challenged by two paras, really dangerous-looking characters. One of them took him to the battalion CP, which was just a hole in the ground, carefully covered with tree trunks. They had crawled most of the way and, as it had rained, Fischer's uniform had lost its "new-boy-look," something he had been very conscious of. A very young major with a bloody and dirty bandage around his neck said, "Welcome, and what can you do for us exactly?" "We can see and shoot in the dark, sir." "Great, I'll tell you what the position is. Across the valley are the Yanks, nothing wrong with that but there's one sore point." Through the observation slit he pointed to a large tree trunk "See that trunk? To the left is a little dip in the sky-line, see it? Behind it is a bunker, an old one of ours, to make it worse. The Yanks have it and they have installed four or five heavy trench mortars, which are giving us hell. We don't have the equipment to take them out; it needs artillery or at least heavy mortars. We have tried to take it the normal way but the bastards have too good a field of fire from the right, and we would never get through. Now, every evening they exchange the crew, I reckon it's about a dozen or fifteen men, they walk out toward the night and the fresh team comes in from there, sometimes they meet in the middle. It would be ideal if you could catch them at that moment. If you dispose of them for us, we could jump the two hundred meters and take the bloody bunker and hold on to it. What are your thoughts?" At this moment machine gun-fire hit the area, bullets were whistling overhead or thudding into the tree trunks. Fischer needed all his willpower not to crouch against the wall of the dugout, his heart was thumping. Nobody else was batting an eyelid. Scanning the target area with his field glasses gave him time to pull himself together. "We shall position the gun on the brow behind us, sir, we are too low here. Once we have taken the two groups out, I suggest we'll give you a signal, three short bursts across the bunker? We have tracers. We shall then scan the frontline left and right and see how they react. If they do, their flashes will give them away and they've had it." "You seem to be very sure of yourself, corporal." "Yes, sir, the gun is terrific. Permission to mention one more thing: during the time before our signal, your men must keep their heads down, as we cannot differentiate between friend and foe, we only see silhouettes." "Lieutenant, see to that, this man is dangerous! Why aren't you a general yet, corporal? How old are you?" "Seventeen, sir." "That must be the reason." He grinned. "If that works, we'll be bloody grateful." "So will I," Fischer thought. "God, what an act I put on, but I got away with it. I think. And God be thanked he did not ask how often I had done this kind of thing before!"

He was halfway up the hill on the way back to the others when mortar fire set in, they must be the ones the major had been talking about. Luckily, there was a dugout and he dived in. "Hey, who are you?" said one of the two paras inside and Fischer explained. "Well, I'll be damned, do you think it will work?" "I know it will." He had to stay a while, the fire continued. The shelter looked very safe, the whole area must have been a mature forest once, the fallen trees made great hiding-places, ideal for defense, lethal for the attacker. The paras, audacious-looking characters, told him that they were used to this kind of warfare from Cassino. They had been holed up for months in the ruins "and nobody would have got us out if it had not been decided high up to clear out." In the half hour or so he had to stay, Fischer learned a lot about this special breed of soldier, because that's what the paras were. They were an extremely close-knit and tough formation, ranks seem to be of little importance, shown by the fact that they all wore the same uniform, a kind of grey anorak, halfway down the thigh, which could be buttoned between the legs for jumping. They called it their body-bag. Epaulettes did not exist, very small rank-insignia were worn on the sleeve. Fischer had the feeling that no other soldiers worth their salt existed beside paras—as far as they were concerned, well, he would show them!

The fire subsided as quickly as it had started and he was on his way. He filled in Brink and Müller, and then they looked for a place to position the gun, as night was beginning to fall now. Blink found an ideal place, a little hollow which had to be extended only a bit. It was right on top of the hill, suicidal in daylight but just right for their purposes. Fischer sent Blink down to the CP to report they would be ready in fifteen minutes, and what time did the major expect the change over?

"Between 1030 and 1100 was the information Blink brought back, but it was a quarter past when figures appeared on the scope, very clear and blight. The bunker-crew ambled along from the left, the fresh group from the right. Fischer was dripping with perspiration by now, "They're here!" he hissed. "Rolf" came from Blink, "it's just like the firing-range, let them have it!" The right word at the tight moment, Fischer pulled the trigger. The tracers hit a little low; he corrected that at once and the shots disappeared into the group and it turned it into something lifeless in seconds. The three signal bursts aimed a little higher and then he swung the gun right, true enough, flashes appeared along the edge of the wood and the gun travelled along the line, extinguishing one after the other.

Fischer was still dripping with sweat and to have time to recover, he said: "Do you want to have a look, Bert?" They changed places and the No. 3 (he was the only smoker) held out a lighted cigarette to him. Fischer took it and, although he did not inhale, it seemed to help. Suddenly, the undergrowth was rustling, Müller cocked his MP and just brought out: "Who goes..." when a voice came back: "Machinegun 22nd this is Major Heide." "Here, sir." "You know," said the major, having nearly stepped on them, "this garb makes you all but invisible. I came to tell you myself that it went beautifully. We're sitting in that bloody bunker now and didn't lose one man. That was a great job you did. Can I have a look?" Brink rolled to the side: "The medics are out now, sir, we are not firing."

"I should hope not. Well I'll be damned, this is amazing, I can see every detail!"

He asked a lot of questions and what was that at the end of the gun? A flash-suppressor, he thought so. And how are they going to play it from here? "We shall stay here for the rest of the night, sir, and watch if they are doing anything stupid. At daybreak we shall disappear into the village, there is our radio-link. We hole up for the day, we have strict orders not to jeopardize this equipment. If we are not called away, we shall come back at nightfall, but not to this location, in case they took a bearing on us, it'll be a few hundred meters up that way, but we can still cover you well." "So you will watch over us tonight? Like Guardian Angels?" "Yes, sir." "Great, my men need it, they haven't had a decent night's sleep for weeks. Thank you all very much! How long can you stand looking through this thing?" "About one night, sir, then we have to have a night's rest, our eyes, I mean. So we alternate, I was No. 1 today, Corporal Blink will be in charge tomorrow." "Clever, well, I'm off, I brought you some fags to keep you awake, oh, and give me your bottles, I'll send you up a hot drink, good night, men." Good night, sir, and thank you." Not long afterwards the lieutenant turned up with two second lieutenants in tow, they brought the bottles back, and "Could they have a look?"

The radioman had not been idle, firstly, he had fetched a bale of straw from a farm and made a wonderful bed in the cellar and, secondly, he had found, at the same farm, a large hidden store of bottled meat. There were about a hundred jars, he said, and they would eat as much as they could, take with them as much as they could, and hand the rest over to the paras.

The radio kept quiet, so it was another day here. The gun was taken to pieces and cleaned lovingly and the belts re-arranged. Brink had loosened a few burst during the night, and he and Fischer found that they could do with fewer tracers, remembering the lieutenant's warning in Kliplev. So instead of every ninth round being a tracer, they changed it to every thirteenth.

The afternoon found them nosing around in the village, what was left of it. The odd shell fell, but more on the far, eastern end of the houses. Attached to the ruins of a larger house, stood a long, low shed and in it they found racks with stacks and stacks of new, thick woolen pullovers and also what must be knitting machines. The pullovers were in vivid colors with high rolled necks and rather crudely done. Perhaps they were made for fishermen? Fischer and the No. 3 chose a green one, Brink, of course, red. "You look like a bloody pirate!" said the No. 3 to him. "Good!" replied Bert. Back in the cellar, Fischer sent Sparks to kit himself out (he, rather surprisingly, chose yellow).

At 7:00 came a message for them to head back to base next morning as quickly as possible. When dusk fell, Brink and the No. 3 set off to find a new location for the night, and Fischer crawled down to the CP to report. The lieutenant put a finger to his lips and waved him back outside: "The major is asleep." Fischer told him that they would leave next morning and also about the meat and the pullovers.

"Bless you, that'll be a change from that bloody Gummiwurst!" He beckoned to one of the runners inside and said: "Kaufmann, go with our benefactor here, he'll show you something nice for a change."

The night was relatively quiet. On the light wing of the sector was some activity, but Blink could not get a clear picture what was going on. In the end he discharged a whole belt into that spot and that ended all movements. Interesting to see was that some of the paras who had taken the bunker were seen coming back with the mortars and many boxes of bombs. Obviously, the major was going to set them up so they could be turned against their former owners. While this was going on, Brink kept a sharp eye on the sector nearest the bunker and indeed some flashes appeared, which he silenced immediately. This was truly a terrifying weapon.

After breakfast in the village, Blink and Fischer went down to the CP to let them know they were leaving. The bunker was empty except for the major sitting on a box in the middle and the medic, putting a fresh bandage on his neck. Brink said, “Sorry, sir,” and they were going to wait outside. But the CO waved them in: “Don’t be silly and come in! Are you leaving now? Thanks again for the backup and also the meat and the pullovers, you were very useful to have around.” “Permission to ask the major a favor?” It was obvious that Brink felt very uneasy about this. “Corporal Fischer and I were wondering if there were any spare helmets around? Because they are not so deep at the back, it would be much easier to hold our heads up all night. But it’s probably against regulations, sir?” “Bugger regulations, of course you can have them, there’s one around here somewhere and,” turning to the medic, “when you have finished butchering me, find another one outside!” As part of the deception program Fischer asked for “permission to thank the major for giving us a free hand.” “Isn’t that always the case?” “No, major, (implying they had to argue with obstinate commanders more often than not), we carry a permanent order from division but we’d rather not use it.” “Have you now, let me see it.” While Fischer unbuttoned his tunic and held the case out to the major, he was putting his back on. It showed the Crete-stripe on the sleeve and the Knight’s Cross dangled from the collar. Having read the order, he said: “Your CO must be a good organizer, how large is your unit?” “Fifteen guns last count.” “Well, I mustn’t keep you, I would like to, though! Thanks once again and good luck to you all, good bye, lads.” “Good bye, sir, and thank you for the helmets!”

Out of earshot Brink said, “Do you think he saw through us being such greenhorns and all that?” “I think we were very convincing and apart from that, it was dark anyway,” said the No. 3. Having convinced or not, the four were feeling a lot more confident.

CHAPTER 10

Rangers

"I have called you back here," Wagner addressed them, "to hear personally how things went on your first mission and to see whether we can make things easier or better in any way. But first I want to know if anybody laughed about you or were the Paras perhaps even grateful?" "You were right, sir, nobody laughed and they said they were very grateful." "There you are! Now for changes, any suggestions?" "We changed the belts from ninth to fifteenth for tracers." "I'm very glad to hear it, anything else?" "Any news about the maps, sir?" "Sadly not, but I was able to get a batch of radio telephones, that might be useful. They transmit to about fifteen kilometers. We shall have to code the locations somehow; these will be open lines." It was amazing what sophisticated kind of equipment was still available at this stage of the war, if only that would apply to petrol and ammunition as well. "Now tell me exactly what happened. What line did you have to shoot to get hold of these helmets? And as for your pullovers!" "Actually, sir," said Sparks, rummaging in the cart, "we took the liberty (Sparks words) to bring three back for you, green ones." "How thoughtful of you, Müller, I am glad you and Brink don't share the same taste!"

While having an overdue wash, Feldwebel Wörner came past. "What the hell is this smell, Brink?" Bert answered with a perfectly straight face: "It's Lilac, sir, it's our soap." "Lilac? Soap? Aren't you afraid the enemy will pinpoint you from this stink? You smell like a brothel on Sunday morning!" "I wouldn't know about that, sir, but the smell will have worn off in a couple of hours." Sparks had picked up the box in a ruined chemist shop and it was bliss to wash with it after the issue soap which by now consisted mostly of fine sand, held together with just a little bit of soap. It was like washing with sandpaper. "Lilac! Men of my unit smelling of Lilac, Jesus!" Wörner muttered, walking away.

After a number of sunny days the weather had changed once again. It was drizzling and safe for marching. The road wound its way to a railway line, which it crossed in a tunnel, very wide, and there must have been a number of tracks above. It then straightened out and, according to the "youth hostels," it should lead to a bridge. Two marched on either side of the road, with a good distance between the pairs. At the approach to the bridge were MPs, this time supported by a captain. The usual challenge was followed by the usual un-buttoning of tunics and expressions of surprise on their faces. "So where are you heading?" "We don't know yet, sir, our orders are to await further instructions at this bridge." "What instructions, soldier?" "We have our own radio link" Fischer pointed to the trailer, "which will go on air at 7:00, then we can tell you." The officer was slowly coming round to the fact that they must be something special, own radio-link indeed! "Who are you, if that is not a secret?" "Night-sight machine gun unit attached to 22nd Division, our orders come from divisional headquarters only, sir." It would not do any harm letting that drop, although, strictly speaking, it was not quite correct.

Only a few steps away was a small overgrown hollow, like an old sandpit, a good place to set up the radio and wait. Sparks made a real show of it, taking the radio boxes off the trailer, making sure they did not see the meat jars, and laboriously putting the telescopic aerial together. The captain ambled over. "Corporal, that badge on your arm, is that not AA?" "It is, sir." "I wonder, you might be able to help me a great deal." He was quite human now that he wanted something.

"The situation is this: you were almost the last one to have come this way, there are only stragglers behind you, walking wounded and such. This part of the front has collapsed two days ago (as if they didn't know that!) and a new line of defense is being put together on the other side of the river. The bridge has been destroyed a few days ago, but the engineers have made the river fordable; it's not very deep unfortunately. On the other side was an AA battery which was bombed or shelled at the same time, but one gun still seems to be in position and it could cover the road tunnel, you see. I'm afraid of tanks. I don't have a thing to confront them with. Did you notice the ground on either side of the road being swampy? So they would have to pass through the tunnel and if we could block that." He left that sentence banging in the air. "I would like you to come with me and give me your opinion on that remaining gun, it could save us, perhaps."

The battery was a sorry sight, three guns were smashed but the fourth looked indeed unharmed, but the main thing, it was a 10.5 and it greeted Fischer like an old friend. He opened and closed the breech a few times, that was ok, elevation and traverse were working (by hand of course), ignition would have to come from the night sight batteries. The captain stood by anxiously. "This gun is in working order, sir, only two things wrong, I could not depress the barrel enough to aim for the tunnel, the enclosure will have to be dug out about half a meter, but secondly, there is no ammunition. The racks are empty except for a few star-shells. Now what they would do to a tank, I have no idea. They may well be effective, they're meant to go up 10,000 meters and the tunnel is what, 1,500? So they would pack quite a punch on impact. And containing a combustible charge on top of that, it might work, sir." The captain was hanging on his lips, "But you realize, sir, these guns have no ground sights? I would have to lay it by aiming through the barrel, can be done, though. Permission to make a suggestion: I will go back to my group now to see what they want us to do. If we have to leave now, I would try to delay until the gun is at least set up and ready for firing. The four of us will come back and get her ready. Could some of the men dig out the enclosure from, say, here to there?" He put two stones on top of the earth wall. There were plenty of infantrymen digging in on the left and right, so that should not be a problem. The captain took all this very seriously, that was quite obvious.

Sparks reported that they should hang on until next morning, apparently the situation was extremely confused and Wagner probably did not know where to dispatch them to. The trailer was reloaded and they set off for the bridge, or where the bridge had been. Artillery fire had set in and they spent more time in the ditches than on the road. It was heartbreaking to leave the trailer on the road every time they took cover; after all, the radio was their lifeline, apart from the meat jars. The relief on the captain's face was immense when he learned that they were staying on; he had seen to the lowering of the enclosure, that was fine now. Laying the gun was next. To the right of the breech was the emergency box, a kind of first aid kit for the gun, it should contain a roll of insulation tape and it still did. Fischer tore off a foot, ripped that down the middle and taped a cross over the muzzle and the open breech, as precise as possible. He had two cross hairs now, once they were brought in line with the tunnel mouth, that's where the shell would hit. After adjustments to elevation and travers, the tape was taken off again.

The 10.5 pulled its own shells in, with the aid of rubber-rollers driven by a motor. The gun was of course without electricity, the provision made for this situation was a ring protruding from the motor housing on top of the gun, attached to a steel cable which could be pulled out, rather like starting a lawn mower. One full "pull" should be sufficient to draw a shell in. The pull-rope was strapped in its proper place! Two men were supposed to do the pulling, but Brink, in his usual style, said he would do it on his own.

"So, what is the procedure now, corporal?" the captain asked. "Brink and I will load the gun, we will set up the machine gun in such a way that the captain can observe the tunnel and give the firing order. Our No. 3 will be next to you, sir, on your order he will touch this cable to the night sight battery, as these guns are fired electrically." Two of the MPs had taken up position in the tunnel, having pulled out a telephone cable with them. Very likely, this would be cut by artillery, in which case they would try and race back on their motorbike. At the moment the phone was still working. Fischer had commandeered two infantrymen as ammo-carriers and had told them what to do. Four rounds would be available. It seemed sensible to eat before the circus started and they received their share of meat. They could not work out what kind of outfit Berta was, the camouflage gear, the para helmets, the radio, and the way they told the captain what to do, it was all a bit much.

"Bert," said Fischer, "we may as well load while there is still a bit of light. I'll tell you when to pull." Swinging the loading-tray under the breech was hard work, he had to overcome the dead hydraulics, Brink just about managed to pull the shell in. "Christ" he said, "I'll do the four for you, but that's it! This is worse than shifting bricks!" The phone rang, so the line had held. "They're coming!" the captain called across, "They're about a kilometer from the tunnel, the MPs are returning now." He was lying behind the machine gun, it was almost dark now, but he seemed to enjoy himself hugely. "Please sing out when you are about to fire, sir!" Fischer called back. The motorbike came down the road at breakneck speed, weaving to avoid the shell holes.

"Here they are!," that was the captain again; "I don't believe this, there are two abreast, what idiots! I'm firing now, corporal!" The gun sounded and bucked just like in Habichthorst. "Wonderful, bulls eye!" "You want the others in, sir?" "Yes, let's make a real mess." "Keep the cable on the battery, Hans!" The shots would now break automatically when the breech closed. These were the last rounds this poor old girl would fire, but what a swansong! A huge fire was raging in the underpass, with a few explosions thrown in. The captain came over to the gun: "Well, men, this calls for a drink." He passed his water bottle around; it was full of Calvados.

When they were alone again, Brink whispered: "I don't feel good about this. I reckon we should piss off as soon as possible. I can smell trouble!" "I was just about to say the same," Fischer answered, "I'm sure they're for it in the morning. Let's hang on another hour to see if they try anything with their Infantry, but I doubt it, they will rely on the heavies." He turned to Sparks: "Make to Wagner: Changing position to crossroads four kilometers northeast present location due to imminent bombing." "How do we know about the bombing?" he asked. "You're right, add 'probable.'"

They stuck it for another two hours, but nothing happened. By then Brink was "in charge," and he went in search of the captain to tell him they had to leave. "I feel sorry for that man," he said on his return, "did you notice the so-called soldiers he's got? They're nothing but children, I'm sure none of them is older then sixteen! Wagner was right, the country is running out of men." From their new position the drone of aircraft could be heard and the skyline disappeared in smoke. It had not taken long to develop this self-preservation instinct.

Wagner came through on the telephone, not too well, a lot of fading Brink said afterwards. The new destination lay to the south, but when the lieutenant spelled out the approach, he said, "Go south from the crossroads you're at to D." Brink had to interrupt: "It's off this bloody map, sir!" So Wagner had to describe the route even more laboriously like "going from Fa to De," it was absolutely pathetic.

Anyway, when this was done, he said: "Be very careful, Brink, the frontline has been described to me as 'fluid.' March long distances apart and don't have the trailer at the end. Let me know when you get there, good luck!" They had to cover perhaps twenty-five kilometers and it was slow going. One of them went ahead to sniff out the situation and then waved the rest on, if the coast was clear. After a couple of hours like this, they heard small-arms fire on the right, not too close but not to far either. "That's Yanks!" said Fischer, "No answering fire either, better have a look." They squeezed through a dense forest of young pines giving first class cover, having left Sparks and the trailer just inside the trees. The noise grew louder and they came upon an extraordinary scene: the pines petered out and changed to a grassy vale with a flock of sheep grazing at the far boundary. Along the right-hand side ran a track and on it, stopped, two Panzer IV guns pointing down. "Dead elephants, no petrol!" whispered Brink. Forty to fifty yards into the paddock stood and kneeled a line of Americans, doing something completely idiotic, firing at the tanks with their rifles and a machinegun, laughing and shouting while doing that. Behind them, on their knees, were two of them taking a tank rifle apart, or so Fischer thought, as he had never seen one before. Perhaps the troopers wanted to prevent the tank-crews from escaping before they had their weapon going again? Further back still three men were crouching over a map spread out on the grass. They had no look-outs posted! Brink shrunk back into the trees, very slowly inserted a belt and very quietly pulled back the lever which fed the first shot into the gun and set the bolt. Then he did a typical Brink: he stood up and called out: "Hey, you arseholes!"

He had put the sling around his neck and held the gun by the bipod, it swung across the map-readers, the tank-rifle repairers, and the line firing at the tanks. It took just seconds, none of them had a chance. Fischer was furious: "You crazy bastard, if you ever pull a stunt like that again, you're on your own! What if the gun would have jammed? We'd be full of holes!" "Our gun does not jam." "Rubbish, you forget this lousy ammunition. I mean it, Bert, next time I'll go into hiding and you can stand there and bang away all you like! Give me some bloody cover now, I'm going over to the tanks." He kept well out of the line of fire, picked up a stone, and knocked against the side. "In the tank!" he shouted, "German infantry!" Cautiously, the turret-hatch opened, the crew clambered out, slid down the side, and had a pee against the tank. "Thanks, mate!" The commander was a sergeant, "We've been cooped up for a whole day." "No petrol?" "No petrol." "Any MG ammo left, sarge?" "Plenty, help yourself. I will have to blow this poor girl up anyway, have you any spare hand grenades?" "We can let you have two, are you all right for food?" "Haven't eaten since yesterday." "We can fix you up later." The same happened at the second tank, "Crikey, you're good shots, where is your gun?" asked the commander, a corporal. "Up there in the woods, and can I have your ammo?" "Sarge," Fischer asked, "will you give me a hand with the belts? If you could take them with you up the track you came and wait for me by the road? I'll go back through the woods and meet you there." One man climbed back into the tanks and passed the pouches out; they would not run out of ammunition for a long time.

On the way back to Brink, Fischer walked past the tank-rifle, still in pieces on a rag. He picked up the bolt and threw it into some bushes. One of the men with the map had fallen across it, and he had to roll him over with his foot to get to it. At last they had a decent one, if with a bloodstain in one corner. On the map lay a packet of cigarettes, that came along as well. It showed the same camel he remembered from the packets the airmen left in Habichthorst. "I'm really glad my old captain can't see me now," Fischer thought. "He would be disgusted with me! The SM wouldn't, though! He used to say that he wouldn't piss on the Yanks if they were on fire. I would just say, military manners have fallen by the wayside, captain, sir." This home-spun philosophy carried him up to where Brink was waiting, who looked decidedly crestfallen, something remarkable in itself. "I'm sorry, Rolf," he said. "That was stupid of me, but when I see these bastards acting as if they don't have to have a care in the world, I just see red! Won't happen again."

"Where are you heading now, sarge?" Brink asked. They did not know, in the twenty-four hours of captivity they had lost contact with their unit and without the engine charging, the batteries for the radio had run out of steam quickly. "We can try find them for you, what's your unit?" "Panzer Lehr." Both Brink and Fischer whistled through their teeth, this was one of the most successful divisions with a reputation second to none, providing they had petrol, of course. Before the war, the division had started life as a teaching/training formation for all new tank crews, hence the name. Quite a while ago they had come down to a normal fighting unit, but they had maintained their first-class leaders at all levels. Without having to be told, Sparks was setting up the radio which caused the tanker to ask, "Who the hell are you?" When told, it was his turn to whistle. Fischer said: "Have two panzer crews with us contact location known for them?" He could go straight into Morse without having to take it down first. Wagner replied he would be back in thirty minutes and to stay switched on.

"Have something to eat now." Brink suggested and they fell on it. There was plenty of bread and they had sacrificed one of the precious meat-jars. On top of that there were two cold chickens which Sparky had shot the day before. When the No. 3 had seen them he said in disgust: "You can't eat them, they're much too old!" Apparently he saw that by the legs. "Bloody farmer," muttered Brink, "always knows best." So it was decided to turn them into chicken soup, a large pot was found, carrots and onions in the farmhouse garden and the pot was kept on the boil all night, the one on sentry-duty keeping the fire going. The tankers had their pen knives out and said it tasted great. "It has been bloody years since we had chicken!"

Wagner came back with "Your supply unit is at Derise-sur-Pont, 15 kms east." That impressed the tankers no end, "Thank you for everything now, we had better push off. If you let us have the grenades? We all have to go back to pick up the Yank rifles, we only have a couple of pistols between us. Stay alive and thanks again!" Two muffled explosions came through the woods when the tanks went up. "Shit!" said Brink, "That was an easy victory for the others, bloody war, we'll never make it!" Nobody disputed that. The No. 3 spoke up: "Wait on, Bert, you shot about thirty of them, doesn't that count?" "That is supposed to make me feel better, is it? Thirty of these jokers for two perfectly good tanks?" Brink was getting noticeably bitter about the whole thing.

The situation in the sector they had been ordered to was volatile, to say the least. Wagner had contacted them again on the march to warn them "they are only just holding." The CO, an artillery major (why artillery?) gave them the gloomy picture. He had been put in charge of one of the latter days inventions, an air force field regiment. These units were made up from flying personnel and their groundcrews, in other words highly specialized men were being wasted here, but then they did not have to be specialized anymore as there was no petrol for the planes. They were issued with a rifle, a few hand grenades, and panzerfausts, but there had been no time for infantry training. “What can I do with men like that?” the major asked. “They are simply not up to it; they are doing their best but my losses are horrendous. On my right wing I have two Infantry companies, good lads, and we’re holding without trouble, but here and on the left wing we are in deep shit, I tell you! If I had at least infantry officers or a handful of old sergeants—no, bugger all!” The man was at his wits end and who could blame him?

The lay of the land was like this: the township, in ruins, crawled up the easterly and westerly slopes of a valley, dividing them was the main highway running north to south. The western side was American, the eastern side German. “The only good thing is,” the major explained, “we are so close together, they would not dare bomb us, even artillery is being used sparingly. My main concern is, they cross at night, early morning rather, in small groups, neutralize a few of our positions, and go back to their lines. I almost think they’re doing it for training or even entertainment! They are Rangers, we know that from the bodies they left behind, so they’re not easy to deal with at the best of times.”

“We will be able to help, sir. The way you describe their tactics—that is right up our alley, done it lots of times. Permission to leave you now, we have a look around and dig in for the night. We shall report back to you when we are ready. Where will we find you?” “My CP is in a cellar this side of the church. And be very careful, they have some really good snipers!” The lay of the land was ideal with the township rising up a gentle slope, providing their favorite conditions: firing from above the area to be defended. However, the distance was approaching the limit of the gun’s range. Brink and the No. 3 crawled to the left to find two more positions in case they had to scarper. Fischer and Sparks did the same on the right wing. Strictly speaking, this was against orders as the radioman was a protected species but time was not on their side and night was falling quickly. They ended up with a string of five pits covering about 500 meters.

The CP cellar looked very safe with the strong arched ceiling of an old building. “Have you room for our radioman, sir? He should actually hole up well behind the line but there’s absolutely no cover outside the town.” “He is welcome, and we have some really good barley soup left.” That was a favourite with army cooks; it was either very good or very bad, and this looked a good one. It was dubbed “calfs teeth” by the soldiers. “We have double rations here because of high losses.” What a reassuring thought that was! They had their mess tins filled to the top, to be balanced uphill again.

There was quite a bit of movement on the other side now, the Yanks walking about nonchalantly, "as if there wasn't a war on, you just wait until later," Brink muttered. He held his fire so as not to give away their secret, which was revealed only at 4:00 a.m., when six groups of about ten men each slatted to come across the bottom of the valley towards the German lines, not particularly cautious either, they were walking upright! "Stupid buggers!" said Brink. "All right, here goes." The gun was fed tank-belts so as not to risk any jamming. The attack collapsed within seconds and the six slowly moving sections had turned into six untidy heaps of bodies. Brink then trailed the gun across the edge of the town for good measure.

The Rangers were indeed a different kettle of fish compared with the normal trooper; within minutes mortar-bursts were marching up the hillside toward the gun pit, as they had obviously taken a fix. Brink disconnected the gun from the battery, Fischer grabbed ammo boxes and spare barrels, and the No. 3 shouldered the battery. They darted to the most northerly position, 250 meters to the right. "Take over, Rolf, a bloody twig hit me in the eye!" It didn't look good, blood was gushing from it. While Fischer was setting up the gun again, the No 3 put a dressing on it and Bert looked more of a pirate than ever. No sooner had the equipment warmed up that Fischer made out two mortars still firing at the position they had just left. They were an easy target, but he kept the gun on them a bit longer in the hope to destroy the laying mechanism. Suddenly a bomb hit the ground about twenty meters in front of the pit, they were found again! Fortunately, the ground rose sharply and the slope absorbed the shrapnel, almost. For some reason Fischer was not wearing his helmet, an absolutely stupid thing to do. He felt a slap against the right side of the head but took no notice of it; there were more important things to do, the position had to be changed again. They hared to the left end of the line and dropped into the pit, the mortar fire was now on the previous foxhole. "Where the hell is he? There were definitely only two of them!" "Visible, you mean," said Brink and he was of course right. "And I think I've been hit." The right side of his head and neck were covered in blood, running black in the first morning light. The No. 3 investigated: "You've got a hole in your ear, you silly bugger." "How heroic!" said Brink. It was about the size of a thumb and bleeding profusely. How could an ear bleed so much and how could one bandage it? "How about" the No. 3 cut in, "we fold the dressing over and sandwich the ear in it?" "You do that with your cows, do you?" "You're right, when they rip a teat on barbed wire." When they had finished with Brink, he resembled not only a pirate but a pirate with a bad tooth ache. "I'll have a look at your head now, you're bleeding as well." Hans said to Fischer. He found a number of small shrapnel, ten or so, sticking out of his scalp and wiped them out with a dressing because his hands were filthy. It was bleeding a lot now and it took two dressings to stop it, their last ones.

For the way back to the CP, Brink and Fischer untied the camouflage covers of their helmets and put them on their heads, the helmets themselves would not fit and the white bandages would have made a perfect target for a sniper. All the same, the No. 3, jumping last, yelped "Been hit, arm!" "Can you make it to the cellar? Leave the battery, I'll pick it up later." The cellar was empty apart from a runner and of course Sparks, who took over straight away. "Somebody help me undress him!" When he had examined Hans, he said, "Man, but you've been lucky!" The bullet had entered the arm just above the wrist, traveled upward, and left it just centimeters below the elbow. "We've no more bandages, Sparks," said Fischer. "Yes, we have." He went to the trailer, rummaged around and came back with a pack "50 Field-Dressings Size A" printed on it. "Where the hell did you get those?" "Found them. Now this won't give you a lot of trouble, the bullet did not go in through the uniform, so no infection and the bullet itself is sterile from firing, get it?" "This man is full of wisdom," said the runner.

Sparks sprinkled some sulphonamide powder on the wounds and finished off with two very professional bandages.

Brink and Fischer looked on in awe. "Where did you learn that, Sparks?" "Paramedic in the auxiliary fire brigade in Frankfurt." It was good news for Brink also, the eye was unharmed, there was a long gash in the upper lid, but it had stopped bleeding and Sparks cleaned it with something from a bottle. "We leave it open for now, the eye will probably be swollen shut for a while, though. Who is next? No, I'll do a fresh one on your ear first." He washed Brink down like a baby, an extraordinary sight! The wound was clean, bleeding minimal, powder, fresh dressing, all in under five minutes. He then pulled three more splinters out of Fischer's head ("good job you have such a thick skull!"), washed him down, powder, bandage, "finished!" "Well, Sparks," that was Brink, "I'm speechless, thank you very much." "I don't know what to say either," Fischer added. "Fancy having our own medic, that always troubled me, being out on a limb like we are."

It was seven now, the radio had been turned on and started to chatter immediately. Sparks listened intently and when the signal died, said, "Leave today, no new destination, march northeast." He had also scribbled something on a bit of paper, which he showed to them when the runners were not watching; it said "Get out soonest." Fischer turned to the runners: "Is there anywhere near where we can have a few hours kip?" "We have the cellar in the next house, plenty of straw, you'll be OK there." "Thanks, will you tell the major where we are and also that we have to leave today? And please wake us at eleven."

All stayed calm, only the mortar, or was it two now, kept up a desultory fire. The major was back, brooding over a map. "I'm sorry to hear you have to leave us, I admit I felt a lot safer with you in the background. Goodness, but you did a lot of damage! When I was doing my round this morning, the Yanks came out under a white flag to collect the dead, that must have been forty or fifty!" "They came in six groups, sir, ten men each plus two mortar crews, plus a few who were hanging around, probably getting on to eighty, sir." "It's taken a lot of pressure off my men and they are grateful, they had a collection, and I'm suppose to give you this." He handed Fischer a grubby paper bag full of cigarettes, some in packets, some loose. "I heard about your bad luck, how are you all?" "Not too bad, sir, the No. 3 has stiffened up a bit, but we'll be fine. What's the best way to get out of this place, sir? We can't risk crossing the field above us, but we can't wait until it's dark." "That's easy, the streets run parallel to the slope of the hill, go along the top one, it has enough left of the houses to give you cover. You can use it right to the North end of the town, go uphill there, and you are in a forest. The street is full of rubble, but you take my two runners to help you across with your cart." "Thank you very much, sir, and could we perhaps take a refill of that soup with us?" "You're very welcome, and thank you for your help, take care and good luck!"

The Yanks must have noticed something, a few shots whistled past them or whined off the bricks, but they could have been visible only fractions of seconds, too short for even a good sniper to take aim. In the forest, Brink said to Fischer: "That was a bit dramatic, 'get out soonest'?" "Wagner must know something we don't."

The forest led up to a road running the right direction: northeast. They did not dare use it, the day was clear and the danger of fighter bombers always present. Burned-out vehicles along the roadside were evidence enough. It was heavy going dragging the trailer through the woods, particularly as the No. 3 was of not much use, but fortunately heavy clouds drifted over from the west and when drizzly rain began to fall from early afternoon, it was safe to go back on the road. Having covered about ten kilometers, they arrived at a hamlet, or the ruins of it. It was getting on to 6:00 and time to find a place for the night. The boulangerie looked good ("perhaps they left sausages behind?"); a solid old building once, it had neatly collapsed onto the cellar, giving it a good protective layer. A large empty window was facing the road, just right for Sparks to stick Iris aerial out. A column of infantry trudged down the road, followed by a few lorries at breakneck speed. At the very moment when a car appeared, artillery fire set in and it skidded into a crater. “In here, sir!” Brink shouted through the window and the two men, a captain and a seargent, shot into the cellar. “Good evening,” said the captain. “And to you, sir.”

By the color of his epaulettes, he was a panzergrenadier; his right arm was in a sling. He looked at the four with more than normal interest and after a while he said: “I’ve just been to the field hospital down the road and met up with an old friend. He told me he had invaluable help from some weird outfit and the way he described them it could be you.” “Who is your friend, sir?” “Major Heide.” “Paras?” “Yes, and he was full of you.” “Has he been wounded?” “Nothing big, shot through the arm, just like me. Actually, I could do with a bit of help from you!” “Well, sir, we can only act on orders from division, but we are between two operations. What exactly is your problem?” “We are attacking at first light tomorrow, we have a very strong line facing us and no artillery for softening them up to speak of, only a couple of assault guns and one of those has a dodgy engine. If you could thin out the American positions before the attack, my men would appreciate that.” Brink had got the map out, “Where is your sector, captain?” It was not far, about six kilometers due west. Fischer had written out a message for Wagner: “PGs requesting presence south of Davilon tonight can we assist?” He came back immediately: “Affirmative leave morning for Avigny 25 North signal when near good hunting.” “Your chief is a nice man, corporal!” The captain was rubbing his hands, which was not easy with the bandaged arm. “There is one thing, sir, can you lend us a No. 3, a strong man? Ours is not fit at the moment.” “No problem, you all look a bit shop soiled!”

The artillery had increased and the house was hit several times. It had been a good choice, the cellar shook but the ceiling held. After a short while the firing stopped as suddenly as it had started and the captain was getting restless. “Hope they didn’t hit the bloody car, help me push it out of the hole, will you?” It had lost all its glass but the engine started. “I’ll see you later, go along this road about another kilometer, there is a chapel on your left, turn into the road there and that will take you straight to me. See you, lads!”

There was still plenty of time. Sparks had started a fire in one corner of the cellar and the barley soup was warming over it. “You know,” said Fischer, “just before we left for Denmark I saw my old AA captain and told him what they had in mind for us, small independent groups and all that.

He told me to consider myself lucky, because that was much better then being part of a large outfit. The man was certainly right. We all loved him by the way." "Alright, alright," said Brink. "But do you know what I really like? I would like to take my stinking boots off and put some house slippers on." "I'll keep my eyes open, Bert." said Sparks. After dinner the gun was taken apart and meticulously cleaned; Sparks was charging the batteries. About 9:00 they set off, all having had the bandages changed. Fischer had no complaints, the wounds were doing fine. Sparks had cut the pad out of a dressing and the helmet fit again. He promised himself never to be without it ever. Brink's eye was closed completely and he was of no use at the gun. The No. 3 was not feeling too clever, he was running a high temperature. Sparks produced some tablets and promised him he would be 100 percent the next day. "Where did you nick all this stuff?" Fischer asked. "From a shot-up ambulance." Rain had started again.

They had obviously arrived: on either side of the road crouched an assault gun, looking twice its size in the dark. The crews had buttoned groundsheets together and tied them to the side of the tank for a shelter. The commanders were two sergeants who looked curiously at the new arrivals. "We are looking for the PGs, a captain with his arm in a sling?" "That's Captain Henschel, his CP is over there, the chinks of light. Who are you?" Brink told them while Fischer walked over to the dugout that was sunk into what looked like a railway embankment. "Hello," said the captain, "why are you looking so pissed off, corporal?" "It's this damn rain, sir!" "You should complain in your fancy uniform, look at us, we only have a groundsheet! Anyway," he pulled a bottle from his pack, "have a swig to warm yourself up. The lieutenant here will show you the way; afterward come back here and we'll plan the thing." The second lieutenant looked very young, younger in fact than Fischer which, of course, he couldn't be. The old army-ditty came to his mind: "The whole company has pubic hair except the lieutenant, he is too young." "Is your chief always so jolly, sir?" asked Fischer. "Not really, but he is very excited about you joining us, we need your help badly!"

It was a railway line and the embankment was exceptionally high. The enemy-side and top were pockmarked with shell craters, offering instant positions for the machine gun. The night was not too dark, enough light for the lieutenant to explain the lay of the land. The long gentle hill opposite, covered in trees or what was left of them, was to be re-taken because it formed a salient into the German lines threatening the flanks on either side. The center of the attack was about where Fischer cowered and his field of fire would, hopefully, cover the whole sector. "I'll set up the gun, sir, and if you could point out the details to me?" There were three machine gun pits and a few mortar positions. "Thank you, lieutenant, I'll just pop down the embankment another 200 meters to look for a second position. I don't know whether this lot is clever enough to get a fix on us (we use tracers) in which case we have to move, and fast. I'll report to the CP later." "Before you go, corporal, can you spare a cigarette? We ran out a few days ago." "Keep the packet, lieutenant, I'll bring you some more." He took two packs from the paper bag on the trailer, which made the lieutenant very happy. "I will give one to the chief, that will make him even jollier!" Fischer found another suitable shell hole easily enough, there were so many of them, and he marked the spot with a large broken branch at the bottom of the embankment.

One could have cut the cigarette smoke with a knife, they must have really missed them! "Thank you, corporal, the fags were really appreciated. So, what do you think?" "Field of fire perfect, sir, but they'll need stirring up before the attack or I won't have any targets." "Right, the assault guns will fire a few rounds and we'll drop a few mortar bombs. Runner, get me the two tank commanders!" When they reported, he said, "Can you fire across the embankment or will you have to set back?" "No problem, captain." "Good, I will leave you where you are because if you," he had turned to one in particular, "break down altogether, you're dead meat in daylight. You fire ten rounds at 500, you at 800, and spread them over the whole sector. Commence firing at 0445 until 0455, then it's over to you, corporal. When you've done give us a shout, there will be someone outside this entrance. Check your watches: 1106. Questions?" "The No. 3, captain?" "Hell, I forgot! Runner, you know this big chap in A Company, he has a scar on his forehead?" "Hollmann, captain." "Go get him!" "Hollmann," he said, "for tonight you take your orders from this corporal here, they lost their No. 3 and you are taking his place, right?" "Right, sir." "Let's go and fix the bastards!"

Fischer took Hollmann to the runner's shelter to introduce him to the others and pick up the batteries. Brinks swelling had gone down a little but he was still in no position to aim a gun. "How long is the cable from the gun to the battery?" Hollmann asked. "About four meters, why?" "We had bean soup for three days and the whole battalion is farting as if there's no tomorrow. I'd rather stay in a hole of my own." "How considerate of you," said Fischer. He was given his fags for the night and happily set about deepening his hole. "I know where there is a pine tree down, want me to get some branches? I think the tankers have an axe." That was a great idea, a few of those on top of each other made a perfect mattress, soft and dry in the rain.

From about two Fischer was experiencing difficulties with his eyes, spots flirted across the field of vision. He switched the sights off and massaged the eye with his thumb, which helped at once, but the symptoms returned after twenty minutes. Well, that was all right, if he rubbed them just before 0450, he should be fit for the fray

At 0440 he woke Hollmann, who was snoring in his hole, to cover his ears as the assault guns would shoot very closely above their heads. The plan worked like a dream, the Yanks were running around like chickens, it was ridiculous. The machine gun quietened the whole sector in no time apart from the very right, which was out of reach. Brink shouted down the embankment: "All done!" and immediately came the short blast of a whistle. There was little firing on both sides, and the German shapes disappeared quickly between the trees.

Half an hour later the captain turned up, happy but his bandage was blood soaked. "Well, men," he said, "great success, we got the bloody hill, five men lightly wounded and we took eighty prisoners. The Yanks were completely spooked. It's all down to you! My word, that gun did some damage!" "Permission to suggest, captain, our radio man is also a medic and he would be happy to see to your arm." "That is excellent, I say, you couldn't stay with us for good? Well, silly question but thanks, lads, we are in your debt! When will you be making tracks?" "About nineish, sir." "No, don't show yourself before half past or so, we have a spotter plane coming over every morning at the same time and he calls down the artillery on anything moving." "Want us to bring him down, sir?" "What, with this gun?" "With this gun, providing I'm in the right place." "I'd like that very much, not that it will make much difference, they'll just send a new one, but it would be something personal for us." "If it is alright with you, sir, we shall snatch a few hours sleep in the runner's shelter. Could somebody wake us in time?" Fischer connected two belts and removed the tracers, having first found a good position only a few steps up the line, a tree with a strong fork halfway up the embankment, which provided cover.

The captain came himself, "I must see this!" he said. When Fischer wanted to shake Brink, he stopped him: "Leave him be, he is not fit." "I need him to feed me the belt, sir." The captain waved him outside. "Don't you think I could manage that?" "Of course, sir, but ..." "But what? Because I'm the captain? Don't be silly, man!" Well, there were surely not many captains in the German Army feeding machine gun belts to a corporal! Normally the gun pulled its own belt in but when shooting at such a steep angle like a plane it would catch on the housing, hence it had to lifted up and guided by the No. 2.

No sooner had Fischer loaded it and cocked the gun, the captain said, "Hear him? He's early!" The plane appeared above the trees, a small one-engine model, quite slow and heading, what incredible luck, straight for their position, perhaps a bit high, but perhaps not. Fischer aimed well ahead of it and pulled the trigger. Not half a belt had left the gun when the right wing dropped and the plane nose-dived into the woods behind them and not very far either! Fischer released the belt and lent the gun against the tree. The captain just stood there with the belt dangling from his hands. "Bloody hell!" he said, "What happened? Bloody hell! Where did they teach you to shoot like this?" "I must have hit the pilot." Fischer said and then pointed to the badge on his sleeve. "That's AA, isn't it? You must have been pretty young, no hang on, were you one of those auxiliaries? I heard about you. So what will I tell my gunners? They've been trying for weeks to shoot the bugger down." "It is really quite easy, sir, they must not aim at the plane but well ahead and not change the aim! It's then like a curtain and he is bound to fly into it, it's a bit hit and miss, though." "But it seems to work, thank you, I will pass that on at once, I'm glad I came along!"

Fischer went back to the runner's dugout to get their stuff together. Brink had been seen to, and he could actually open his eye a little. The No. 3, miraculously, was on the mend, he also had fresh bandages. Sparks could be generous in that respect. Fischer was just having his renewed when the captain stepped inside. "I'm moving the CP forward and I came to say farewell and thanks again, also for my men. And here is something for a cold night!" and he held out a new bottle of brandy. "Take care, lads!" When he left, Fischer shouted, "Tenshun!" and the captain turned around and waved.

The road to Avigny was straight for miles, with high poplars on both sides. There was a slight fog, more of a mist really, but probably enough to keep the planes away. They had a system now, whereby one man was marching well ahead, who was responsible for directions and also kept watch for planes. One pulled the trailer, the other two kept to either side of it. If they were attacked, they grabbed a wheel each and the cart could be lifted quickly into the ditch. If the cart would get damaged, or rather the radio, they would have been completely lost in the true sense of the word, they could not get in touch with Wagner, nor could he issue new orders. "I'm your only lifeline with civilization," Sparks insisted.

It was getting toward lunchtime and they saw a kitchen-unit parked in the forest, well under cover, emitting its typical smell of cooking and woodsmoke. They were of time-honored design, probably not having changed from the last century: a basin the size of a copper with a screw-down lid, the firebox underneath which was able to take anything combustible, and a stove-pipe chimney at the side. It rolled on two big cart wheels and was, more often than not, drawn by a horse. They worked very close to the frontline and the units picked up their meals from there in cannisters. The soldiers called it the "Goulash Cannon." The No. 3, who was leading today, walked across and, after some discussion, waved the others on. The cook was a sergeant and not all that willing to cooperate, but the divisional order and a packet of cigarettes changed his mind. "You will have to wait, not ready yet, half an hour." "What are you cooking, sarge?" "Pea soup, will that suit the gentlemen?"

Continuing their march after lunch, they were joined by a column of American prisoners on the other side of the road, dejected looking, like all prisoners. "I wonder if they're from last night, they would not appreciate our company, if they knew!" Suddenly, the No. 3 blew his whistle, the signal for an air-attack. Within seconds they were in the cover of the road-ditch, which was full of nettles. Brink grumbled, "Bloody French, why don't they keep them clean?" A Thunderbolt—they could recognize the types by now—raced along the road, guns blazing, and two explosions shook the ground, as they carried two rockets. One must have hit quite close, stones and earth rained down on them. Fischer still had his head buried in his anus, when Brink shook him. He pointed to something on the edge of the road and then crossed himself! It was an arm, an American arm, complete with wristwatch. It was sitting there, the fingers curled under, but the fore-finger outstretched, pointing at Brink. "I didn't know you were religious, Bert." "I'm not, it seemed to be the right thing to do." When Fischer got over his shock, he grabbed the tiling by the sleeve and threw it into the bushes but then he thought, "Hang on, that was a German watch, the bastard stole it!" He got up—the plane had long since disappeared—and rummaged around for the arm, he took the watch off, and went back to Brink, who had not moved and was as white as a sheet. "Here, Bert, wear it, it'll break the spell!" It was what was called an officer's watch, large black dial with strongly luminous figures. Brink had smashed his on a stone a few days ago. "I don't want it!" "Oh, for God's sake, don't be superstitious." But then all soldiers were—in the end, he did strap it on. The rocket had torn a big hole in the POW column, but they didn't have time to bother with them; they had to get to Avigny and time was running short.

About three kilometers before Avigny, they left the road for the woods and Sparks set up shop to report to base as Wagner ordered. The reply was ominous: "Situation changed, new orders at 8:00." "Let's look for a place for the night," said Fischer, "if we can stay put that is, the next side-road leads to a village, not too far out if we have to carry on." The inhabitants had deserted it, it was teeming with soldiers, being the headquarters of some regiment or other. Brink was disgusted: "This is no good, they'll get clobbered sooner or later, we can't stay here. Did you see that chapel on the way here? Perhaps God will hold his hand over us in there." They doubted it but turned around, it would be safer than this place.

It was a charming little church, completely untouched and still smelling of incense. Fischer and Sparks crossed themselves coming through the door, an absolutely incongruous gesture in the circumstances, but habit was too strong. Sleeping would be difficult, the only furniture being pews. The No. 3 would "scout around a bit" and came back with two lengths of rope: "The bells have gone, but they left these. How about lashing two pews together, that'll be like a double bed." And so it was.

"Would you like some potato cakes for dinner?" asked Sparks. "We have some spuds in the trailer and a bit of bacon, no onions, though!" He also fetched a flattened piece of tin, which must have been a bucket once, with holes hammered into it. "A sergeant who holed up with me the other night gave me the idea. Always carry a nail on you, he said," and there it was, stuck through the inside of the pocket flap. "I got three more for you." Grating the potatoes was a dangerous job, but the result was first class. They had laid the fire behind the church out of sight from the road and, when the cooking was finished with, a few large stones went on the embers. They had washed the "foot-rags"—a rainwater butt stood conveniently by the wall—and they were later wrapped round the stones to dry. Sparks had set up his charging contraption in front of a pew; he also brought a bundle of bright pink oblong pieces of thick blanket material and started to sew. "What on earth are you doing?" Fischer asked. "I'm making leggings for us, winter will be on us soon." "Will they go over or under the uniform?" enquired the No. 3. "Idiot!" said Sparks, "I finished yours anyway, you can try them on." They were great, covering the whole leg with a longer "front," which showed over the trousers. "Make holes and button your braces through them." There he sat, sewing and pedaling. "I wonder what the lieutenant would call this, 'Defenders of the Home Soil' perhaps?" Brink suggested. "You are always good for a surprise, Sparky." "You shouldn't be surprised, I'm a tailor." "Will you promise us not to get shot while this bloody war lasts?" He promised.

At 2000 he put his sewing aside and his headphones on, the message was short: "Fischer to ring me!" Sparks threw a few switches and gave the handset to Fischer, who asked for the lieutenant. "You mean the captain,

Behrends, Horn, Jakobsen, Kohler, Fischer

B-17 Flying Fortress brought down by Fischer's unit

Control end of 88 mm antiaircraft guns

The boys who made up the AA battery

Hiwi

Battery boys. Fischer third from left

Loading 88 mm AA shells. Fischer third from left.

Fischer (right) at the smaller AA gun, possibly 40 mm

88 mm AA gun crew. Fischer is first at left.

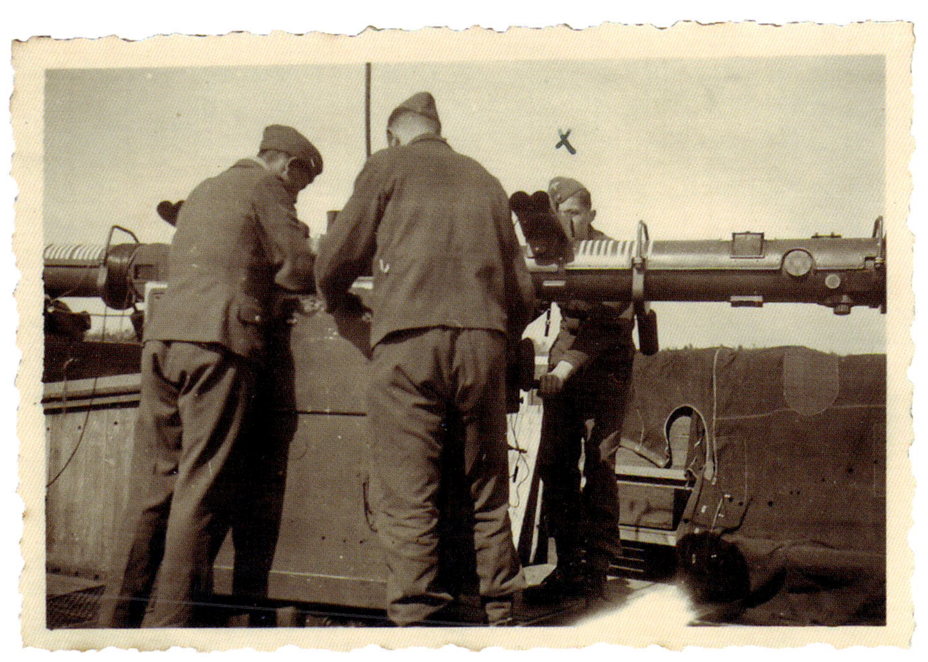

88 mm AA gun crew. Fischer is first at right.

Portrait of Rolf Fischer

Zielgerat ZG 1229 "Vampir" night vision scope

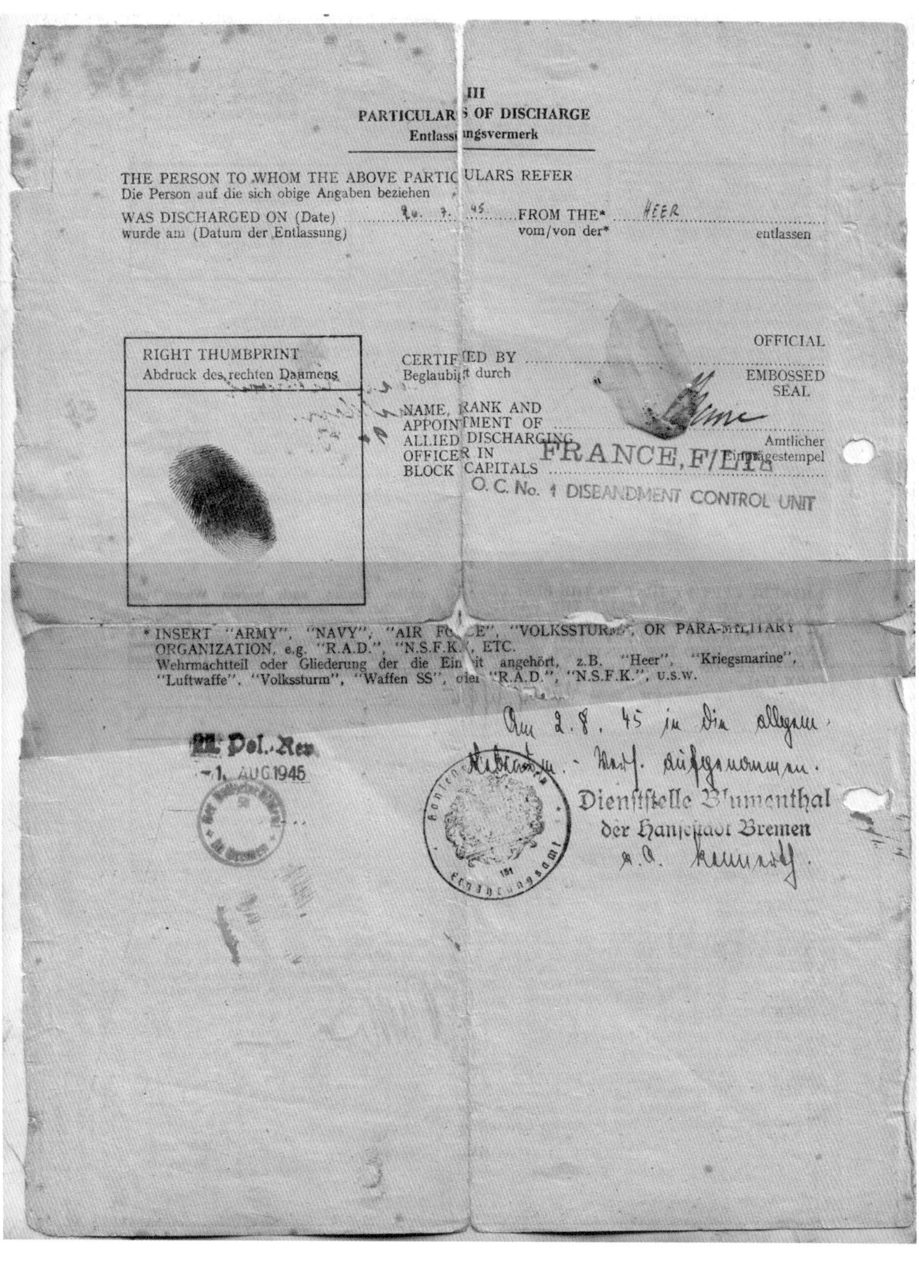

III

PARTICULARS OF DISCHARGE

Entlassungsvermerk

THE PERSON TO WHOM THE ABOVE PARTICULARS REFER
Die Person auf die sich obige Angaben beziehen

WAS DISCHARGED ON (Date) 24. 7. 45 FROM THE* HEER
wurde am (Datum der Entlassung) vom/von der* entlassen

RIGHT THUMBPRINT
Abdruck des rechten Daumens

CERTIFIED BY
Beglaubigt durch

NAME, RANK AND APPOINTMENT OF ALLIED DISCHARGING OFFICER IN BLOCK CAPITALS

OFFICIAL EMBOSSED SEAL
Amtlicher Einprägestempel

FRANCE, F/

O. C. No. 1 DISBANDMENT CONTROL UNIT

* INSERT "ARMY", "NAVY", "AIR FORCE", "VOLKSSTURM", OR PARA-MILITARY ORGANIZATION, e.g. "R.A.D.", "N.S.F.K.", ETC.
Wehrmachtteil oder Gliederung der die Einheit angehört, z.B. "Heer", "Kriegsmarine", "Luftwaffe", "Volkssturm", "Waffen SS", oder "R.A.D.", "N.S.F.K.", u.s.w.

Pol. Rev.
-1. AUG 1945

Dienststelle Blumenthal
der Hansestadt Bremen

Rolf Fischer's discharge papers

CONTROL FORM D.2
Kontrollblatt D.2

CERTIFICATE OF DISCHARGE
Entlassungschein

ALL ENTRIES WILL BE MADE IN BLOCK LATIN CAPITALS AND WILL BE MADE IN INK OR TYPESCRIPT.

I
PERSONAL PARTICULARS
Personalbeschreibung

Dieses Blatt **muss** in folgender weise ausgefüllt werden:
1. In lateinischer Druckschrift und in grossen Buchstaben.
2. Mit Tinte oder mit Schreibmaschine.

SURNAME OF HOLDER FISCHER
Familienname des Inhabers

CHRISTIAN NAMES RUDOLF
Vornamen des Inhabers

CIVIL OCCUPATION SCHUELER
Beruf oder Beschäftigung

HOME ADDRESS Strasse ALLMERS. 29
Heimatanschrift Ort BLUMENTHAL
Kreis OSTERHOLZ
Regierungsbezirk/Land STADE

DATE OF BIRTH 4. 4. 27
Geburtsdatum (DAY/MONTH/YEAR Tag/Monat/Jahr)

PLACE OF BIRTH BLUMENTHAL
Geburtsort

FAMILY STATUS—SINGLE † Ledig
Familienstand MARRIED Verheiratet
WIDOW(ER) Verwitwet
DIVORCED Geschieden

NUMBER OF CHILDREN WHO ARE MINORS
Zahl der minderjährigen Kinder

I HEREBY CERTIFY THAT TO THE BEST OF MY KNOWLEDGE AND BELIEF THE PARTICULARS GIVEN ABOVE ARE TRUE. I ALSO CERTIFY THAT I HAVE READ AND UNDERSTOOD THE "INSTRUCTIONS TO PERSONNEL ON DISCHARGE" (CONTROL FORM D.1).

Ich erkläre hiermit, nach bestem Wissen und Gewissen, dass die obigen Angaben wahr sind. Ich bestätige ausserdem dass ich die "Anweisung für Soldaten und Angehörige Militär-ähnlicher Organisationen" u.s.w. (Kontrollblatt D.1) gelesen und verstanden habe.

SIGNATURE OF HOLDER Rudolf Fischer
Unterschrift des Inhabers

II
MEDICAL CERTIFICATE
Ärztlicher Befund

DISTINGUISHING MARKS NARBE RE. KNIE
Besondere Kennzeichen

DISABILITY, WITH DESCRIPTION
Dienstunfähigkeit, mit Beschreibung

MEDICAL CATEGORY Fit
Tauglichkeitsgrad

I CERTIFY THAT TO THE BEST OF MY KNOWLEDGE AND BELIEF THE ABOVE PARTICULARS RELATING TO THE HOLDER ARE TRUE AND THAT HE IS NOT VERMINOUS OR SUFFERING FROM ANY INFECTIOUS OR CONTAGIOUS DISEASE.

Ich erkläre hiermit, nach bestem Wissen und Gewissen, dass die obigen Angaben wahr sind, dass der Inhaber ungezieferfrei ist und dass er keinerlei ansteckende oder übertragbare Krankheit hat.

SIGNATURE OF MEDICAL OFFICER
Unterschrift des Sanitätsoffiziers

NAME AND RANK OF MEDICAL OFFICER IN BLOCK LATIN CAPITALS
Zuname/Vorname/Dienstgrad des Sanitätsoffiziers
(In lateinischer Druckschrift und in grossen Buchstaben)

P.T.O.
Bitte wenden

† DELETE THAT WHICH IS INAPPLICABLE
Nichtzutreffendes durchstreichen

PSS 2324 6.45 500m

Fischer's WWII badges

Fischer in the postwar years

don't you?" answered the radioman. "Congratulations, sir, from all of us!" "Actually, I just wanted to speak to you both, how is it going?" "Quite well, sir, last night went off all right and the commander was happy. But we have a problem, sir." Wagner interrupted: "Haven't we all, Fischer, haven't we all?" "We got knocked about a bit, Brink has a hole in his ear and a gash over the eye, the No. 3 a shot in the arm (on the mend), and I got some shrapnel in the head, nothing serious. But Brink can't shoot for a few days and I had eye fatigue last night. Will we be doing something now?" "No, the unit you were supposed to assist does not exist anymore, so sleep tonight and set off early along the same road heading north. Cover as much ground as you can, but don't go beyond Chardonville; report your whereabouts in the evening. And for God's sake, be careful, there are only nine of you left." "How's that, sir?" "We'll never know; radio contact ceased, can only mean one thing. Take extra care and let me have Brink." "We will, captain, good night, sir."

Brink had found a packet of candles in a cupboard behind the altar and had lit ten. The light was needed for cleaning the gun and, of course, for Spark's sewing, who was determined to finish his invention. As soon as a plane could be heard, they would blow the candles out, there was no danger. The No. 3 had taken all belts from the boxes for checking, draping them over the pews like bunting. When these jobs were done they lit up—all were smoking now—and broke into the bottle of Brandy. "What a life!" said Brink. "To think of those poor sods in holes in the ground, having all sorts thrown at them and look at us, we should be ashamed!" "Just enjoy it," said the No. 3, "we'll be back in the shit soon enough!"

It was Fischer's turn to be in lead. The road was almost deserted, the main traffic going west-east or vice versa; who in his right mind would travel north-south? All the same, a roadblock came up and his field glasses told him it was manned by the hated SS troopers, hated, because they thought, probably with official backing, they stood above the normal soldier and often tried to push them around. Well, not with this lot! Fischer raised the MP above his head, the arranged signal for just such a situation. He could see Brink taking the gun from the cart, loading it with a short belt, and closing the distance. The roadblock would not have noticed these preparations, they were busy with other groups. There were four of them, nice clean uniforms, nice clean boots, just the things to rile line soldiers. "Marching orders!" the senior one, a corporal, barked. "And who are you, you're not MPs?" "Never mind that, we are telling you what to do!" "I see." said Fischer unbuttoning his tunic to pull out the divisional order, but hung on to it. "This is no bloody marching order!" "It's not meant to be a bloody marching order, it's our legitimation to be here or anywhere else for that matter and I expect that you bloody co operate, as the order of my general says!" Brink had arrived, the gun was hanging across his chest, the belt dangling from it. He pulled the cocking lever back and the noise made the roadblock men spin around. "Any problems, Rolf?" "Don't know yet, these self-appointed policemen seem to think we have no marching orders." "But we don't need marching orders, have you not explained that?" "I shall have you escorted to my headquarters, they will teach you manners!" and he started to walk over to a tree stump on which stood a field-telephone. Brink swung the gun around and put a burst through the box, reducing it to splinters. The SS corporal froze, "I'll get you for this!" he screamed. "Oh, shut up, you arsehole." Fischer shouted back. "I'll tell you what to do now!" Brink was at his kindest, but it was the kindness of a large and ill-tempered Rottweiler. "You will hang your MPs by the strap onto the barrel of my gun, we shall take them with us because you would not be above shooting us in the back, would you, comrades-in-arms? You can pick them out of the ditch, up there where the road disappears." "And don't get your boots dirty!" said the No. 3 in a rare display of venom. Fischer had some comforting last words: "Do you know the Yanks don't take SS prisoners, they shoot them on the spot?" The three men knew that Brink was only waiting for an excuse to pull the trigger and did not move. Brink and the No. 3 walked off, Fischer kept the roadblock covered, and Sparks was re-arranging the cart ("something rattles"), when one of the SS men called out: "Hey, don't forget granddad!" pointing to Sparks. Brink put the gun down on the road, walked back, and hit the trooper a vicious blow to the side of the head, a backhander with his fist. The man's feet actually left the ground before he collapsed a few steps away. "You have probably killed him!" said Sparks. "Good, who's going to miss him?" "Would you have fired, Bert?" "You can bet your life!" "It's a fine state of affairs when we shoot each other." "It's called brutalization of the war." Before they threw the machine pistols away, the magazines were taken out.

CHAPTER 11

Kindergarten Units

They marched within five kilometers of Chardonville and reported in. It had been uneventful, low clouds ("the soldier's friend") and drizzly rain. There had been a stretch where heavy calibers whistled across the road, but they were meant for somebody else further east. The reply read: "2 kms before Chardonville road Levalle you will be met by guide 572nd division 2000 hours." "Oh shit!" said Brink. "Another of those kindergarten units!" These divisions, scraped together from sixteen-year-olds, half-healed walking wounded, and old men, carried those high numbers over 500. They were generally barely able to withstand pressure and to be in their company meant skating on very thin ice. "It'll be like the time with the air force field division, only worse. The backbone-providers from the 22nd Division, that's all we are." Brink's utterings were always a mix of sarcasm and bitterness; the longer the war lasted, the more bitterness prevailed.

It was two hours before that time when Brink, whose French was for some reason quite passable, pointed to a sign "To the Sandpit," "Shall we hole up there?" Shortly before eight Fischer walked back to the main road and found the guide, but he was dead (if it was him). A smoldering truck lay nearby, probably a daring pilot had been attacking despite the bad weather. The dead soldier looked very young, so he was likely to have been the guide. Fischer broke off his ID disc and was about to turn back when he noticed a group similar to Berta, trudging up the road. He could not believe his eyes, they were Brand and Köhler, two chaps they had got quite close to in Denmark. "Bloody hell, Rolf, is it really you or is it your ghost?" Brand called out. "It is, you heroes, and it looks as if we've been given the same lousy job!" "How's that?" "572nd Division!" "Shit, we did not know that." "Since there is no guide, you might as well come with me, Brink will be floored!" "Oh, good, so he is still among the living; how is the old bastard?" "He's got a hole in his ear now, but don't tease him about it or he might sock you one!" It was odd that Wagner had not notified them about the rendezvous.

The surprise on Brink's face was perfect, and he sat there with his mouth open. Fischer left them and walked over to Sparks: "Can we telephone?" "Don't know, I'll try," but Wagner was too far away. Consequently, he made out a message: "Found guide killed requiring new instructions met up with gun Dora." Wagner would come back as soon as possible and "to stay on air."

This was a good opportunity to have something to eat, and it promised to be a feast. Brand had a whole ham on his trailer, but they were very happy to have a jar of pork opened for them ("It becomes so monotonous!"). When Brink brought out the Brandy, he stopped him: "Leave it, Bert, is that all you got?" Instead he fetched a demijohn of Calvados from the cart, "Living off the land, by order." Soon Wagner came back: "New guide at 10 you and Dora share frontage 572nd div." The waiting time was used to bury the first guide who was lying forlornly by the roadside. The new one was as good as Wagner's word, and he was there dead on time. He looked even younger than the first and the rifle seemed to be too big for him to carry. "There are so many Americans!" he said in a shaky voice. "Not much longer." Fischer tried to console him. They had to march another four kilometers but made good progress, the track was clear and night had set in. Indeed it turned out to be the same story, weak German troops, clobbered by artillery and confronted by a massive concentration of American units. Whatever were they waiting for? They could have just walked over the rest of the regiment! A plan was worked out with the CO, a soft spoken major, very experienced, judged by his decorations, but with nothing of any substance behind him. Fischer explained how they had worked with the panzergrenadiers and the major thought this to be the right course for him to take as well. He had of course no assault-guns at his disposal, "but I have a few heavy mortars left." He decided that they would, at midnight, lay down a barrage in front of the American lines and when Berta and Dora considered it the right moment, they would take over and thin out the opposition. At that moment the mortars would advance their fire into the woods where the machine guns could not reach. Dora went down to the right wing, and when it was all over they would rejoin Berta for leaving, because they would not stay any longer than necessary.

The result was everything the major had hoped for, and he believed they could now hold for a while longer. He had been promised reinforcements, real troops this time, but whether they would materialize was in question. "I would like to know why the Yanks run around shouting, disregarding cover, when something like this happens, they don't seem to learn." "We have seen it time and time again, sir, and we can't explain it; that's why we usually make such an impact," answered Brink. "I tell you what," that was the major again, "I think losses like just now hurt them like hell, while there is no limit to planes and tanks, they seem to find it difficult to replace men. Anyway, we thank you very much, I feel a lot better now. Take care and good luck."

Halfway to the main road stood a wooden shelter, for foresters probably, where they had left the two radiomen. They had been busy and chopped off a pile of pine branches for bedding and they slept until dawn broke. New orders were coming in and, sadly, both groups had different destinations, meeting like this were a real shot in the arm.

The road was perfectly straight for at least two kilometers, sunk into quite high hills. The marching order was different, three with the trailer, one followed walking backwards so there would be no surprises. After a few hundred meters this man changed over, as walking backward left one disorientated. They caught up with a platoon of very young Infantry, stumbling along and looking utterly dejected. In charge was a second lieutenant of the air force who matched his men in appearance. "Hallo, sir, where are you heading?" Brink called out. The officer pointed forward "They are coming." "Who's coming?" "Many Americans!" This man was clearly under shock and useless. "This is a good place for an ambush, sir!" Fischer threw in, but the lieutenant just made a vague gesture with his hand and plodded on, as he had no magazine in his MP! Brink did the right thing and shouted "Alles hört aufmein Kommando!" ("All obey my command.") From that moment on, the officer ceased to exist and his men straightened up. "Gather round, men, we are going to ambush these arseholes, right?" "Right, sir!" Sir indeed! The steep sides will protect us from them sneaking up on us, so we'll catch the buggers on the road. I want a good runner, I mean really fast." A lanky chap stepped forward, "Take off your belt, leave it with a mate, also helmet and rifle. Hare back to the bend and warn us, you'll hear them a mile off, nattering, stand in the road then and wave your arms, your mate will watch you all the time. Then run back here. Who's your mate?" "Here, sir!" "You take my field glasses and don't think you can make off with them! Walk backward and don't let him out of your sight for one second! Next, are you the gunner?" "Yes, sir!" "Are you any good?" "I'm very good." "That's what I like to hear." "Oh, Brink!" Fischer thought. "Run to that bend, dig a position in the left ditch, and camouflage it. Chop off branches with your spade and be quick about it! Have you shot tracers before?" He hadn't. "Never mind, off! Who's the No. 2?" "I am, sir!" "You run to the bend, on the other side is our radioman, ask him for a handful of tracers, tell him I sent you, I'm Brink. Replace every tenth round in your belt, got all that? Show me your ammo!" Fortunately, they were mostly brass. "You other lot! Dig positions in both ditches ahead of the MGs, we'll be opposite yours, camouflage them! Hop it, we don't have much time!" They were changed boys; there was someone telling them what to do and they would make a stand now.

Fischer still had a job to do before the fighting started: the gun's rate of fire had slowed down, there must have been some obstacle in the breech. While Brink was digging the pit, he took the gun to pieces and found the fault quickly, a bit of wood had got under the bolt. When the gun was re-assembled, he shouted: "test-firing!" and loosened a short burst off into the air; it was fine now. "You haven't told him about the radio and crossfire, Bert?" "Shit, I forgot, I'll go across." The Americans carried portable radios, easily recognizable by their long whip aerials, and these men had to be taken out first to prevent them from phoning back. Fischer would aim at the opposite side of the road, the other gun would cover his, as crossfire was always useful. "No. 1!" he shouted across the road, "Your camouflage is too high, chop it down!" Perhaps it was better to check them all, and he walked up the road some distance. He made out some un-natural looking ones and when they were corrected, he called out to the riflemen: "When the look out comes back, get right down into the ditch but leave the rifles on the road, only when the machine guns start firing, you come up and blast away!"

Quite some time passed before the chap waved his arms like mad and came galloping back. A Jeep was leading the American column and the radio was on that. Fischer called across: "No. l! See the aerial? Change of plan, we concentrate on the car first and then you shoot down your side of the road, no crossfire, the Jeep will be in the way!" Having now come around the bend, the Yanks did not even hesitate to scan the road and went blithely on. As a result of the tracers the Jeep went up in flames almost at once. The riflemen were banging away as if a whole regiment was confronting them, even when there was nothing more to shoot at. "Stop firing," Blink barked. "Up you get and round the bend. We'll stay a while and cover you!"

They marched together for a couple of kilometers, always leaving the look out at the bends in the road, and arrived at a new line of defense. It looked good, a few tanks, a few assault guns, and reasonable looking infantry. Fischer went to the captain in charge: "Sir, we met up with this platoon, they are leaderless, but OK, the gunner is very good. Can you give them a home? They wanted to come with us but we can't do that." He showed the divisional order to the officer, who said: "Of course we will have them, how far are the Yanks behind you? We heard small-arms fire not long ago and not far away?" "That was us, sir, we ambushed the leading platoon about three kilometers from here, nobody has been following us since." "Can you tell me who you are?" "We operate at night, sir, with night sights, we are directed over radio by 22nd Division."

When they said good-bye to the riflemen, Blink remarked to the gunner: "You were right, you were very good" and the chap looked as if he had been given a medal. "I wonder what they thought who we were? Anyway, I enjoyed myself." "We know you did, Bert," said the No. 3, "you were a right little Napoleon." "Arsehole!" said Blink.

CHAPTER 12

Hürtgenwald

Rain. That made it safe on the road. They sloshed along the slimy surface, everybody occupied with his own problems. "What an odd band we are," Fischer thought, "we couldn't be more different from one another. There is Sparks, a middle-aged tailor, not very talkative, caring and resourceful. I bet he is worrying about his family all the time. The No. 3 says even less, but then he is from Oldenburg and they have a reputation for that. The absolute image of steadfastness, can't imagine anything shaking him up. Being a farmer, he loves the land, I have often seen him stroke the soil and trees, I bet it hurts him seeing the damage done to it. And then us two schoolboys, Brink aggressive and hot-tempered, a brilliant soldier from instinct, but wouldn't last long in normal combat, takes too many risks. Born 200 years too late. So where am I on that scale? Somewhere in the middle, I suppose. I feel responsible for the lot of them, don't know why, probably because Brink is a bit reckless and needs reigning in quite often. The main thing is I'm happy to be with that lot and would be desperately unhappy if something should happen to them or if we would be separated, oh well, Wagner will see to that. And this bloody war must end soon. We've been fighting it knowing for two years now that we can't win it, that should really be enough! So what's keeping us going? Orders, of course, but that's not all. Self-preservation comes into it, and you mustn't let your mates down because they think the same way. What an un-holy shit!" A lot of it had to do with routine, the missions which were an adventure, if a dangerous one, at first, became the purpose of their existence, the memory of those encounters run into one another, it was generally the same: called upon for help, marching, ducking the planes, shooting as many as possible on the other side and marching again to the next location, and always a bit more toward the east, retreating. It would have been soul-destroying if the rest of the group would not have been in the same position; they propped each other up mentally.

"Do you realize we have been together five months?" asked Sparks. "And never a cross word!" said the No. 3. They were in a cellar awaiting fresh instructions, for two days now, which was most unusual. "Two possibilities," said Fischer, "either we are winning now and they don't need us anymore, or the shit is really steaming and Wagner doesn't dare send us places." "That's an easy one," said Brink. "Do you also realize, we haven't been out of these clothes for five months?" "Anybody can smell that," said the No. 3. "At least we haven't picked up lice, yet. What I would really like is to have a shit on a toilet, one of those where you pull a chain and water comes down, do you remember them?" It had turned winter and the camouflage-suits had been reversed a while ago, they were in white now, well, off white. Not one day went by when they did not, silently, thank Sparks for the leggings.

A motorbike stopped outside and a dispatch rider came stumbling down the steps, caked in mud and a bleeding arm showing through a torn uniform. "I saw your aerial, perhaps you can help me?" Then he collapsed on the floor. "Hans, help me undress him!" This was Sparks's department. Brink and Fischer dragged the motorbike down for safety. While Sparks cleaned the wound, the No. 3 collected a few small splints. The man was coming round again and he was made to swallow a brandy. "I'm not sure, but I think the bullet grazed the bone, it's clean and bandaged but I shall put splints round the arm, just in case. Have it seen to when you can." The sergeant was worried about the messages he carried, and Sparks suggested he would radio them through "if you can give me a frequency?" He could and a string of coded groups went on air. All the same, he was restless and thought he should carry on, which got Sparks very uptight. "Don't be stupid, sarge, you'll never make it, you lost too much blood, at least sleep here." They broke out the last of the meat jars, a large one, and the sergeant was glad he stayed. "It must be great to be so independent, what can I do to be transferred to your outfit? Oh well, it can't last much longer!"

While they were eating, Wagner came through, and for the first time the destination was a German name. It was not as much of a shock as they had thought it would be, for months now their orders had brought them ever closer toward the German border, there had been ample time to get used to the idea. The place was off the American map, and the old youth hostels came out again. "Christ," said the sergeant, "is that the kind of equipment they sent you out to fight a war with? Look in my left saddle bag, there's a pile of maps, I'm sure I can let you have one." They were going to leave at first light. "It would be very silly if you pulled the bike up the steps yourself," Sparks warned the sergeant. "You'll start the bleeding again and that will be the end of you." He promised to get some help. "Listen," he said, "you are going down the road to Monschau, aren't you? Eight or ten kilometers from here is a village I've forgotten the name of but there is a bridge right by the entrance. At the other end is a depot and the old feldwebel there is happy to give things away; he said he had orders to blow the place up once the front came nearer. I got new boots there and yours look as if they could do with replacing." He was right, the months of marching, mostly on hard roads, had worn the heels away almost completely, so it would be a godsend.

It was snowing heavily now, which meant no danger from the air. Finding the depot was no problem and the feldwebel was as cooperative as the sergeant had predicted. They got their boots and, another blessing, two sets of winter-underwear each. They changed there and then, and the old disgusting stuff went up in flames. "Can we have some of those iron rations?" asked Sparks. Here the NCO was hesitant, but when Fischer pulled the divisional order out, it put him at ease. "You see, sir," Brink tried to make it even easier for him, "we are on no automatic rations supply because of the irregular jobs we have to attend to and so we have to fend for ourselves." "Oh well," answered the feldwebel, "this order practically tells me to supply you, doesn't it? Help yourselves, the Yanks have their own rations." These tins were of exceptional quality, liver sausage and pork, and they stacked as much as the trailer would hold.

The assignment was one of those "a guide will meet you" efforts and, sure enough, he was there on time. Only face-to-face it became apparent that they were awaited by a second lieutenant, most unusual. "65th Regiment, 22nd Division?" he asked. "Welcome to the shit, I came myself to fill you in on the way." All of a sudden shells came whistling across from the West straddling the crossroads and there was only just time enough to dive into the ditch. Only ten shells came down and the fire wandered on, but after the last burst there was a tinkle on the trolley: a solitary shrapnel or stone had smashed into the generator—the gun was blind! The cursing was something to behold; even the lieutenant, who was no novice, was speechless. Sparks was already setting up his aerial to report the disaster.

"He wants to speak to you." Brink was nearest and took the handset: "No, we are all right, captain, oh, good!" "What is the name of this town?" "It's Bergenbroich, sir, there's a damaged pylon at the entrance, somebody will be waiting under it. Thank you very much! Are you ok, sir?" Apparently, Wagner was not far away and he would send a replacement tube straight away by motorbike. It should be with them in an hour, depending on the road, Sparks would stay behind to wait for the messenger. "It will be easy for you to meet up again," said the lieutenant, "we are going down this road for two kilometers. There are a few houses there and you will find a good cellar. The frontline is another two kilometers west of that. You haven't any fags to spare, have you?"

What the lieutenant told them on the way did not exactly make them feel good; it was just as well they had such confidence in the equipment and each other. This was the situation: Since September, the Americans had launched attack after attack at a forest area across the Belgian/German border, the Hürtgenwald. It was generally densely wooded, old pines grown, in parts, into an impenetrable mass of trees; never forestry-controlled, perhaps it had been some kind of nature reserve. In most areas, according to the lieutenant, the only way through was on one's stomach. A lot of the soldiers could not get used to those claustrophobic conditions and had panicked ("I'm one of them."); they had been sorted out and were now stationed in sectors more suited to them. It was defender's country, cut by deep and steep valleys running more or less north-south, in other words with frontline. The Hürtgen had no roads to speak of, only a few trails, mostly cut into the hillsides. The Yanks had suffered enormous casualties, but they kept coming, "like it must have been at the Somme," said the lieutenant. As their aircraft could not get at the defenders and tanks could not be deployed, it was infantry against infantry, "and we are holding easily."

Their final destination was a firebreak where the lieutenant had his command-post at the highest point. "These lanes are the weak spots, the buggers try to infiltrate here at night and as we have Rangers facing us, it's quite nerve-racking night after night. I was told you could help us." "Don't worry, sir, we had dealings with them before and they are good but we are better!" "Bighead again," Fischer thought, but the CO was pleased to hear it. "We are going to have a look around to get the lay of the land, sir. We leave our No. 3 with you, if we may, be back in an hour at the longest." "One thing to watch out for: The frontline is not straight, it follows the contours of the hills, many bulges and gaps in it. If you see white pegs—don't go beyond them, mines!"

The Hürtgen was crossed by the old Westwall, which the Yanks called the Siegfried Line. The bunkers and pillboxes had been built in '37 or thereabouts, and their fate had been cruel once France was overrun. They would not be needed again, and consequently they were stripped of armament and furniture; even the steel doors were shipped to the coast to be used in the new Atlantic wall.

Having crawled quite a distance under the pines, Fischer said, "You know, Bert, I can't stand this either. I would be going mad in this cave, and I don't know where I am!" As there was no snow under the trees, the camo uniforms were reversed once again, lying down. They were nearing the edge of the wood and the ground dropped away. Small arms fire flared up below and after another few meters they were looking down onto the back, with the entrance, of the an old bunker, about hundred meters away. The defenders must have done well, scores of bodies were spread out in front of it. Suddenly screeching tank-tracks came nearer, very surprising, as this was certainly not tank-country. A Sherman appeared, a weird looking thing, the turret was reversed with the gun pointing to the back. To the front a bulldozer-blade had been attached and that was pushing soil toward the pillbox. The tank reversed three or four times and the filing slits were buried. The men inside kept firing until that moment but, obviously, infantry weapons made not the slightest impression on the Sherman. They could not use a panzerfaust; firstly, the firing-ports were too small, bazookas did not exist when they were designed, and anyway, a rocket launcher could never be fired from within, the blast would have burnt the crew. What an elegant way to neutralize a bunker!

Suddenly, movement in the doorway, the crew came out to give themselves up. A dozen soldiers stumbled out, two of them carried a wounded mate between them on crossed arms and the last one carried a wounded on his back. By now a number of Americans had climbed onto the roof looking down at the sorry procession, suddenly they brought their rifles up and shot the German group down, shouting and grinning as they did so, then two jumped down among the bodies and stripped them of their watches, handing them up to their mates.

For the first time in his life, Fischer felt cold with anger. Up to now, all the shooting had been done in, if that was the right word, a clinical way with no hatred involved, and then there was still the old doctrine valid "You will kill me if I don't kill you first," but this was very different! He cocked the gun slowly (Brink whispered: "Leave the tanker to me!") and pulled it across the Yanks who were still admiring their new possessions. Brink had fired a whole magazine into the unfortunate tank commander who was now hanging lifeless in his hatch. The shot men screamed, none of them were dead. "You aimed low, didn't you? Well done!" said Brink. Whatever one might have thought about their infantry, the American medics were brave men. Very soon they were crawling toward the stricken group, the large red crosses on the side of their helmets would have made ideal targets. Although never shot at, a lot of them did get hit, there was simply too much lead flying about.

On their return to the line, the lieutenant asked if it had been them causing the commotion. When they told him what happened, he said, "It's a sad state of affairs, high time this bloody war ended." The task for the night was simple: Troops attacking up the firebreak were to be eliminated. The gun had to be positioned in front of the CP because this was located just behind the brow of the hill. One thing they were not happy with was that the two positions, the primary one and the other to escape to if pinpointed, could not be far apart, no more than the width of the firebreak. The lieutenant had riflemen stationed at the edge of the forest on either side, who would be withdrawn after dark. Their foxholes were expertly done, deep and well covered. Apparently they had learned that in Russia and were happy to pass it on: "Don't just dig a hole and cover it, look for cover first and dig in under that, saves work and looks more natural."

After informing the CO, Brink and Fischer set off to, hopefully, fetch the new generator. Sparks had arrived at the ruined hamlet, announcing his presence by the aerial sticking out of a cellar window. Feldwebel Wörner had come himself, not only bringing the generator but a spare sight as well "just in case you bugger that up next!" Furthermore, Wagner had sent a bottle of Korn and twenty packets of cigarettes, which delighted the lieutenant who received three of them. "Your captain must be a nice man!" "He fusses over us all the time," said Fischer. "Lucky you!" said the lieutenant.

It was dark now and the riflemen had been recalled. The gun was in position with the sights working, and from now on, it was waiting for things to happen. The lieutenant came and stayed a while. "Come and get me if anything is stirring," he said. The night was very quiet, so quiet in fact that they grew quite jittery. The only distraction was foxes, scores of them, passing through the firebreak and back again. It was bitterly cold and windy and occasional snow flurries did not improve matters. About 4:00 three silhouettes appeared, one on either side of the forest and one in the middle. "What a stupid arrangement!" said Brink. Fischer crawled back to fetch the CO. Brink did not fire, the Yanks worked their way up the hill, stopped short of the minefield, and then retraced their steps. The lieutenant reckoned they would be back in force at dawn. "That's often their time; they seem to think we are still asleep." He was wrong, nothing happened at all. "I don't get it, sir," said Fischer, "if they were reconnoitering, which they were, why didn't they attack? They couldn't have seen anything alarming, there was nothing to see!" The lieutenant had no answer either but he had stopped "searching into the American military mind long ago." "Anyway, they are up to something and I hope you will stay another night?" Of course, they would stay until the job was done.

Sparks had seen to the pine-branch mattresses in the cellar and even had a fire going. He had cooked something like porridge from milk powder and noodles that the No. 3 had nicked from the depot. It was almost like home, "But I would like a bath!" said Brink. When they came back the following evening, they saw that the entire firebreak had been plowed up. The craters were not deep; it must have been mortar fire. The lieutenant stuck his head out of the dugout, "Welcome back," he said, "we had some fireworks as you can see, we had pulled right back into the forest, no casualties, but the minefield's gone, exploded. Your position had a few hits, but the cover held." Now that was a comforting thought. Apparently, the countryside, with hills and deep valleys, was not suited for positioning Artillery of any kind and probably the Americans did not want to use guns from further away because the lines were so close together. They would no doubt send planes in when the weather opened again; hopefully, it would stay cloudy for a long time yet.

"I think we should take more tracers out," said Fischer. "Let's try every fifteenth because we are quite exposed here. They will still have the mortars in place and we have nowhere to scarper to really. Come and help me, Bert, I saw a short tree-trunk just behind us, we roll that up on top of the bunker, that'll cover the gap between these two." It felt a lot safer afterward. The gun was set up, it was snowing heavily now, and a bitterly cold wind was letting the flakes dance. Fortunately the snow did not affect the sight much; the picture was perhaps a little on the hazy side, that was all. Sparks had had an ingenious idea: he had rigged up the new spare sight to the battery and two men could scan the ground now or take it in turns.

"God, this cold makes me hungry!" said the No. 3. He opened a tin and made sandwiches for all of them: "And here's a special treat!" He had Calvados in his water bottle. "Where the hell did you get that?" asked Brink. "Sparks has an iron ration on the cart." Where would they be without Sparks? The lieutenant slid down the entrance: "Just checking on the situation, my, you are living well, this smells great." "You want some, sir? We have enough," said Hans and prepared another slice. The lieutenant took a long pull from the bottle and sighed deeply. "Let the buggers come now!" he said.

"Some movement, sir!" Brink was the gunner. Fischer passed the spare sight to the CO, who literally gasped. "Why didn't we have these bloody things a couple of years ago, the Ivans forever came at night to slit our throats! Yes, I can see it now, looks like the real thing. Don't get me wrong, but can you handle that, on your own, I mean?" "Easily, sir." Brink and Fischer replied simultaneously, and the lieutenant had to grin. "I don't know what to think," Brink carried on. "First they send this recce-group, then they mortar the place almost a day later, and then, when the ground is white again, they come walking across it, sticking out like dog's balls, they really don't deserve better! I shall wait until they are all on their feet. Looks about a company, do you agree, sir?" He did and Brink cocked the gun. "I think they're all out in the open, I'm firing now!" He pulled the trigger with the usual devastating effect, after three belts Fischer asked: "Barrel, Bert?" "In a second, no, it's OK now." The barrel would be almost red hot by now and needed to be exchanged for a spare one, or else it would be ruined. This machine gun beat any other for the speed with which that could be done. Near the bottom end of the barrel was a flap in the housing.

When opened, it pulled the barrel end out with it. That could then be slid out completely by the No. 2, he had an asbestos patch for that, the fresh one was thrown in, flap banged shut, time: five seconds. There were no more targets and soon the medics came out to set about their grim task. "I'll go back and shoot a Very light," said the lieutenant, the signal for the Yanks that they would not be fired on, that was the custom at this part of the front. A little later he sent a runner back with the Very pistol and a red cartridge (the first one had been white), "The chief wants you to let that off when they have finished, they'll signal you." After that the normal killing would resume; it was sickening.

A few hours later Brink kicked Fischer, who had dozed off, "Hear that? What is it?" It was like snarling or growling and a sound like tearing material, but there was nothing on the scope. "I'll pop down to the CP," said Fischer. "I don't like this." "I'm sorry to waken you, Lieutenant. There's something going on and we can't make out what it is." Back in the bunker, it took him only a second to identify the noise: "They're foxes going for the bodies, the Yanks will probably collect them in morning, what's left of them. You know, we found that the buggers prefer American dead to Germans; they are probably fatter." The war in the Hürtgen certainly held some revelations in store!

At first light stretcher-bearers appeared. The Very pistol was still in the dug-out, the lieutenant had left another white cartridge, and Fischer fired it.

"Fischer to ring me at eight," came over the radio. "That sounds ominous," said Sparks. "He is not usually so laconic." 8:00 came and the chief was loud and clear, he must have moved closer. "Fischer," he said, "from now onward, until I tell you otherwise, it's *freie jagd*, things are too muddled for anything else. If the situation gives you any choice, operate towards the northeast. Use your head, not only your firepower! That goes in particular for Brink! Bartels and Jansen, they were hotheads like him and they were the first ones we lost! You are defending, Fischer, not attacking, understood? I will give you your coordinates later over shortwave. Keep an eye open for Frieda, they are operating in the same sector. Good hunting and give me Brink!" He must have told Bert in no uncertain terms, Brink was only heard to say, "Yes, sir, understood, sir," several times. *Freie jagd*, "free hunting," was an order rarely heard and used in the infantry. Fighter pilots and submariners were familiar with it in the event when no particular target had been singled out and it was up to the men themselves to locate one. It meant absolute freedom of action, responsibility had to be taken later.

Their contact was 54th Regiment's headquarters, whom Wagner had notified of Berta's arrival. If they had any specific problems, Berta would of course assist; if not, they were on their own. It was difficult to find the command post because it was so unassuming, just a radio van and a few tents tucked well away under trees. The CO was a colonel and he talked to them at length. He had heard about Wagner's unit but, understandably, he wanted to know more details. The sector was fairly quiet at the moment, he said, but he would appreciate it if they would take over a gun position, the most important one, for a few nights. "The crew are on their benders, for weeks there has been trouble at night apart from the usual action during the day; in short, they have not slept for weeks." He detailed a second lieutenant to take them to the spot and acquaint them with the frontline.

The MG position turned out to be one of the old bunkers, and Brink, who was in command, protested violently. "We won't go in there, sir, the concrete interferes with our rays, we'll dig our own position under those trees, field of fire will be the same." "Suit yourself, corporal, as long as you shoot the buggers, we don't care from where you do it." The ray-story was of course complete nonsense, just an excuse for not wanting to shelter in the bunker. It was an ideal spot, a lot of trees were piled up like a giant bonfire. The heap was high enough to provide cover for tunneling under them in daylight and in no time at all they had a secure dugout, just like the paras taught them. No mortar shell would make an impression on that cover. Sparks moved in with the bunker crew, he did not mind. Food was brought up and with the bread came three herrings per man. It was late afternoon and a good opportunity to snatch a bit of sleep before night fell. When it turned dark, Fischer crawled over to the bunker to tell the crew to knock off, and they were immensely grateful.

The lieutenant turned up with a bottle of Korn. "I came to watch this if there is room for me." Fischer handed him the second gunsight and he whistled like others before him. "Here we go!" he said. "They are setting up the mortars now, they have to come out of the woods for that, which they can't in daylight. Cost us a lot of men over the weeks, they have some heavy tubes." "Not for much longer, sir!" said Brink and swept across the figures milling about among the trees with the usual grim result and then focused on the mortar crews, four of them. When they were down, he was about to go for the mortars once more in the hope to disable them. "Corporal," said the lieutenant, "let me have a go, I'II never get this chance again." Brink moved over and the lieutenant fired, way off the mark. He tried again and again, it was no good. "Shit! I fired machine guns before, what am I doing wrong?" "We did the same when we started and it took three weeks to get on target properly. I can't tell you what makes it different, nobody could tell us either!" Fischer consoled him.

The following three or four days were quite comfortable as far as it went. Food came up regularly, the Yanks were licking their wounds and kept quiet. it was raining heavily, but since the soil was porous, the dugout stayed dry underfoot. It felt strangely disquieting not moving back in the morning and returning for the night. Anyway, the MG crew was getting back in to shape again and it was time for Berta to get off their backside. They would leave Sparks and his equipment behind, also the gun, and the three of them would go out and do their own reconnoitering. Toward the evening they planned to return to see if fresh orders had arrived and to pick up the rations. The lieutenant had drawn a crude map for them, covering 3 kms on either side. The minefields were marked in red.

During the night they heard a short machine gun burst on the left, that could well have been Frieda. Working along the frontline toward it, it showed itself solid, good troops, deep dugouts, certainly a positive change from the recent past. When asked whether they knew of a MG-gang operating at night, they did. “You from the same outfit with your fancy uniforms?”

Frieda’s position lay about two kilometers to the south. “Hey, you heroes!” Fischer called out. Winter was speechless for a while. “My God, it’s good to see you, and all in one piece.” He must have been one of the best looking soldiers in the German army. His father was a Lutheran minister of the church, a particular austere and strict creed, but that never stopped Gert from being “human” as he called it. The number of his girlfriends was legendary and rumor had it that his father had caught him in an extremely compromising situation with a more mature female member of the congregation in the bell tower of the church! He was brother to three sisters, one more beautiful than the next.

Although he lived, like Fischer, in Blumenthal, they did not share the same school. He went to Lesum Grammar because an old friend of his father was headmaster there. That was the reason why they did not serve in the same AA battery.

“Listen,” he said, “are you on an assignment?” “We’re on *freie jagd*.” “Oh, good, if you help us we could really hurt the buggers!” They were covering an old stone-arched bridge over which American supplies would roll at night. “There is a similar one down the river, you can’t see it, it’s round the bend. If we block one each they won’t be able to move and we can let the whole column go up in smoke. Agreed?” “Sounds good, we’ll get our gear, back in a couple of hours. But what a bloodthirsty bastard you turned out to be! What would your old man think of you now?” “Oh, sod him and his sermons about loving thy neighbor, where has that got us, tell me that?”

A good position facing the second bridge was quickly found later on, but the No. 3 did not like it. Brink and Fischer had learned to accept that Hans had developed an uncanny feeling whether a place was safe or not. Brink reckoned it came from him growing up so close to nature; anyway, if he objected, there was no argument and another pit was dug. Close to midnight a line of trucks nosed forward and no sooner had the leader reached the bridge, a machine gun chattered on the right. Winter had closed the backdoor, so to speak. The belt composition had been changed to every second round being a tracer, guaranteeing a fire at the receiving end. The column was close enough for Fischer to make out the petrol tanks underneath the lorries; they blew up at once and the vehicle with it. Working their way down the river and when they met Winter in the middle, thirty or forty lorries must have been ablaze, the ones carrying ammunition ending in a spectacular explosion. "Now that was ammo well spent!" said Kätner, Gert's No. 2. "Usually their bloody planes do that to us." The Yanks, understandably, poured heavy small arms fire across the river but it was harmless, fired blind and in frustration. Now and again a ricochet whined past and sometimes clattered against some equipment or helmet. "Well, Gert, it was great meeting up with you lot, we must do that again sometimes!" "God willing. And keep your heads down! Even you can't win this bloody war, Bert!"

Daybreak saw them back at the CP reporting to the lieutenant on the events of the night. Sparks was also informed because he, on account of his meticulous handwriting, kept the war diary. All units down to company level and all independently operating bodies were under strict orders to keep this record, and only the most severe battle conditions were an excuse to write it up later. Wagner had left a message to hang on for the duration of the bad weather (rain had turned to thick snow); if a change came along, they were to head east to a certain crossroad. "You know what he is doing, don't you? Keeping us away from the bombers."

At the north end of the regiment's sector the troops were thinner on the ground away from the center; on the other hand the terrain turned more mountainous by the yard, making the defense a lot easier. The end of the Regiment's line presented itself as a sergeant and five men in a dugout, which had been built for "hedgehog," all-round defense. Just beyond it the ground dropped sharply away. The rise on the other side was already responsibility of the next unit. "This is a bloody windy corner," said the sergeant, "and what makes it worse, we buggered up our gun barrels with that shit steel ammo, if they were to try in earnest, we've had it." "We can let you have a new barrel and some decent belts, sarge," said Fischer. "Can you spare a man to go back to the CP or rather the old bunker near it, do you know the one I mean?" He did and singled a man out. “Go to the bunker and find our radio man, I’ll give you a message for him, he’ll fix you up.” He scribbled a note for Sparks on the dispatch pad and the grenadier hared off with it. They could afford to be generous, three spare barrels had been confiscated along the way and there had been plenty of petrol-less tanks around. “Very grateful!” said the sergeant. “We should be all right after tomorrow, a platoon from SS-Wiking is to move in here to shore up the defenses on either side of the valley, there’s a trail cut into the side of our hill and the Colonel thinks the Yanks might try something here.” The Wiking Division consisted of volunteers from Denmark and Norway, and they had a fearsome reputation as fighters. “I’d rather we didn’t have anything to do with them,” Brink said.

Along the valley ran a strip of pines, the Hürtgen kind, very old with branches reaching right down to the ground, refusing entry or offering shelter, depending on the situation. Although still early, it was getting dark, mostly on account of the thick snow clouds. Before returning to base, they wanted to have a look at the valley and so they started to worm their way through the trees. Halfway, on a less dense patch, they stumbled on to two German infantrymen, very young, very frightened, and very relieved to see them. The story was that they were from the next unit, across the cutting, and they had been sent to make contact. While on the way, they were cut off by American tanks, or so they claimed. “Rubbish!” said Blink, “Where should there be tanks? They can’t move here, that’s the beauty of the place. Where did you see them?” “Down in the valley.”

There was nothing else for it, Fischer and Brink continued on their stomach towards the drop. The boys had been right: a column of five Shermans were parked on the trail the sergeant had mentioned, almost below them. The engines were running, but the forest had swallowed up the noise completely. The leading tank was in trouble, its weight had caused the roadway to slip downhill and it was hanging there, supported by two huge oak trees. It was doubtful if it would ever move again unless pulled out by another tank, but it was highly unlikely that there was one on that side available. Five Yanks, presumably the commanders, stood around it, having an animated discussion. Two of them were smoking long fat cigars. Cigars! The hatches of the tanks were open and Brink whispered: “Can we do it?” “Easy!” Fischer whispered back, which was really silly against the background noise of five tank engines. The plan was simple, Hans would stay on the right wing where the commander stood, which was the shortest distance, the tanks stretching back to the left. He would give the others five minutes to get into position, one above each tank. After that time had elapsed, he would shoot the commanders down, which was to be the signal for the others to jump the Shermans and drop a grenade into the hatch.

"We take the belts off. Have you thrown hand grenades before?" Fischer asked the two boys. No, they hadn't. "Push the grenade down your tunic, you need both hands to climb the tank. Before we leave the trees, unscrew the cap but pull the cord only just before you drop it, can you do it?" They nodded, both sweating profusely. "Put your foot on the track, plenty of handles you can pull yourself up on, watch me! And you," to the other one, "watch the corporal! Off we go!" Bert was taking the last tank on the left, he had the longest approach, but five minutes should be ample.

For some reason the tanks had not driven close to the hillside of the trail, which was absolutely stupid as the danger of the surface slipping under their weight would have been considerably reduced. Unfortunately, that meant they had to drop down to the road first and jump up again onto the tank. One last check showed no lookouts. The No. 3's MP rattled on the right and the four jumped out of the trees, down the slope, up the tanks, and back again, like pulled on a string. Unfortunately, Fischer had jumped onto a stone coming off the Sherman and the ankle was twisted. "Help me up!" he called to the boy next to him, who might have been young, who might have been frightened initially, but he was there, almost throwing Fischer up the slope. The grenades were exploding and out of each hatch erupted a fireball like little volcano, all four tanks started to bum immediately.

"You have done well!" Brink had turned to the boys who were looking extremely proud of themselves. The one who had helped Fischer had the tell-tale patch between his legs, he had wet his trousers, but who cared? "How long have you been out here?" "Four days, corporal." Now that was certainly throwing them in at the deep end! "What's your unit, by the way?" "65th Regiment, 22nd Division." "Hell, that's ours too, you from Delmenhorst or Bremen?" "Bremen." The regiment had always been housed in two sections, the infantry was stationed in Delmenhorst, the regimental Artillery and support units in Bremen.

On the way back, slow because of Fischer's foot, artillery fire set in, a rare occurrence in this sector because the lines were close together and there was definite danger of hitting their own men and, secondly, for a considerable distance, the ground was simply not suited for artillery pieces, too hilly at best, mountainous in parts, heavily wooded, so God knows where they had placed those guns. Normally the job was done by mortars, much more unpleasant as the bombs approached silently, the only warning being the "plop" of firing them off. They had just dived into a large shell crater which was still smoking from the detonation, when two more bodies rolled in from the opposite direction. It was the lieutenant on his daily inspection tour accompanied by a runner. When told "what they had been up to" as he put it, he said to Brink: "Take me there, I will verify it." The single-handed destruction of a tank "by Infantry means" which came down to hand grenades or a mine put on the top above the engine (the weakest spot) carried automatically the Iron Cross, if confirmed by an officer. Bazookas and any other kind of gunnery did not count towards the medal, the tank had to be jumped, which was not everybody's cup of tea. The tank, although a symbol of power; was quite vulnerable to such attacks, the crew being blind to a high degree. A German tank would, if at all possible, never operate alone; they tried to keep each other in view to give protective fire. In the early days this role was taken by panzergrenadiers, infantry which advanced with and among the tanks, but they had been mostly used up by now. The Americans never prescribed to those tactics, the Sherman was supposed to be invincible and consequently a high number of them fell prey to such individual attacks. Also the British suffered severe losses. Not that it mattered much, as new machines came to the frontline in unlimited numbers.

Along with the Iron Cross came a badge to be worn on the lower sleeve, a tank on a silver ribbon, which was actually more valued than the medal itself. Some soldiers had three or four of those, in fact, the lieutenant had blown up five, which meant he wore a gold-colored badge, not five silver ones. There were not many of those around. When he and Brink were back, he asked for their pay books for the decoration to be entered into, a runner would come and fetch them when it was time for the "lametta" to be handed over. The Iron Cross 2nd Class and the Tank Destruction Badge could be given out by the regiment, anything higher came from division. "I saw something really weird," Brink confessed, "you know the commanders you shot, Hans? Well, one still held the cigar in his fingers and it was alight. I could see the trail of smoke quite clearly! Made me shudder!"

The two boys were going to find their way home early the following morning. They were told to give last night's wreckage a wide berth, that would be the best way to avoid the Yanks. They breathed a sigh of relief; now they would not have to face the bodies again! Before leaving they asked: "We were wondering—were there any men in the tanks we blew up?" "Certainly," said Fischer, "the driver, the gunner and the loader, why?" No answer came. "Listen," said Brink, "just imagine if the boot would have been on the other foot and you would have been in the tank, do you think the Yanks would have knocked first before throwing the grenade down the hatch? Stop being soft, that's what you're here for, remember?" "You cannot afford to be soft, anyway," Fischer added, "you have a medal now!"

As the days wore on, the feeling became stronger that they should join up with the old regiment.

If all of them were as young as the two lads who strayed across the boundary, Berta was bound to be of help. Wagner agreed, *freie jagd* was still on and the weather continued to be atrocious. The colonel was told orders had come in to move on, he said he was sorry to see them go, thank you very much and good luck.

At the first outpost of the 65th they were told that the CO was a major Weber and where to find him. Brink and Fischer went together to introduce themselves and, again, he had heard about them; consequently, he had a lot of questions. "Permission to ask the major where we can set up the radio, ideally a kilometer behind the front line?" "We can offer you a bunker, it's been hit a while ago but it will give you cover, a runner will take you." The bunker, like all bunkers, stank. It was this unnerving smell of dank concrete, moss, rats, and God knew what else, but it offered shelter from the continuous rain. "We are not going to stick this for long, are we?" muttered Brink, expressing everybody's feelings.

The following days, or rather nights, were routine. There were no particularly weak or dangerous spots in the regiment's sector, so it was patrolling along the line, setting up the gun from time to time, scanning for movements and eliminating them, a cushy job. They had just started on their way "home" one morning, when artillery shells fell. They dived into a trench where a sergeant was having a shave, unperturbed. "How can they set up artillery in this terrain, sarge?" asked Brink. "That's not artillery, son, they're our assault guns, recognize the bang anywhere." He was obviously an old hand. "I know three or four went in not long ago, then they ran out of petrol and that was that. The bastards turned them round and now they're firing our own shells at us. Until they've used them up, we'll get clobbered!" It made sense, the shells came over "singly," not as carpet from a battery.

They had almost reached the bunker when Fischer heard Brink cry out, then everything went black. When he came to again he saw the No. 3 dragging Brink into a shellhole; he was losing blood at an alarming rate. The shrapnel, or whatever it was, had sliced through his bottom, so deeply that the white of the pelvis was visible on either side. It must have been the same one that hit Fischer's helmet (it had a deep dent in it), knocking him out cold. "I will see to him, Rolf, my hands are cleaner!" said Hans. There was no disputing that Fischer's, and Brink's, hands were ingrained with gun oil and powder-residue from the gun, they were of a uniform grey. "I have to stop this bleeding, give me your dressings and if you could fetch Sparky." Brink had passed out, which was just as well because Hans started to clean the wound with a dressing pad. The wound looked like cut with a knife, no torn tissue. "That's good, isn't it, Hans?" The No. 3 shrugged his shoulders, "Just get Sparks, I'm trying to press his arse together to stop the bleeding, don't be long! I called for a medic but of course there's none around, never there when you need them!" That was not quite fair, the German medics were by far not as plentiful as their American counterparts, probably only two were attached to a company. "I'll take the gun and the ammo back with me now, I'm off!"

Fortunately, the radio was parked not too far back, a machine gun and two full ammunition boxes were no great fun to carry. After about 100 yards he reached a trail leading east and Sparks was near that track, a kilometer on. Fischer looked around and not far away lay an empty hand grenade crate, which he dragged to the point where he had joined the trail, as a marker for Sparks to turn right.

Sparks had raced off, having thrown a lot of things into his pack; Fischer stayed back to man the radio. An hour later the two returned, carrying Brink on a make-shift stretcher: two groundsheets buttoned together and two young trees pushed through them. Brink wore a weird looking, cross-shaped bandage, to hold his bottom together, so to speak, anyway, blood was only seeping out now. Sparks took over, "Let's carry on east, there was, at least a couple of days ago, a field dressing-station perhaps three kilometers down the track. Bert needs operating on, and soon, and I haven't got the equipment." Fischer changed places with Sparks at the stretcher and they went off down the track. "Sparks," said Fischer, "pull your aerial out, we have to impress, we are very important and have to be attended to at once." Fischer went to the medic feldwebel who was in charge of reception, it seemed. "Sir, we have a wounded man here, member of our team, we need him urgently and I was wondering." "You want to jump the queue, is that it?" "Yes, sir, and what's more, we would like to take him with us again, if that's at all possible." "Well, that's rather up to the doctor, don't you think? But you're in luck, it's quiet at the moment, he can go straight in," and two orderlies took Brink away. "We are not making this up, sir, here is our legitimation," and he pulled the divisional order out from under his tunic. The feldwebel read it carefully and, without a word, followed Brink in. Coming back, he said: "The chief will talk to you later about your man, is this a radio-link? You could help us out, ours has had it and we need plasma urgently. All right with you?" he turned to Sparks, a bit belatedly Fischer thought.

The doctor came outwearing a long blood-stained rubber apron, like a butcher. He held his hands in rubber gloves aloft; they were probably his only pair. The feldwebel came across, lit a cigarette, and put it between his lips. "Your man should heal quickly, it was a good wound. I would have liked to have given him some blood but we haven't any. It would be irresponsible if you took him with you; perhaps in two or three days, can you wait for him? Over there is another bunker we use for storage, you can hole up in there." "Thank you, sir, we'll do that." "Permission to ask the doctor," Sparks piped up, "why can't we give blood?" "No reason, show me your dogtags." The blood group was embossed on them, Sparks and Hans had A, Fischer O. The doctor called an orderly over: "That bum T just operated on, what blood group?" "A, sir." he came back after a minute. "Coming now?" he asked Sparks. "I'd like to go half!" said the No. 3. The next step was to put Wagner in the picture and, as was to be expected, he was very concerned about Brink. "Have you been up to something heroic again?" Fischer thought he had better not mention the tanks. "Take up the doctor's offer and stay until Brink can move again."

The bunker made a very nice change, it must have been used as an overflow of the main wards. There were beds in it and a heater, also piles of blankets. "We should try and stay here afterwards, if the doctor has no objections, we are not in the way, are we?" Fischer asked. "I doubt if Bert will be able to march four kilometers there and back every night, certainly not before the stitches are out."

That was Sparks the expert. A long message came over for the hospital saying when and what would be delivered and he was to take it across. "Bring Bert's trousers back!" Hans shouted after him. They were soaked in buckets overnight, the bunker had yielded a liquid disinfectant, which dissolved the blood nicely. Then they dried over the heater and next day Sparks set to work repairing them. The camouflage was no problem, he could mend the straight tear easily; more difficult were the trousers, the whole bottom was missing. "I'll have to think about it," he said.

The rain had stopped and it was warm all of a sudden, a good opportunity to take the gun apart and give it a good clean. Fischer and the No. 3 sat on a groundsheet outside the bunker, the gun between them, when they witnessed an extraordinary scene. The doctor came out for his customary cigarette and seven men filed out after him. When they passed him, everyone said "Thank you, doctor" but in English! The last one to come out was an officer by the look of him, a small chap with a large moustache, and he did not say thank you. Every single one had a part of his anatomy bandaged, arms, legs, one had the upper half of his head hidden under bandages and he was led by a mate. They were not Americans, so they must be an English bomber crew, and a damn lucky one at that. Waiting for them, probably to take them to a camp, was a small civilian lorry (a potato merchant), with the loading space thickly filled with straw. When the airmen were pointed towards it, the little officer started to complain loudly that they would not lie on straw, they were soldiers, not cattle. His crew tried to stop him but he would not have any of it. He spoke very good German, but with an atrocious accent. Now, a bomber crew could not be certain of a friendly reception in Germany in the best of circumstances, but if they started to throw their weight around this came, more often than not, to a painful end. The doctor did the only sensible thing; he turned his back on the man and stepped back into the bunker. The crew had mounted the lorry helped by two orderlies, the officer was still ranting on and his men were looking acutely embarrassed by now. The No. 3 nudged Fischer: "Let's give him a hand up!" Leaving the machine gun, they walked up behind the chap, grabbed his upper arms, half carried him to the lorry and, one hand on his arm, the other on the seat of his trousers, threw him over the tailboard. He yelped (his arm was in a sling) and Hans said to him: "You haven't won the war yet, you silly little man!" His precious cap had fallen on the track. The motorcyclist who had brought the medical supplies was waiting; he was to tail the lorry and act as a guard. Fischer looked at him and pointed to the cap. The man nodded, and when the lorry moved off, rolled slowly and carefully over it, pushing it into the mud. "Did you see some of the men grinning when we chucked that cretin in?" said the No. 3, "He was lucky that Bert's lying in there, he wouldn't have got away so lightly!"

Weeks later Brink's wound started to play up again. "Probably rubbishy blood they put in me." he said. "You don't know about the blood, do you?" Fischer asked. "Course not, how can I?" "Well, it was Sparky and Hans who shared what you needed." Brink was extremely embarrassed because he had never thanked them, which he did at once. Kind old Sparks said: "I was happy to be able to help."

The No. 3 sounded less kind: "I was hoping it would improve you, you old bastard! Fat chance!"

Brink did very well. It did take two days longer than the doctor had predicted but all the same, it was a miraculous recovery. He was still moving gingerly, but at least they were together again. Sparks had had an inspiration as far as Gert's trousers were concerned: he found a torn great coat at the hospital and cut out a patch the shape of the leather on riding-breeches, which covered the damage perfectly. "You know Sparky," said Brink, "I shall rather fancy myself in those, thank you very much!"

CHAPTER 13

"The End Is Nigh!"

After another week in the shelled bunker, which seemed to stink even more after the nice one at the hospital, fresh orders came through. It was another one of those high-numbered divisions and Wagner was not very optimistic about it. "You'll have to see what's left of the regiment, I have the feeling it's not a lot! Liaise with Frieda again, meet at the crossroad eight kilometers north of Wellsweiler." Not very reassuring, but going in with Gert and his mob made them feel a lot happier. "Perhaps we'll get divine protection being near him?" the No. 3 suggested. Unfortunately, the weather had improved, which meant they had to dodge the planes again (and again).

Winter's squad was waiting already, and they set off together, the point where they were supposed to find the guide being four kilometers west. Very few troops were in sight and there was no fire, Infantry or otherwise. The guide had not arrived so they continued in the general direction, west. A holdup came when Brink turned to Sparks: "Would you have a look at my bum, I think I'm bleeding." He was, but Sparks had swiped some special plaster at the hospital, that gummed the gap between two stitches together. "Christ, Bert, I didn't know you caught it, that must have been awful!" Gert sounded really concerned. "You are marching like you are on raw eggs."

Having struggled through the remains of a forest, it became obvious what had happened: the bombers had been and gone. They left the entire sector ploughed up, a kilometer deep and probably the same on either side. This moonscape was without any sign of life, here and there bits of bodies protruded from the soil and out of four Panther tanks two were on their side, one was completely turned over and the fourth had its tracks blown off. "I have to go for ammo, we're getting low," said Winter. "We're coming with you!" Fischer and the No. 3 went. "I hope the Panthers are not full of mangled bodies; that happened to me once before and it wasn't funny!" said Gert. "Let's take the one with no tracks, that should be clean." Fischer was right, there was no sign of the crew and it held enough belts for both guns.

It was difficult to decide where to go from here; it was very early in the morning, but almost full light. But then the Americans made up their minds for them, Brink spotted them coming over the skyline, many of them! "Well, they cannot use tanks and they won't suspect anybody being alive here. What say if we deal with them?" Bert was of course right about the tanks, the churned-up ground was too soft for them. The Yanks has not yet learned what the Germans had been taught in Russia, the normal tank track was too narrow except on hard soil, so their width was increased. “Will you go down the line, Gert?” Fischer asked. “Right, we make for that clump of tree stumps, we’ll cover the whole sector then.” “We’ll wait for you to fire because you have to dig in first. But we’ll be locked on and follow immediately. What, 300 meters?” “300 it is.”

There was no hurry, the Yanks were still about a kilometer away, it looked like Battalion-strength or thereabouts. A groundsheet was quickly rigged up on sticks like a roof, covering faces and the gun, so reflections would not give the position away. All three put the tanks at 200 meters, at half that distance again stood a tree stump, so a fix on 300 could easily be taken. It was unbelievable, the Yanks were walking leisurely towards them, many of them had a cigarette dangling from their mouth (said Brink who had his field glasses on them). Fischer could make out two radios, one right opposite him, and the second in Gert’s sector. They had to be the first to go. Fischer aimed at the bearer, but waited for Frieda to open up, both guns had to shoot at the same time or half the Yanks would go to ground and that was not the idea. Brink was No. 2, he had tried to shoot but the recoil of the gun caused so much pain in his backside that he had to give up. The troops were coming up to the 300-meter line and Frieda fired right on cue. Fischer pulled the trigger within the same second and the attack simply melted away. The barrel had to be changed twice and most of the ammo had been used up, so it looked like another trip to the tanks. Gert must have had the same idea; they came crawling towards Berta. “That was rather effective, wouldn’t you say? I’ll have to go back to the tanks, though.” “So do we,” said Fischer. “Bert will stay at the gun to see that none of these jokers get funny ideas, but I don’t think there’s much life left out there.” “But you can’t shoot, you just told me!” “I’ll go on single,” Brink answered. The gun could be set to single shots, acting as a rifle; however, it was less accurate and only good shots (like Brink) got results. “You have to shoot with feeling!” was his theory. This time they covered the 200 meters crawling, just in case. None of the bodies moved, but Brink got a few shots off, all the same. It felt odd hearing their own bullets whistle past. Fortunately, the on-their-side Panthers were also empty of dead crew, but with a full complement of ammunition. The No. 3s crawled back first, loaded with belts. Winter and Fischer threw hand grenades into the tanks and followed them without interference.

Everybody was getting jittery now; it would not be long before the fighters arrived and that would mean certain disaster in this coverless violated landscape. Luckily, the next woods were only a few hundred meters east and it was an enormous relief to be out of sight from the sky. True enough, only minutes later four or five Typhoons buzzed around like angry wasps, machine-gunning here, firing a rocket there, their frustration almost visible. "We should get away from here," said Fischer. "There's nothing more we could do and the next thing will be another carpet." He unfolded the map, still the one with the bloodstain; it showed the constant use and had to be handled gingerly now. "Let's head sideways from the direction of their attack, either north or south. Wagner will probably want us to go north. How about somewhere near Weissenburg, it looks hilly and well wooded. I'll ask the captain." "You do that" was his answer. "Well done this morning and give me Brink!" who had to report on the progress of his behind.

Their destination was twenty kilometers away, having to use less dangerous side roads, it would, in reality, probably work out at thirty. They were well on their way when Winter made what he called an announcement: "We hit on a food-dump before we met you this morning and you are invited for a late dinner." "Halleluja!" said Brink, "we have been a little short of late." "Before we start (that was Sparks) come with me and I take your stiches out, it's overdue." Brink looked doubtful. "Come on Bert, I'll treat you more gently than they would in a field-hospital!" They were back after ten minutes.

It was unbelievable what Frieda had found at the depot; they had sardines, butter in tins, meat, liver sausage and black pudding, also in tins, condensed milk and a box with twelve bottles of Korn, but they were short of bread, something Berta had plenty of. "Let's crack another bottle!" Winter said, "The end is nigh, I reckon, I can only hope we'll be in the right place when that happens."

Near Weissenburg stood a small brick mill, looking quite out of place amongst the trees. Brink stopped them from making camp in the kiln, which looked so safe. "That solid-looking top part, don't be fooled by it, it's mostly hollow, flues and such, it would collapse like a house of cards if something hits it." The tents were pitched instead and it looked like a quiet night. Which of course it wasn't. At 10:00 the phone rang, so to speak, Wagner wanted their exact position. "You are needed, now, both guns, get your map! Go to the crossroads three kilometers east and turn north there. After eight kilometers another road joins from the west, got it?" "Small river running alongside?" "Correct, follow that road until you meet up with a group of tanks and assault-guns, report to Major Hummel. Enemy has broken through, the major has taken care of the rough stuff but they have nobody like you with them, get me? How are you off for ammo?" "Understood, captain, and yes, we have plenty." "Right, get going and report in the morning, good hunting!" "Report in the morning," grumbled Winter's No. 2, "if we are still alive that is, sounds a right bloody mess!" "Oh, you miserable sod!" said Gert but, turning to Fischer he had to admit, "We don't have a sight anymore, I dropped ours yesterday and we can't get a new one, Wagner is too far." "This is your lucky night, Gert," and Fischer pulled their spare from his tunic pocket.

"Glad to see you!" said Major Hummel. "Our problem is, we haven't a single infantryman near us, let alone with us. The Yanks broke through yesterday, along this valley. We smashed the head of their column, about a dozen or so Shermans so the track is blocked and no more armor can get through, but there is a lot of infantry following and if they descend on us, it's good night! Our orders are to hold until evening and then move to a new blocking position. Any suggestions?" "Can we see the lay of the land first, sir?" Brink was No. 1. The major called a second lieutenant over who was to act as guide for Bert and Winter, the rest of the crews stayed back amongst the tanks, the huge machines creating a feeling of safety, there was also time for a smoke. The CO asked to see the sights and Fischer rigged up a gun for him. "Bloody hell," he exclaimed, "wonderful, if they would have given us those earlier, what a difference that would have made, bloody hell!"

Brink and the lieutenant returned. "The positions of your outposts are ideal, sir, we shall use them both. It seems they have some sort of camp behind the shot-up tanks, we'll get them there. Permission to suggest you put a couple of shots well behind that, it always makes them run around, never fails. Give us ten minutes, we'll be in position then." Watches had been checked, the lieutenant came as well. One position was on this side of the river, the second opposite, accessible by a bridge which was down, but enough still showed above the water to balance across. Three tankers were crouching in each hole, armed with machine-pistols only and they were very, very happy to be relieved. It went like clockwork, the guns locked on, the two shots fell, pandemonium broke out, and the devastation was pretty well complete. Two petrol bowsers made it worse. Their explosion extinguished any life left. "Bert," said Fischer, "I better get on to Wagner, what are we suppose to do when the tanks leave? They can't expect us to hold the whole bloody front on our own! Will you be ok on your own for a minute? I'll come back when I hear you firing." "Leave with the tanks, make the best of the situation, report before nightfall from a safe position." That was it, from a safe position. Fischer knew what to do now. The lieutenant had returned and had reported to the major, who slapped Fischer on the shoulder that his knees buckled (he was a big man). He walked to his Tiger and came back with two bottles of brandy: "We're in your debt, lad."

A little later he decided "to speak to your captain, what's his name?" Sparks made the connection and gave the phone to the major. "Captain Wagner? This is Major Hummel, I just wanted to thank you for sending me this bunch of lunatics. They destroyed the American advance in minutes and, I don't mind telling you, saved our skin. I only wish I had their equipment!" He listened for a while before saying, "Thanks again, captain, and Good Luck." When they were getting their things together, Brink asked Winter "Where is your No. 3?" Gert just shrugged his shoulders "mortar" and walked away.

The "safe position" decided on was a hamlet, not more than five or six houses and a chapel, off a major road so tanks would not appear at the doorstep—the only thing wrong, it was occupied by a field hospital. The Stabsarzt, a doctor of captain's rank, did not want them there. The whole place was decked out in Red Cross flags and he refused to have any fighting troops near, well, understandable.

So they carried on to another village, just as small, not far away, having argued themselves through a roadblock first. In a way it was even better, the road led to the village more or less straight for two kilometers and it ended there. If it was kept under observation twenty-four hours a day, they could feel safe, unless the planes decided to flatten it, but the rain had returned. The village was of course deserted, but really weird was the almost complete absence of soldiers in this sector. "I honestly don't think there are many of us left," said Winter's No. 2. It certainly looked like it.

The kitchen of one of the houses looked out onto the approach road, one gun was placed on the kitchen table, a chair behind it, comfort! And sentry duty every seventh hour for an hour wasn't bad either. Somebody had lit the copper and there followed a long washing orgy, the grime of months came off only reluctantly. Sparks and the No. 3, true to form, had been foraging through gardens and cellars, but only came up with the usual potatoes, carrots, and onions, anyway. Sparks started a soup in another copper in another house.

After dinner, when the brandy came out, Gert started to talk about his No. 3. "Let's drink to him, you know the poor bugger had to have a shit, sardines always gave him the trots, and when he had gone, there came this big mortar-bomb, only one and he was in the way. We were going to bury him but there was nothing left. Here's to him, he was a good chap." He took his mouth organ out (he was an expert with it) and started to play the age old lament "I once had a comrade," playing single notes only, sounding like a wail, all hummed the melody. Halfway through the second bottle, Fischer said, "We'll be alcoholics by the time this is over." "Maybe," answered Brink, "but it makes this shit much easier. Let's not get soft," he continued, "Gert, give us the old favorite of Sergeant Wiegert in Delmenhorst!" "My God, that's years ago!" but he knew immediately what to play: "Once we were moored off Tampico, and Tampico was wonderful. Dolores from Mexico, when shall we meet again? Dolores, I said, Dolores, you are so beautiful to look at, your feet are as black as your eyes, I shall never forget you." The melody lent itself to many variants within the chords and when the company marched along singing it, Wiegert used to say: "Boys, you sound just like an organ!" Wiegert with his poor smashed face, he was like a father to them.

The song had a second verse, worded in the most beautiful German but so vulgar that they were not allowed to sing it marching through built-up areas. On the open road again, somebody would invariably call out: "Second verse, sarge?" and Wiegert would answer: "If you feel you have to!"

Very early in the morning a shot broke. Winter's No. 2 was on duty. Everybody jumped up but he said: "Don't panic, I only shot a pig." "You shot what?" "A pig, you know, you can eat them." "Well," said Winter, "that was the first sensible shot this gun ever fired." "I suppose it's up to me now." The No. 3 took out his penknife and started to sharpen it on the kitchen sink. "Who's going to help me hang the thing up?" "There's a ladder behind the house, I'll get it!" Brink was quite excited. "Man, wild boar! I wonder if we'll find any cranberries?" "Get a grip, Bert, let's see if they give us time to cook it first. And you won't find any bloody cranberries at the end of winter!"

The pig was hanging on the ladder ("What an ugly bugger!") and Hans cut into the neck to bleed it. "Are you not going to skin it?" somebody asked. "You don't skin pigs, you chuck boiling water on them and scrape the bristles off." There was of course no boiling water, so Hans carved the meat out of the skin, so to speak, a wasteful way, but there was so much of it. The skin and all the rest was left in the bushes for the foxes and it had disappeared after a few hours. Sparks had built four fires to be able to cook all the meat at once. "I'll tell what I'll do! I saw a smoking-chamber behind the house, tonight, when the smoke can't be seen, I'll get it going and hang in the meat we can't eat straightaway. It'll be too short for a proper smoking but it will keep the meat a bit longer."

Fortunately they were left in peace the whole day. The rain was heavy and Sparks had to stretch a groundsheet over each cooking fire. Winter had discovered an oversized copper in one of the houses, big enough for two, crouching to have a bath. It was an unbelievable luxury, particularly washing the hair after many months. Drying off was the problem as they only carried a hand towel, firstly much too small and secondly they stank as only unwashed towels can stink. Hanging around the warm copper was the only alternative. Sparks had concocted some Wild Boar soup, it was first class and he received a lot of praise for it. The roast meat in the evening was unforgettable, and there was plenty of alcohol to go with it. Brink had a toast: "Let's enjoy the war, peace is going to be horrible!"

The next assignment meant a busy night. They were expected to divide their attention between two units: on the left a depleted infantry battalion held on to a low range of hills by the skin of their teeth, on the right one of those unfortunate air force field units was trying to do the same but that could simply not be expected and it was only a matter of time that the front would collapse here.

"Those poor sods can't even dig in properly!" said Brink disgustedly and, consequently, their losses were enormous. What had avoided a catastrophe so far was a group of heavy mortars, operated by old hands and set back in a very good position, they were able to keep the Yanks at bay, as they had an observer with a telephone in the frontline. Also, there was a machine gun at each end of the air force sector, manned by tank-less tank crews and they were holding their own.

To cover the area of both units, Berta had been forced to change position at least ten times, and they were washed out when they returned to Spark's hideaway in the morning. However, just as they had dropped off, a runner from the captain in command of the flyers brought a message. Apparently, they had lost one machine gun ("direct hit, nothing left") and the CO asked them for help. This put Berta in a spot: it was strictly against orders to fill in for "normal" gun-crews, "but we can't leave these poor buggers in the shit now, can we?" said Fischer. "We just won't tell Wagner," Brink suggested. "If we come back to tell anything at all!" the No. 3 threw in. "That's what I like about you, your confidence, you miserable sod!" Brink answered.

The night equipment was left with Sparks, the belts exchanged for the reserve in the trailer because they were tracer-free. After a quick wild boar breakfast, they were slogging it back to the frontline, the rumble and screeching of tank tracks grew louder behind them and three assault guns lumbered up. The driver of the first one stuck his head out of the hatch and shouted over the noise of the engine: "2nd Air Force Field Division, know where they are?" "We're going there, it's three kilometers, give us a lift?" "Hop on!" They were the old types with open fighting compartments, not the safest of their kind but the weather was such that no planes could operate. The gun-commander told them they were called in to deal with a concentration of tanks, apart from that he had no details. “I think we were a bit hasty, what the hell are we going to do against tanks?” Brink muttered under his breath. Anyway, the situation was not all that threatening. Since they had left early morning, the woods about 400 meters in front of the German line had filled up with Shermans, they were difficult to count between the trees, there could be anything between thirty and forty. It looked as if they had sent two machines ahead to test the ground and that was when things started to go wrong: both of them were sitting there in no-mans-land bogged down, rendered harmless at an angle of 45 degrees.

The previous machine gun had been sited in the cellar of a small collapsed house, they remembered Wagner saying: “Stay away from landmarks!,” it was too easy for the others to home in on them. A new position had to be built, lying down as it was daylight, they were tunneling once again under some fallen trees, Para-fashion. Suddenly, the assault gun tracks clanked and screeched on the left and the machines blithely rolled up the hill in full view of the Yanks. Not that they could do much about it, being stuck among the trees, their gun movements were greatly restricted. The German guns were the dreaded 88s, which no tank could survive, and within ten minutes the Shermans were nothing but a blazing scrapyard. The time it took was too short for the mortars to lock on to the assault guns; they would have been in real trouble because of the open fighting-compartments. Before that happened the two machines reversed and rumbled out of sight. “Bloody hell!” said Brink.

The Americans were furious and they threw everything they had at the German positions. Berta’s cover was hit several times but the fresh trees gave perfect protection, at least against mortar-bombs, but hopefully they had no artillery. “God help the poor sods outside,” said Fischer; he had the gun and Brink and the No. 3 were scanning the woods opposite, passing the targets on to him. They were hard to make out, only the mortar-muzzles were showing and the only way for a machine gun to subdue them was to try and hit those few inches of barrel, in the hope that the ricochets would wound or even kill the crew. Sometimes it worked, mostly it didn’t, it was simply too small a target. Tracers would have helped with this precision work but they would, of course, have given the position away. “Sorry, lads,” said the No. 3. “I have to crap.” There was nothing else to do but “go on the shovel,” which was no problem but when it came to throwing the stuff out, Hans went up and down the entrance several times. “For God’ sake, do it, you’re making me nervous!” said Fischer. “Waiting for a lull in the firing, want to chuck it in front of our hole for the Yanks to step into when we retreat next.” “Now, that’s good thinking!” said Brink.

Toward evening the No. 3 began to fidget, Brink and Fischer knew the signs, he felt it was time to move out of the present position. As before on a number of occasions, there was no argument or discussion. At that very moment a 2nd Lieutenant slid down into the hole, which became rather crowded. He had been sent by the Major to thank them and to tell them reinforcements had arrived: "Two companies regular infantry, would you believe it?" Quite obviously, he could not believe it himself! "And the chief sends you some fags for helping out, good luck men!" "And to you, sir." The question was, should they wait till nightfall to make their way back or now? "Now!" said the No. 3 and so they zig-zagged across the open ground like rabbits. "This is a dodgy spot, lets go back a bit further," said Brink. It took Sparks no time at all to pack the cart, and they were on their way within minutes. Covering the first kilometer with long distances between them, they closed up when the mortar danger ceased.

"Are they biting again?" Brink asked the No. 3 who was scratching a lot. "I could do with some treatment as well," said Sparks. "Tonight then." Lice, the scourge of the frontline. It was odd, with all the experience in the German army, there was no insecticide available to kill them. In the old days when soldiers could go on leave, they were treated at de-lousing stations first: all clothes were placed in metal cupboards and exposed to overheated steam while the owner had a shower with carbolic soap. Brink and Fischer hardly suffered from this pest, they had obviously components in their blood the lice did not like. Sparks had come to the rescue once again. One day, for some mysterious tactical reason, the frontline had to be corrected and the Yanks were pushed back two or three kilometers. When the fighting had ceased, looting for food and cigarettes started in the deserted American positions and Sparks came across a large tin of DDT. He had, God knows where, heard about it and took it. Later he sowed small bags from bandages and filled them with the powder so they could ""dust" themselves regularly. It looked ridiculous but worked like a dream.

This mission had a reassuring feeling about it, good troops, albeit a little thin on the ground, however, with experienced, well equipped men, that did not matter all that much. They had to shoot only once during the night, taking out a recce-unit. Returning to last night's position next evening, the place was deserted, not a living soul in sight, only two dead Germans nearby. Not even Brink felt like going forward into this vacuum, particularly as the next 500 meters offered very little cover. Then voices could be heard and when the owners came nearer, it was unmistakably Hessian dialect. They were two sergeants, both wounded, one of whom

Fischer remembered from the night before. Attended to already, they were in a happy mood, their wounds were not too bad but bad enough to be sent back. “Where is everybody, sarge?” Fischer asked. “You missed all the fun, mate. The Yanks broke in early and we had to counter-attack, threw them back a couple of kilometers and that’s where we are now. Here, have some fags, we’ve plenty. Right lung-torpedoes they are, I tell you!” Their pockets were bulging with Lucky Strikes, a brand new to Berta. It was impossible to look for a new position now in the dark, so they just buried the two dead and headed back to Sparky. When Wagner was informed later he agreed. “Actually, I wanted you at some other place but go back for one night or else they think you have scarpered!”

Judged by the increasing volume of small-arms fire, they were nearing the new frontline when they stumbled onto a large shell or bomb crater. Seven dead German soldiers were lying in it in grotesque contortions, no arms, no equipment, and riddled with bullets: shot POWs. This time the Yanks had not, as they often did, dropped hand grenades on the bodies to conceal the execution. To the right a bunch of prisoners staggered along, watched over by two guards. “I have an idea!” said Brink and ran over to them. After he talked to the guards the group changed direction. “They will bury them!” His face was contorted with anger when he pushed the Americans roughly over to the crater. Obviously they expected to meet with the same fate and three of them were wetting their trousers. The crew had taken the spades from the sheaths and asked the guards for theirs. Fischer threw them at the American’s feet and shouted: “You dig! Seven graves, there!” He was so angry that the English words came out without hesitation, although this was the first time he used the language in earnest. The prisoners understood, eagerly grabbed the spades and started to dig furiously, happy to have been spared. Two of them, officers by their uniforms, hung back and Brink was just about to kick them into action but Fischer said: “Leave them, Bert, they can bring the bodies up later.” “Brilliant, I will tell them!” Digging the graves took a while, the ground was not too bad but, as the spades were only about two feet long, they had to dig on their knees. When they had finished, Brink approached the officers: “You! Down there and bring bodies!” and Fischer thought that Bert’s English was not much better than his. They did not want to do it, their response was completely incomprehensible and they could only make out “officers.” “Oh dear,” said the No. 3, “they should know better than argue with Bert, this will not have a happy ending.” Brink led them to the edge by the scruff of their neck and kicked them up their backside, sending them flying onto the bodies below. They had the sense to bring them up without further protest. "We shall fill the graves in," Fischer had turned to the guards. "Take the bastards away before we get tempted and thanks for your help!"

Sparks had a nice surprise next morning; he had shot a hare and a rabbit. Shot but not skinned them, that was the No 3's department. Odd, that was actually something Sparky could not do. "I'm running short of salt, keep your eyes open, I have only enough for these two," he said.

The next job was a long way away, it meant marching all day but under low clouds. Late afternoon the road rose sharply and consequently the ditches became deeper. "Good place to have a bit of kip," suggested Brink. "Couple of hours," said Fischer. Their sleep was brought to a sudden end by an almighty crash; blood streamed from noses and ears, and they were almost deaf. An empty shell case came down on the No. 3, cutting his cheek deeply. Above them, not more then a meter away was the muzzle of a gun, heavy anti-tank probably, smoke still drifting from it. "What the hell are you doing down there? I could have killed you!" a voice came from above. "You bloody nearly did, you berk!"

Fischer shouted back, "Sir." He added this somewhat meekly, as it was a second lieutenant looking down. "Come away from there, I'm firing again." This was the amazing setup: a heavy anti-tank gun manned by the said lieutenant, nobody else in sight, its tractor with two wheels in the ditch a few meters down the road. He was carefully laying the gun and fired, now they looked what he was firing at, a Sherman coming round the bend about 1,500 meters up the road, another one was blazing already. "Well, this is it, that was my last round!" It was well spent, as the tank blew up. Sparks had found a packet of cotton wool in the trailer and Brink and Fischer plugged their noses. The No. 3 had been scanning the area where the tanks were blazing and called out: "Infantry to the left of the tanks!" The target was at the very limit of the gun, so it was Brink's turn; he was the better shot due to his phenomenal eyesight. "Start from that big twin-tree to the left, Bert." Shooting at that distance, one could actually see the tracers flying in an arch, not a straight line. But Brink had got it right again, the arch disappeared into the large group of Americans emerging from behind the tanks. "Brilliant shooting, corporal!" said the lieutenant, who had also watched. There was no more movement at the far end of the road. "Well, men, I'll be on my way, there's nothing more I can do here. I'll just disable the tractor, which is out of petrol anyway. I'm afraid I have to declare myself bankrupt. Can't do much with a pistol, can I?" "Will you join us, sir? It's not healthy to be on road on your own these days. If we're stopped, you can be in charge of us." He accepted gratefully, "Where's your crew, sir?" Brink asked. "Dead or wounded, we got air-attacked." Sparks had been rummaging around in the trailer and came up with the spare divisional order Wagner had supplied them with in case one got lost. "It might be advisable (Sparks actually said that!) that you carried that whilst with us, sir." "You are an amazing bunch, who are you, or is that a secret?" Sparks had offered him a Lucky Strike, "I think I just have to sit down for a moment, for Christ's sake what are these, opium?" said the lieutenant. "If the Yanks smoke these all the time, it's no wonder they do funny things!"

It had started to rain heavily, thank God, and they made good time on the road, although with an uneasy feeling in the back, with nothing between them and the Yanks. The lieutenant had carried the breechblock of his gun with him, which he threw away now, also the sights. Then the screeching of tank tracks could be heard, a noise which never failed to send shivers up Fischer's spine, but at least it came from the German side. Three Panthers and one of those huge assault-guns, nicknamed Ferdinand, rumbled towards them, a company of Infantry on either side. The lieutenant went up to the captain who led the formation and explained the situation and then they plodded on. Close to seven, they pulled off the road for "radio-hour" and something to eat. The lieutenant had no rations of his own and he was very happy to be invited. "A bit of cold hare, sir?" Sparks asked with the perfect manners of a head waiter. "Have you any idea where your unit is, sir?" asked Brink. "In heaven very likely, if there are any left amongst the living—I haven't a clue." "Shall we try and have them found? What is your unit?" The regimental number was passed on to Wagner, but he could not offer much hope; anyway he would come back before eight. He was as good as his word, but all he could find out was that a workshop-company of 12th Panzer Division (to which the lieutenant belonged) had been in Hermfeld until the day before, present whereabouts unknown. As it happened, this town was quite close to the route Berta was ordered to take and he would leave them there and try find out more. "It was an experience meeting up with you," he said when they parted company. "Try and keep out of trouble!"

"You know," said Fischer, "what the lieutenant said made me really think, we are bankrupt, aren't we? We have to find or nick our ammo, we don't know where tomorrow's rations are going to come from, and yet we are so much better off than all the others, at least we have a certain amount of freedom. All the same, I think we should keep out of trouble as the Lieutenant put it, not take any risks, I mean, we've done some daft things, haven't we? Of course we won't leave anybody in the lurch, that's not what I mean. But Sparky has his family to think of, Bert, you have to take over the mill, Hans the farm, you are both only sons, aren't you? My excuse can be that my family lost one son already. What do you reckon?" "My word," said Brink, "what a speech! But I'm with you, I've had this stupid war up to my eyeballs, what about you two?" Sparks and the No. 3 just nodded. Sparks went to his trailer and returned with a bottle of korn. "If this is the beginning of a new life, we had better drink to it!" "You crafty devil," said Fischer, "how often have you told us that our lifeblood had dried up?" "I was lying, too many alcoholics about."

One day disaster struck. It was not an attack from the air, or artillery or tanks, but the radio went dead. Sparks was crestfallen when he told the news. "Can't you repair the bloody thing?" Fischer asked. "No, I'm just a simple signaler, but I think I know the cause." In those days radios were running on valves, small glass-tubes which, amongst other components, contained a filament which heated up, red-hot it had to be to be able to emit electrons. The most common failure was this filament burning through, just like light bulbs. What Sparks had done was switching on the set and, after a few minutes, he pulled out the valves one by one and held them to his cheek, to feel if they were warm. Two stayed cold. "Didn't they give you any spares?" asked Brink. No, they had not. "I can only think of two things to do, either we find a depot of sorts, which is highly unlikely, or I vandalize an abandoned set, like in a tank. The good thing is that all parts in Army sets are interchangeable." "There was a wrecked Panther a few kilometers back. Shall we have a look if the Yanks have not caught up with it?" said the No. 3.

At that moment a Kübel, the German equivalent to a Jeep, came toward them at breakneck speed, heading for the front. Brink stepped out into the road and the car stopped; only one officer, apart from the driver, was in it. "Permission to request a lift, captain!" Brink had the divisional order out and the captain studied it. "I bloody can't take you all!" "It's only for our signaler, sir, he'll explain." "Hop in, then!" "You are not going on your own!" said the No. 3 and followed Sparks. Brink and Fischer (and the cart) waited in the road ditch. After an hour two small figures appeared. "They look about as dejected as I feel," said Fischer. It was indeed a very unhappy state of affairs, being cut off from Wagner. Nobody to fall back on, no advice, no orders, like living in a vacuum. He had been right: they had no valves. "All shattered by the impact!" said Sparks. An internal explosion had occurred inside the gun barrel, which was peeled back like a flower. "I think a rocket attack from a plane," said Hans, "more craters nearby and a freak hit in the barrel."

All that was left to do was to march east, this time actually hoping for a roadblock, where MPs could, perhaps, supply some information. “Let’s hope they won’t be those SS bastards,” said Fischer. For once, they were in luck. A roadblock came up and two infantry sergeants manned it. Brink (in command) went over and talked to them flashing the order. “Do you belong together?” Three more pouches came out. They listened to Brink’s story with interest but could not supply the whereabouts of a depot. “But,” said one of them, “not far from here is a Regiment HQ of 12th Panzer. For some reason they have a large signals section, they might be able to help. Have you got a map?” It was no big deal, ten or twelve kilometers. Sparks made the MPs very happy with a packet of English cigarettes.

Two officers were standing between the tents, a colonel and a captain. “We may as well go straight to the top!” said Brink and “requested permission to talk to you, sir!” The colonel listened without interrupting. “You have to see our officer signals. That big tent, ask for Lieutenant Werner, tell him I sent you.” They had just performed a crashing salute, when the colonel said: “It just came to me, men, do you know one of my commanders, Major Hummel?” “Tiger company, sir?” “The very same. A few weeks ago he was assisted by an outfit like you, know anything about that?” “It was us, sir!” “Good, I can thank you personally then. The major reckoned you saved his bacon and, consequently, mine as well!” He came and shook hands.

“Which valves do you need?” said the lieutenant. “Two KV23M, sir” (or something like that). “Always the first ones to go. How long were they in use?” “Eight months.” That’s quite good really. Well, we have plenty; I’ll let you have two and two as spares. That should see you through to the end of the war!”

CHAPTER 14

Hill 237

"Fischer," said Wagner when they were able to ring in again, "you will be the death of me! What the hell has happened? I've been trying to radio you for hours!" With his force getting smaller and smaller, he must have been very relieved not to have lost Berta. "Who's in command?" Wagner asked. "Brink, sir." "Brink, this is special, I can't say more this being an open line, you'll get your orders later. Get your map! I know where you are, we needn't mention it. On a line north/northeast you'll see Hill 237 where you'll meet up with Anton (on the German maps all hills and mountains carried their heights in meters, the hill in question was therefore 237 meters high, a simple identification system, hardly ever were two hills of the same height). A main road is overlooked from there running east-west, got that?" "Yes, captain." "March west about eight kilometers, there's a unit of the arm you and Fischer belonged to before you came to us, you with me?" Brink thought a second: "With you now, sir." "Captain Bertram is the CO, he will fill you in. Ring me then from there, the battery has a scrambler." "What's a scrambler?" "A gadget that distorts the speech and conversations can't be listened into. And Brink, hurry, this is urgent, leave at once, force a lift, at gunpoint if you have to!" "He never sounded like this before. I think he is worried,." said Bert.

An armored scout car passed by and offered them a precarious lift on top, the two carts were tied to the aerial ring and the whole thing looked like a Gypsy caravan. Luckily, there was no danger from the sky, light fog on the ground and low clouds above. Hill 237 was quickly reached and the Anton crew was there already, sleeping peacefully under a tree, Meinert and Nuthmann, both very nice chaps who had received the same cryptic message. Together they were now looking down onto the "main road running east-west" and what was happening on it: an army in retreat, soldiers, walking wounded, the odd horse and cart. "We'll never push though that mess going the opposite way!" said Meinert, but there was no alternative: a river close to the road on the right and steep hills on the left restricted movements completely. What made it even more unpleasant was the sight of engineers mining the verges on both sides.

Squeezing through the frightened soldiers, they heard more than once: "Wrong way, you idiots!" Two ambulances followed in the distance, and since they were going toward the front, they would be empty. Fischer hung back and took the divisional order out. Having jumped on to the running board of the first one, an angry sergeant faced him who refused his request for a lift. Apparently, they had orders to evacuate a field hospital and "had no time to bugger about." The order changed his mind though, and he asked how many? "Eight and equipment." "Where to?" "There is supposed to be an AA battery along this road." The driver interrupted: "I know it, it's a kilometer beyond the hospital, 88s, three guns." "Hop on then!" said the Sergeant with a sigh. Traveling this way would not be quicker but pleasanter then pushing through the dispirited troops.

Captain Bertram's face showed relief when they reported. "So why did you abandon us then?" "Sir?" He pointed to the AA badges on their sleeves. "Auxiliaries, captain." "Of course, what guns?" 88 said Brink, 10.5 said Fischer. This was the situation: The stream of beaten soldiers had slowed down to a trickle, the otherwise empty road was stretching about 2,000 meters to a bend where it swung to the right. "As you can see, their armor has to come this way and I intend to destroy the column after the curve. Infantry following is your responsibility, consequently you must be positioned behind the bend, out of sight from here. I have a signaler out there with a telephone, just follow the cable. I have intelligence that the tanks will arrive in an hour, plenty of time to dig in." "So there will be nothing in the way of neighbors, sir?" "No, lad, you will be the last hope of high command!" "Sh-sh-shit!" said Nuthmann, who always developed a slight stammer when he got excited. "I could not have put it better myself, corporal," said the captain.

The guns were cleverly placed, close together under two enormous trees. The gunners had attached ropes to the lowest branches, pulling those down concealed the guns completely, only the muzzles were showing. Three gun tractors and a small lorry hid under other trees. "Ring your CO, telephone's in the first tractor!" They all came with Brink and stood around him. "This is a scrambler," said the signaler, "hold the red button down when you talk, the white one when you listen." Wagner told Brink that, once the 88s had destroyed the armor, they would retreat to the next blocking position under cover of darkness. "However, I have the captain's word that he will leave the ammo lorry behind waiting to pick you up and take you back as well. There will be no other troops on either side of you, so don't miss it! I will give you your destination for after this later, keep reporting to me and good luck!" "Now," Nuthmann said, "that really f-f-fills me with c-c-confidence." One of the gunnery sergeants came over to them: "I better tell you how we are going to do it. See that curve at the end of the road? The tanks will drive into it, and since they never learn they'll be very close together, for company I suppose. Usually they do this sort of thing in company-strength, that is ten to fifteen machines. The captain measured the bend and it should easily hold twenty tanks, if you know what I mean. Obviously, we shall be shooting at a very small angle, but if a shot bounces off, we'll get him with the next one, not to worry. Fortunately the road is curving to the right, or else we would be on the wrong side, wouldn't we? When all tanks are in the trap, we blow up the first and the last one, the rest are hemmed in then and all we have to do is to shoot down the line and take out one after the other. It should take not more than five to ten minutes." "J-Jesus!" said Nuthmann.

"Well, we had better be going," said Fischer and Sparks came across with a bottle: "Would this be an occasion for a little backup?" When parting ways with Frieda, Berta had inherited half of their loot from the depot. The AA sergeant was overwhelmed: "It's been many months since I had one of these, bless you and good luck!" The two radiomen stayed behind and the others followed the telephone cable for about twenty minutes, as the sergeant had warned the signaler of their arrival. The lay of the land behind the curve was absolutely ideal for an ambush. On the other side of the road the hills retreated and formed some kind of large lay-by. On the river side the land had risen to about twenty feet above the water, but what was even more important, the water had washed out a horseshoe-shaped small bay and that meant the field of fire was not restricted to a 90 degree angle towards the road, in fact the road could be covered for about one or two kilometers without trees being in the way. Old pines were standing on top and the signaler had used the same trick as the gunners: on bits of telephone wire he had pulled the lowest branches down and fastened them to pegs in the ground. Because of the restricted frontage both guns were placed together in one shallow pit, Fischer on the right, Meinert on the left. From here a line to a high tree on the other side of the road divided the ground into a left and right sector. The two No. 3s were on either side, seeming the wings. Everything was ready now.

Several cigarettes later dusk was setting in, it was very quiet, only from a long distance came a continuous rumble of artillery. Brink and Anton's No. 2 had nodded off, the signaler tried to look alert. The night sights were switched on now, suddenly something was moving at the end of the road.

Here they came! Fischer gave the signaler a kick and changed places with him because he had to give a running commentary to his battery. He gasped when the tanks stood out so clearly and he counted them off as they came around the bend, sixteen of them, the sergeant had been right. They were followed by two cars, not Jeeps but something bigger and bristling with aerials. "Will your mates be able to draw a bead on the tanks in the dark?" Brink asked. "The layers are picked for their night vision, anyway, it's all illuminated once the first tank is on fire." The Shermans took their time, sending this terrible squealing and screeching of the tracks ahead of them, a noise which could give even old soldiers the jitters. They were below them now, blowing up choking exhaust fumes. "First tank entering curve," the signaler reported back. When the two cars had appeared on the scene, Brink and Nuthmann had quickly prepared two belts starting with twenty tracers and removing the others spaced along the belts. The guns were too close to the enemy to be able to afford this luxury. "I'll take the one on the right," said Fischer. "Bert, give the firing order, we both shoot at the same moment."

"Last tank entering curve!" went down the wire and only seconds later a loud explosion and, an absolutely amazing sight, the complete turret of the Sherman came sailing back through the air, crashing between the two cars. "Hit in ammo-storage!" the signaler commented. "This is the time!" came from Brink, "Fire!" The tracers streamed from both guns and the cars burst into flames at once. The Infantry had caught up now, probably company strength. Before they could react, the guns swept their sectors, the tumbling ricochets from the road surface causing no doubt heavy damage. Brink slapped Fischer on the shoulder, the signal that the barrel needed changing. Anton's No. 2 had the same idea and into the sudden silence the No. 3 called out from the right: "Bert, below you!" Brink threw the fresh barrel in and the gun came to life again, then he ripped the two hand grenades from Fischer's belt (they carried them on their backs), pulled the cords, and dropped them over the edge. A scream confirmed the warning, fortunately the No. 3, concealed to the right around the horseshoe, so to speak, could see the slope in front of the guns.

Before the guns became overheated again, Meinert called out: "That's it, then, isn't it?" "Looks like it," said Fischer. "Can I have a look?" the signaler asked. "Good God!" he said, nothing else. After a while he continued: "When we go back, will one of you walk ahead of me with the cable over his shoulder? It would make it much easier for me to wind it in." "I'll do it!" Nuthmann volunteered. Berta hung back to cover their backs, but nobody really expected any trouble. All the same, Brink carried the gun on his shoulder, the No. 3 walked behind him with the battery connected and every few minutes they stopped and Fischer scanned a half-circle. Nothing stirred. The track which run more or less parallel with the tank graveyard on the right was eerily lit up by the burning machines, even more so as fog was descending. The constant crackle of machine gun ammunition made for a fitting background, every now and again a bigger explosion could be felt through the trees, shells being set off by the heat. There was no evidence of any survivors.

The battery position was deserted; the crews must have worked like madmen to shift the guns. To everybody's relief, the ammo-lorry was waiting between the trees and Sparks came over with another bottle which, this time, was shared with the signaler and the driver. "Tell me," asked the former, "do you get this stuff with your rations?" "Don't be silly, whatever makes you think that? It's nicked." "Well, I thought with your job? You know what I mean." "Go on," said Brink, "You didn't do too badly either. How many tanks were there? Sixteen? That makes about seventy crew, so what's the difference?" "I think I know what our friend here means," said Fischer. "If you think back to when you downed a bomber, you didn't say 'I just killed eight aircrew,' you thought 'I just shot a bomber down.' There you have the difference, the poor sods inside don't count somehow." "Quite a little thinker, aren't you?" said Brink.

The evacuation of the field hospital was still going on, and the driver had the brilliant idea to stop and ask if there was any food to be left behind. They were in luck and a large thermos container of pea soup ended up on the lorry. The next blocking position for the guns was eight kilometers east, and the gunners were working like devils to set them up again. The captain was one of them and his hands were as oily as those of his men. "Did everything go well?" he called over. "Better ring your captain, he's been fussing like a mother hen!" Fischer gave, again over the scrambler, a short account of the events and Wagner was pleased. "I don't mind telling you, I was worried about you!" "We know that, sir, thank you." "You can leave now, the AA guns are now part of a new frontline of sorts, which will give them protection. Find a place northeast and have a rest. Well done, pass that on!"

They all had a good wash in the river and then sat down to an early pea soup breakfast. The captain ambled over to them. It was exceptionally warm and they had taken the camouflage jackets off for an airing. The CO saw the AA medals immediately on their tunics, not only Brink and Fischer, but also Meinert and Nuthmann had it. "Been busy I see, good lads!" the captain said. He squatted down with them while they were eating. "How are you off for fags?" "So-so, captain." "Henze," he addressed the radioman, "see them right and don't be your usual stingy self, you wouldn't be standing here without that lot!" "Come with me then!" He rummaged around in the gun tractor and said: "I can let you have 400 each, that do you? They're English, not as lethal as the Yanks." He disappeared again and returned with an armful of tins. "Here are two each of orange marmalade, don't eat too much or it will give you the shits. You can have three each of this steak and kidney, it's very good, like goulash. And here's some powder coffee, one tin per gun." The captain enjoyed their utter surprise. "We shot up a supply column up north in the British sector. Well, you will be making tracks, thanks a lot for your help, take care and good luck!" "And to you, sir, thank you very much also." They marched off into the welcome fog, not without having their mess tins refilled to the top. "What a profitable night!" said Sparks. "I have been thinking," he continued. "I don't like you lighting up at the gun in the night, somebody will take a pot shot at you one day!" He produced a piece of broken cup, with a long chard still attached to the handle. Around that he had wound some thin wire, a piece of telephone cable was attached to the ends of that. "Touch this to the battery and it will glow like a car cigarette lighter, see?" This weird looking invention worked until the end of the war!

The next mission started off with a long march. A group of assault-guns offered a lift, but Berta declined. It would have been much too dangerous; they attracted planes like a honey-pot flies. Fischer was covering the rear, and he noticed Sparks falling back more and more, which was not like him at all. "What's the matter, Sparkie?" "It's my ankle, I don't know what's wrong with it." Fischer called for the others to stop and told Sparks to take his boot off. He looked aghast at the damage, the ankle had swollen up to nearly twice its size. "My God, why didn't you say something before?"

"It will go down when we get a break." "And when will that be?" "I know a bit about massage," said the No. 3. "I'll use my last margarine ration, I can't bring it down anyway, it's so vile!" It helped (said Sparks). "Let's go on, I'll be all right." Brink had meanwhile cut a crutch from a young tree and that made a big difference, so they plodded and limped on. When darkness fell they turned off the road into a densely wooded area for a few hours sleep. It must have been about 11 when Sparks, who had the first watch, shook them. "I don't like this," he whispered, "there's small-arms fire right and left, but ahead of us, they must have bypassed us!" Under a groundsheet the map was consulted (the one inherited from the dispatch rider) and the situation became transparent at once: more or less parallel to the road they had come on ran another one, roughly three kilometers north. Between them meandered a small river with woods on either side of it. What was more important, these woods were marked with the symbol for "boggy." "That'll be our salvation," said Fischer, "they can't drive here and they will not want to get their feet wet." Brink suggested that he took the lead with Fischer carrying the battery. Every few meters he would scan the ground for movements. "And don't you dare fire that bloody gun!" whispered Fischer. Every twenty minutes they changed places, that was the limit for lagging the battery. It worked quite well, but the scanning slowed them down no end; all the same, they seemed to get nearer to the infantry fire. Suddenly, Brink froze: "Something's there! I think they're German helmets, you check, between the two larger trees!" The shape of helmet was the only distinguishing mark in the night-sight, the body showed up as silhouette only. But here was no doubt, they were German helmets. Brink left the gun, crawled forward and called out: "We're German infantry!" and a voice came back: "When's Hitler's birthday?" "20th April." Brink answered. "All right, come on in." A second lieutenant was in command of a small company or large platoon and the men looked as if they were about to move off. "We have just been ordered to pull back, join us if you like, but it's going to be dicey, we don't know who we are going to bump into." "This is your lucky night, sir," Brink said. "We have a night-sight, you want us to lead?" "Go on, will that work?" "It showed us where you were, sir." "You could help us a lot, lieutenant," said Fischer. "We've been on the march three hours and we are bushed. Would you give us a strong man to carry the battery?" "Bartels, you are volunteering!" Forward stepped a giant of a man who shouldered the heavy battery like a box of matches. "Stay close, the cable is not very long!" A long single line of soldiers snaked through the trees, no talking, no smoking, the only sound, sometimes, the squelching of the bog. The lieutenant was in front with them. The ground rose slightly and became less swampy. Brink stopped again. "Germans, I'm sure, would you check?" The helmets showed up clearly and the lieutenant made his way towards them carefully. When he called out, the question came back: "Who's your commanding officer?" "Lieutenant Hansen!" "Thank God, Hansen, this is Captain Bernel, I thought we lost you!" The unit was under order to fan out to either side and block the traffic on both roads, but Berta kept on marching east, no way would they stay in that death-trap. Brink had cut another crutch, and Sparks could keep up quite well now. The next thing was to let Wagner know what happened. Fischer phoned and the captain's voice was harsh with worry: "Where the hell have you been? I've been trying to get you I don't know how many times!" "We were cut off, sir, and we thought it better to keep radio silence; The AA signaler told us the Yanks have some very good tracking devices." "Christ! Are you all right now?" "Perfectly, sir." "March east, stay on air, I'll be in touch soon. And, Fischer? Good to have you all back! Tell the others!"

"Bloody hell, look at this!" Brink called out. Behind a rickety table under a tree sat an elderly, if not to say old, corporal from the paymasters corps, a crude sign in front of him: BACK PAY. Since the group had received their last money when leaving Denmark, it was about time too! Not that it mattered much, there had been nowhere to spend it. When the notes had been handed over the corporal asked: "Need condoms?," pointing to a battered box. "Now what the hell would we want those for?" said Fischer and Brink added: "You joker; we haven't even seen a female for nine months and things are not going to improve now, are they?" "All right, I'm only doing my duty." "We know you are, we are all a bit nervous," said Sparks placatingly. "I would not hang around here too long if I were you." There was actually a serious side to the corporal's question. Condoms were always readily available in the Army. Consequently, if someone did pick up an infection, there was no excuse for it and it counted as a self-inflicted injury. There was only one penalty for this: transfer to a penal unit, which meant an almost certain death warrant with the jobs they had to do like lifting mines under fire.

Despite the exchange with the paymaster chap, the No. 3 asked for three packets. "How do you do it?" asked the former. "It's a gift," said Hans. The real reason was the clever idea he had a few months ago: to pull a condom over the muzzle of the gun during rainy marches. It did not matter to the gun if the breech was awash, but water in the barrel was a different matter. It always caused wise cracks to flow when they arrived at a new destination. The first time they used this invention, Fischer made a mess of the gun. They had to shoot quickly and he had not taken the damn thing off. The muzzle brake became of course extremely hot and the rubber burnt on to it. It took hours to clean it.

"You will probably enjoy this!" said Wagner over the phone. "It's your friends from the AA. The problem is I don't know where they are. Their scout jeep got separated from them in fog, and it has the maps on board. Fortunately the feldwebel is from around there, and from their description, he has a rough idea of their position. I am not far away, he will come on the bike, take one of you with him, and search for the battery, he also has mail for you all. Who is in command today?" "I am," said Fischer. "You stay behind. Brink will go with him."

About an hour later Feldwebel Wörner arrived; he pulled two bottles of Korn and a carton of cigarettes from his saddlebag (Don't drink it all at once!). Sparks had just brewed some coffee, he had a quick drink and then disappeared with Brink in a cloud of dust and blue exhaust fumes. Luckily, the clouds were hanging low and they would be safe.

The letters from home did not cause any alarm. Neither Brink, the No. 3, nor Fischer lived in a big town, so the danger of air raids was minimal. Only Sparks had some really good news: he had been bombed out in Frankfurt a couple of years ago and his family now lived outside the city in the Taunus mountains. Apparently he had a sister somewhere in the east, she fled from the Russians with three small kids to join Spark's lot, and now she had safely arrived after a string of grim adventures. It was quite amazing how mail still arrived in the present situation, unbelievable really. "Let's have a bit of shut-eye, I'll take the first watch," said Fischer.

It must have been after a good hour when the whine of clapped-out gears came nearer. It was a small lorry, but what a sight! The top of the cab and the windscreen weremissing, as were the doors, and the sides were full of holes. The signaler they met last time was driving it and Brink was sitting with him. He got slowly out of the cab. "It's off," he said. "They bombed the shit out of the battery. Everybody killed except him. Only little bits lying around and those lovely 88s, just scrap! The nice captain! Bastards!" The signaler just sat there, obviously under shock. Sparks ran to the trailer and poured a cup from the newly arrived bottles for him. "I'm in shock too!" said Brink. It was decided that everybody was shaken up and that was the end of the first bottle.

"There a lot of the English tins in the back," said Brink. "Wörner told me to pick them up, but I said I wouldn't, I'd feel like a bloody grave robber. Don't be so stupid he said, think of your mates, they will only go to waste, I'll take some myself. He's gone back to base on a direct route."

Fischer rang the captain and thanked him first for the supplements. "We could not follow orders, sir, battery was bombed out of existence, nothing left!" He wanted to continue the sad story when Wagner interrupted: "Does the feldwebel know all this?" "He went there with Brink." "Right, he has just arrived back; I'll get the details from him. That was a close shave, lad."

"Anyway, we are all right, captain, but there is something I wanted to ask: with us is a signaler from the battery, he's the only survivor. He also drove back the lorry which was to take us there. He's pretty shaken up and doesn't know where to go." "Leave it with me, I had obviously been in contact with his regiment, I will come back to you soon."

The regimental HQ was still quite near, about thirty kilometers to the east. "He'll be welcome there, particularly if he brings a lorry; they lost most of their transport. You all go with him, tell him to drop you off at Singen, that's about three quarters of the way. Hole up there for the rest of the night. I will give you further orders tomorrow. And I'm very glad you did not get caught up in this mess!"

It was nice in Singen. At the eastern end of the township stood a sawmill, deserted of course, but high stacks of tree trunks filled the yard and it was easy to build a good shelter. On the other side of the town was a depot, or rather, had been a depot because it had been ransacked. All the good stuff had disappeared, left was only a large stock of dried vegetables (quite good if steeped long enough), potatoes, and bread, although mildew was taking it over. Some of that could probably be toasted.

Wagner had told them to make the most of it. It would be their home for a few days. "Keeping us out of harms way, no doubt," said Winter. Apparently, all operations on the American side had come to a standstill, they had run out of petrol, the supply lines being overstretched now, and the infantry would not move an inch without the tanks. "The frontline is about thirty kilometers west of you, so I can give you plenty of warning. Make it look as if you have a right to be there!" Sparks took that literally and he found a white board on which he wrote with charcoal: ASSEMBLY POINT 65th REGT. "You crafty devil!" said Brink and helped him put it up in a conspicuous spot. That and the two radios (aerials out) made it look really official. Sparks could get to work with his cooking now. The sawmill's kitchen was undamaged and fully equipped; all it needed was some absolutely dry wood to avoid the chimney smoking. Vegetables had been soaked the night before, potatoes were added, and a few of the English tins, it wasn't at all bad. As they were eating three MPs arrived. "Jesus, here we go again!" said Fischer, but it turned out to be different this time. A second lieutenant waved the "tenshun!" aside. "I saw your aerials, men, perhaps you can help us, who are you connected to?" "22nd Division, sir." He looked as if he did not believe that until Winter pulled his order out from under his tunic and handed it to the officer who said, "Blimey! Our problem is we have just arrived from the northern sector and I can't find anybody familiar with the situation, frontline and such. Can you fill me in?" "Yesterday the Yanks were thirty kilometers away, but we can get you more detailed information from our HQ." Sparks was already pushing his buttons. "Berta here, Peter, is the chief in?" "Right, we'll ring back in thirty minutes, we need the exact frontline, we have MPs with us who lost contact with their HQ." "The captain and Wörner have gone to find some petrol." "Spot of lunch, sir, while you are waiting?" Sparks was really a scream! The MPs accepted very happily, also a packet of cigarettes afterward. Actually, Wagner rang back, the lieutenant introduced himself and started to draw lines and circles on his map. "Not very reassuring, sir, is it? But I'm grateful there is still some organization left in this mess! Thank you very much!" When the men left, the lieutenant did a funny thing and shook hands all round. The evening mist swallowed up their motorcycle.

The only disturbance during these almost idyllic days was two Mustangs racing along the main road, very low, only a few hundred feet up. They came with first and last light in the hope to catch something moving, either too late or too early. The road stretched for miles absolutely straight, an old Roman one, no doubt and burned-out wrecks on either side were a clear signal to avoid it. During the day it was deserted, but in the dark it came to life. "Shall we have a go at them?" Winter asked, "What do you think of this?" One of the piles of tree trunks, close to the road, had a top layer much longer then the rest underneath, forming something like a roof over a porch. "How about forcing two trees apart so the guns can go into the slit, they would point into the right direction." "We shall have to rope or wire them to the bottom one, or else they'll kick all over the place," said Fischer.

The preparations were done in half an hour, the No. 3s had removed the tracers from two belts. If they turned up the same evening, it would be Brink's and Winter's turn to shoot, but both were old AA-hands and knew their stuff.

It was only mid-afternoon and the No. 3 said: "If you don't need us now, Walter (that was Winter's No. 3) and I will go and see if we can shoot some meat. It won't be easy, not having rifles, but I heard some pheasants calling and they are stupid enough to be shot with a machine pistol." He was as good as his word and after a while returned with four birds. "Not very fat this time of the year," he explained. Sparks snatched them away: "They can hang overnight, I'll do them on the spit tomorrow."

They sat behind the guns when it was time for the planes to show up, smoking and drinking, of all things, peppermint tea! The No. 3 had brought back a big bunch of wild mint and it made a nice change. The two radiomen scanned the end of the road with field glasses. Winter played his mouth organ, an unreal scene. Until Sparks shouted: "They're here!" A few more seconds and both guns opened up together making a frightful din. Brink's plane wanted to gain height but fell back and crashed at the eastern side of the sawmill. Winter's target (the one behind) lurched violently to the left to avoid the first plane and his right wing fell off! He smashed into a burned out assault gun by the side of the road, perhaps it was one of his victims? Oddly enough, the plane did not explode and its tail was sticking out of the tank. "That looks positively obscene," said the No. 3. "Rest in peace, you bastards!" said Brink. Winter added, "Amen, I know what happened, my aim slipped to just that little bit left of the fuselage and at that low angle the gun sawed the wing off. A glorious sight!" "You pervert," said his No. 2. Sparks had vanished from the scene, and he came back with a bottle. A bottle! "This is absolutely the last one." "Sparky," said Fischer, "there is absolutely only one of you in the whole bloody army!" The planes were back in the morning, three of them, but they flew a lot higher and were out of reach.

Wagner phoned early afternoon, "Only wanted to know how things are going, did the MPs give you any trouble?" It was Fischer's turn now: "No. Sir, they were the nicest we ever came across. And we had a good day yesterday, Brink and Winter shot a plane down each!" "My goodness, what next? So when are you going to have yours?" "I had mine, sir, when we were with the panzergrenadiers, but it was only a spotter plane." "You know, Fischer, I have the feeling you lot are telling me only half of what you get up to, probably just as well. How is the ammo situation?" "Good, sir, we met some lorries on the way to supply a tank unit, but when they got there it did not exist anymore. They gave us as much as we wanted and we will be alright for a long while." "Have you enough to eat?" "It's a bit tight at the moment, but we'll make out, sir. Although tonight we will have pheasant." "You ought to be ashamed of yourself! Now give me Winter and good luck."

Sparks had set a fire in an open shed and when it had burned down to the coals, the birds went on it. They took it in turns to turn the spit and the smell was unbelievable. The rest were grating potatoes, as Sparks had discovered a drum of cooking oil in the kitchen and potato cakes were on the menu. The distant desultory artillery fire had crept nearer and had become more intense, but the mountains of tree trunks gave off a feeling of safety. In any case, Wagner would alert them in case of any real danger, that was good enough.

Wagner came through on the telephone: "Go on scrambler, Fischer!" "I am now, sir." "Winter is in trouble, his radio broke down, he's got only the phone and that is dodgy! So I cannot be sure if he receives my orders. I tried to make him understand to join up with you or Hartmann who is to the south of you. We don't want to lose him, Fischer! Are you still on the same road you reported from yesterday?" "We are, captain, road is good and it is raining, we are making good headway east." "Good, I told him, or rather tried to tell him, to follow this road where you would wait for him or, if this route is closed by the enemy, he will make for Hartmann.

Find a place where you can watch the road over some distance, if the Yanks are rolling up, scarper, there is nothing you can do and Winter will have gone the other way. At least I damn well hope so! There are no troops near you, so don't play Custer's last stand, do you hear? Good luck and keep me in the picture frequently!" "Custer's last stand!" said Brink. "Isn't he a funny bastard?"

Sparks and the No. 3 would march on five kilometers to a junction where a side road branched off toward the north, petering out as a track in the woods. Hans did not want to leave them but he had to stay with Sparks, whose ankle was still far from normal. He left two full ammo-boxes but the battery went onto the cart since it was daylight. While Fischer was removing the tracers from the belt, Brink had found a first-class position in a bend, probably ten meters above the level of the road. A bit of digging made them disappear into the ground in a few minutes. "Take some shut-eye, Bert, I'm wide awake," said Fischer and settled down with a cigarette and a book he had picked up in ruined house. Actually, it was only half a book, split down the middle, but interesting all the same: *The Ancient Cultures of Mexico.*

The road lay empty, about two kilometers of it, then it bent out of sight. This silence did not, as one would have thought, create a feeling of peace and quiet but an increasing sensation of unease. Suddenly, a horse-drawn cart came creaking around the bend, loaded to capacity with wounded men. When they were near Berta's position, Fischer slid down the hill and asked the driver: "What's coming behind you, mate?" "Nobody as far as I know, but could you spare a few fags?" Fischer handed over two of the English packs and was rewarded by a chorus of "thank you's"from the back. "Can't you go any faster?" he asked. "I will soon, had to give the horses a breather," and they plodded on.

"Just look at it" (Brink had woken up), "that's all that's left of the German Army, two clapped out horses and a load of wounded. It can't last much longer, surely!" After half an hour or so things became more serious: Shermans appeared, ten or twelve of them. Brink had taken the gun, Fischer had his field glasses on the column. "All commanders are standing in their turrets and I can also see the driver of the first tank, he's sticking his stupid head out of his hatch!" "This is what gets me wild!" said Brink. "They behave as if they own the place, like driving across the plains of Montana."

"What on earth makes you think of the plains of Montana?" "Oh, I don't know, read that somewhere a long time ago. I wonder what the drivers will do once I have shot their commanders?" "We better not hang around to find out, being smack in the line of fire! Just do your stuff and then we'll make ourselves scarce!" Brink waited until the first machine had closed up to 400 meters and fired. The leading, now driver-less, tank skidded across the road and stalled, the others bunched up in an untidy heap. The two used this moment of shock among the tankers and slid backward out of the foxhole, dragging their gear after them. It was a safe bet they would get away with it since the tanks had no infantry with them. "They never bloody learn, do they?"

Heading east more or less parallel to the road, they changed loads every kilometer because it was much easier carrying the gun than two full ammo boxes. Sparks and the No. 3 were at the arranged spot, and it was good to be together again. Sparks was warming some soup over a small fire and Hans was brewing coffee. Fischer rang the captain to report in and Wagner told him that Hartmann had radioed in this minute to say Winter had found them and they were all in good shape. The relief in his voice was very noticeable. "I can't help thinking," said Brink, "that I could have set fire to the first tank if I would have a put a belt of tracers into the driver's hatch, why didn't I? Shit!"

"Brink," Wagner said on the phone, "I plan to pull you out one by one and let you have two or three days off, so to speak. The front is static at the moment, they have probably outrun their supplies, I will warn you when the situation changes. Find yourself a place out of sight of patrols. Get your stuff in order and catch up on your sleep. I take it the gun is in top condition?" "Yes, captain, but we are running short of gun oil and nobody seems to have any to spare." "You are not far, I will bring you some myself, it's time I inspected you personally anyway. Let me know where to find you when you picked your hideaway. Make the most of the rest, I hope I will not have to interrupt it!"

Now that was wonderful news for a change! It was early morning and they set off right away so as not to lose any time. It took about an hour to find a good place: a lane off the road petered out into a forestry track that led to a large area of young pines, where it simply ended. An extra bonus was a clear brook whispering by, with good water for cooking and washing and a very rickety old wooden hut, probably a shelter for forestry workers years ago.

Fischer rang the captain to give him directions. "We are between Hailsheim and Burgdorf, three kilometers west of Hailsheim. No landmarks on the road, sir, but I will tie a white rag to a tree where the lane comes off the road to the left; we are at the end of it." Wagner planned to arrive at about 6:00. "How will he control the bike with his bad hand?" Fischer said to the others. "Anyway, with the captain coming to inspect us, we had better do something about our boots!" The mud was scraped off and then they rubbed them down with heather. Sparks had (naturally) a large tin of Dubbin in the trailer that he lifted at some depot and which the boots soaked up happily. "Do you remember that burnt-out farm a couple of kilometers back?" said the No. 3. "I think I will go back and see if there is anything useful left. Coming with me, Sparky?" "Don't use the road!" "What do you take me for?" he said. The other two started to collect dry, smoke-less wood for the cooking fire, because Hans and Sparks were bound to find something; Hans with his knowledge of where a farmer would hide things and Sparks applying his ferret's instinct, they would not come back empty-handed. The gun was cleaned next. "We leave it in bits on the rag for Wagner's benefit," said Brink. The ammunition boxes were lined up, the spare (and cleaned) barrels on top, the MPs standing up in a pyramid; it looked quite smart.

Fischer was asleep in the tent when Brink shook him: "Get up, Rolf, you must see this!" Sparks and the No. 3 were returning. Both their back packs were full and looked heavy. Sparks had stuck the handle of a large frying pan into his. In his left hand he carried three or four chickens (dead); in his right, a sack. Hans struggled with a large stone-ware demijohn; his other hand held an old-fashioned wicker basket full of eggs! There must have been fifty of them! "But" he said, "they will not all be good." "How will you know?" "I'll show you in minute. These are all right, though." Out of his assault pack he tipped ten salamis and twelve liver sausages. Sparks opened his and a whole ham fell out. "Now this will have to be eaten first, it has not been hanging in the smoke long enough. See how soft it still is? But alright for frying." Brink and Fischer just stood there open-mouthed. "I will show you about the eggs, you might learn something for later," said the No. 3. They walked over to the brook where he scooped out a little basin in the riverbank, under water, and dropped an egg in it. It floated on top. "Bad." said Hans and pushed it into the river where it bobbed downstream. "We don't want them breaking here, the stink is awful!" The next three were behaving the same way, then a few sank to the bottom. "They're good!" "This is great, will you let me do it?" asked Brink. Sparks was already plucking the chicken. "We are going to invite Wagner for dinner, aren't we?" "We certainly will, what's in the bottle, Sparky?" "Cider, a very strong kind and would you get the fire going, I shall need a nice bed of coal in a bit." Hans began to clean out the chicken and Fischer started the fire and built the spit (according to Spark's instructions). He asked Hans how the sausages survived the fire. "In the smoking chamber, that's obviously fire-proof. Part of the roof had fallen over it, so nobody had got to it before."

Shortly before six Wagner's signaler came through asking if the chief had arrived and would he ring back immediately? A little later the sound of a motorbike in low gear came nearer and the crew fell in. Bert was "in command" that day so it fell to him to report. The feldwebel had come as well; Wagner was riding pillion. Brink stepped forward: "Gun Berta, crew of four present, nothing particular to report, sir." It felt good to have a bit of drill again. "It straightens you out inwardly," Fischer thought. "Evening, men," said Wagner, looking as if he liked the reception. "At ease and dismissed! How are things?" "We are fine, captain, but your signaler wants you to ring him urgently," said Brink. "Shit, can't I have a few hours peace?" Sparks was fiddling his knobs already and Wagner listened for a while. "Who is nearest? No, we send Winter. Can you cross-connect me from here? Right, I'll wait." Wagner unfolded his map, and when Winter came on he received lengthy instructions for quite a dodgy job, or so it sounded.

The crew had completely forgotten about the decorations, which Wagner of course saw immediately. "Don't you think you should have told me about those? Knocking out tanks was not exactly what I had in mind for you! Oh well, l don't suppose I can change your nature, congratulations!" Then he pulled out two corporal chevrons for Sparks and the No. 3. "Congratulations again." Brink said:" We were hoping the captain and the Feldwebel would stay for dinner?" "How can we refuse, Brink?" Sparks disappeared deeper into the trees where the fire was and came back with the first course presently. It was scrambled eggs (about twenty-five had been fresh), since he had no fat to fry them in, he had squeezed one of the liver sausages into the pan first, which released enough fat for the eggs. Wagner and Wörner just stared when he came back with the pan. "Do you always live like that?" "No, captain, but we had a bit of luck today." "When was the last time you had scrambled eggs, Wörner?" "Can't remember, captain, but whenever it was, they were not like these!" "I am very sorry, but we have no salt," said Sparks apologetically. "I tell you what, corporal, just this once, we shall overlook it. These eggs are out of this world!" The cider went down very well, it was smooth and strong, as Sparks had warned.

Two or three of the missions the captain wanted explaining, but apart from that he did not want to talk about the war, well, what was the point? "It's a long way from your fearing they would laugh about you, isn't it, men?" he said. Anyway, it was time for the main course and Sparks appeared, a little theatrically Fischer thought, with his pan which was now a serving dish. Six beautifully brown and crisp chicken-halves were arranged in a circle. "What have you chaps been raiding?" asked Wörner, "This is friendly territory!" and Hans told the story about the destroyed farm. The bombshell was definitely the coffee. When Sparks brought a mess tin over from the fire, the captain said: "This smells like coffee, real coffee!" "It is, sir, it's English, but I'm sorry, we have no sugar." "Wörner," said Wagner, "you say something, words fail me!" "Well, I see it like this, captain, we should never worry about this troop again. They lead two lives: they're good soldiers but they are also pirates, begging and stealing all the things they need and which the system can't supply anymore. Did you see the spare barrels? Four instead of one! And their boots? They will not go short of anything, not for long anyway!" "I agree," said Wagner, "however, one thing is on my mind: we cannot afford to lose any more fire power, the size of our unit is not what it used to be. Don't take risks, apart from everything else, I want to be able to say farewell to you when this is all over, understood? And don't ask me or the feldwebel where all this is leading to, we simply don't know! The situation has been taken out of our hands, all we can do is plod on, and plod on we will! Come on, Wörner, we have to leave. Thank you for your remarkable hospitality. I noticed a nice clean smell about you, what is it?" "I can answer that, captain." Wörner butted in. "It's Lilac, it's the soap they use! Lilac!" Wagner looked as if he could not take in much more, but there was more to come in the shape of Sparks, carrying a bag, none too clean: "With permission, sir, we would like the captain to accept this, salamis, there's also one for the signaler." Wagner managed a "Thank you," when Fischer asked for "permission to ask the captain if he could bring the gun oil?" Of course he had and the feldwebel got it out of the saddlebag. "I forgot over this opulence!" The crew fell in and stood to attention until the motorbike was out of sight. An hour later the signaler rang to say thanks. The captain could actually keep them out of trouble for the promised three days, which were spent sleeping and washing. The drying underwear and footrags made the place look like a gypsy camp. Sparks and Hans went to the farm again, where they had spared a few chickens, but somebody had beaten them to it and there was now nothing left. "Like bloody locusts they are!" Hans said disgustedly.

"End of leave, Fischer, go on scrambler!" "I am now, sir." "I have something interesting for you, preventing a river crossing. It's your old friends, the paras and you will do this with Winter. He is collecting here a new flash-suppresser first. They are large and heavy, but effective; he'll bring one for you as well. It will lose you a bit of power, aim a fraction higher, try it out first. Go to Hausenheim, ten kilometers north. Meet Winter there at the church at seven. He has a map of your destination. Good hunting!"

Gert was at the church at the dot of seven. Sparks suggested finishing the ham, he was worried about it going bad. Fortunately, Winter had plenty of bread, something Berta was getting short of. They arrived at the para's position about nine, the major was still in command. "I'm really pleased to see you safe and sound, doesn't happen often these days! My men are still appreciating your pullovers." He wore one himself (red). " I'll fill you in: we are holding the bank from here to the large ruin in the distance on the right. Used to be a factory of sorts with large and safe cellars. The Yanks have been shelling it for days, but the more they shell it, the more compacted it becomes. Half of my men are sheltering there, the rest here. Something was started here but never finished, so it's only a heavy slab of concrete with cellars under. Both positions have gun ports facing the water. We became suspicious when we caught glimpses of inflatable boats on the other side; they try hiding them but there are so many. I suggest one gun here with me, the other in the factory; you can shoot then from the left and right toward the middle. A runner will take you, but I'll also announce you, we have a wire across. Questions?" "Is this a river or a lake, sir?" Winter asked. "Neither, it's a flooded valley. Why?" "Wondering about the depth. The quickest way would be to hole the boats, no man in combat gear can swim. The water will do the rest and it'll save us ammunition." "Good thinking, do as you see fit. Want any flares up?" "No, major, we don't need them and the confusion in the water will be greater in the dark." "Right again, I'll leave everything to you. One more thing: when you've done, the whole battalion will pull back two kilometers because this area will be bombed without doubt. Afterward we shall re-occupy it or stay there. We are forming a useless salient here and it may well be the front is going to be straightened. I will leave you to it, men." Fischer said: "We take the tracers out, we can't change position if they pin us down. You take the gun, Bert, we need the better eyes without them!" A man with a soup container on his back stumbled down the steps, "Peter's lying outside," he wheezed when he had his breath back, "shot in the leg!" Three men slapped their helmets on and stormed out, returning quickly, two dragging the wounded para, the other the soup carrier. One of the junior lieutenants insisted on sharing the watch, but all remained quiet. It was the following night that things started to happen.

"This is it!" said Brink, "Get the major!" He was there after a few seconds and gasped when he looked through the sight. "That's about thirty boats!" he said, "Can you handle that?" "Thirty-five, sir, and it won't be a problem.

I'll shoot when they are in the middle of the lake, our other gun will do the same." Four to five shots was the most Bert spent on one boat; he was through them in well under five minutes. Winter's gun also fell silent. "I will sweep the far bank now!" said Brink. "But what about the boats?" asked the major. "What boats, sir?" He handed the gun over to the major, who was silently scanning a peaceful and empty lake. "Well, men," he said after a while, "I'm damned glad we are fighting on the same side!" "That was the nicest compliment we had so far!" said the No. 3 later.

CHAPTER 15

Kampfgruppe Wagner

"Back to base" had been the order, that's what they were doing now, marching. About eighty kilometers lay in front of them as Wagner had shifted his position a good way towards the north. There were hardly any lorries left to catch a ride on and it took three days and three roadblocks, but since they were now masters of displaying an aggressive attitude to the point of looking dangerous to deal with, it did not come to a serious confrontation.

The captain greeted them like lost sons; he was clearly happy to have them back. Sparks had managed a present for him: he had found a small wine bottle and filled it with the rest of the Calvados reserve. Wagner did something quite extraordinary,: he pulled the cork out, sniffed at the bottle, and drank half of the contents down without pausing. "I'll not forget this, lads, I'll keep this for the feldwebel"

Bohlert and Hansen had arrived just before them and, happily, Brand, Winter, and Köhler as well. "I am hoping for Emma and Dora tomorrow, they have the longest way, but that's about it. I am in contact with Anton and Ida, but both are cut off and I doubt if we see them again." Five out of fifteen guns, twenty out of sixty men, what a lousy ratio! Emma and Dora had arrived by the time they got up next morning, both groups looking the worse for wear, they barely spoke. "Gather round, men!" said the captain, "or better still, we'll sit on those tree trunks. I want to fill you in on our situation. The most serious thing is that I cannot get in contact with division any longer and I must assume Headquarters has been wiped out. We are on our own now and we have to look after ourselves.

Well, I think we've done our bit and you have not let me down, not by a long chalk. In the Hürtgen/Eiffel area it's infantry combat only, as you well know, and they can't beat us at that. But with winter at it's end and the good weather starting, they will simply area-bomb their way through it, it's the only way they know and we have nothing to defend ourselves with. To the south, the Yanks have broken through and their tanks are rolling east almost unmolested because there is nobody to stop them. To the north, there is still more resistance, but a similar picture is emerging. We can't confront tanks with machine guns, not while I'm in charge! This is what I have in mind: we march north and break through the American columns in the night, not with force of course. They cling to the roads, also the infantry, they are too lazy to march. We' ll wait for a suitable gap and sneak through, I have done it lots of times in Russia. North of the Yanks are the Canadians, and to the north of them the British. I hope to reach them and we give ourselves up to them. Is anybody objecting to that? I shall leave you for a while and you can talk it over, however, I see no other way!"

So that was it! It did not come as a surprise and yet the thought of surrender, and intended surrender at that, was very disturbing. On the other hand, what alternative was there? Only to get killed for, now, absolutely no purpose at all. The CO returned to a depressed looking group. "What is it to be, men?" Fischer stood up: "Permission to ask the captain if he will stay with us?" "Of course I will lead, what the hell is wrong with you?" "In that case we are all for it, sir." "Right, this is what we will do: We still have a tank full of petrol in the car, so we have transport. You will have to ride on top and we'll lash the guns to the aerial-ring. We leave all radios here and destroy them, Brink will see to that. One battery per gun will go in the car, also the ammo-boxes. The carts will have to be abandoned, also gasmasks and sidearms, we have to travel light, but keep your spades. We shall leave tomorrow night and from then on we shall be known as Battlegroup Wagner."

Nothing unusual in that, a lot of battlegroups were operating, they were thrown together from remnants of depleted units, tankers without tanks, artillerymen without guns. They could range from a brigade down to twenty men and the officer in command lent them his name. More often than not, they operated very successfully. "I know of a depot nearby. We'll go this afternoon, we need food, rifles for the radiomen, and how are you off for hand grenades?" The radios were set down in a square some distance away, and Brink dropped two grenades in the middle. When they were driving across to the depot through a snowstorm ("this is a trial run!"), the radio bleeper sounded, it was Karl, down to the No. 3 and the signaler, direct hit on the gun. "That was Horstmann, that arsehole, pity about the No. 2!" said Bert in a low voice. Wagner gave them a position on next night's route where they would be picked up. The depot was busy but the staff was eager to hand things over; the stocks would only have to be set on fire before the frontline passed over the area. Most importantly, they could lay their hands on meattins, whereas Berta was still well stocked from the last loot of iron rations, none of the others had been so lucky. Each man took five hand grenades. "I could get used to riding round on a car," said the No. 3; marching was not his strong point, he had broken a leg or a foot when little and after about five kilometers he started to limp every time.

The rest of the day was spent emptying the carts and splitting up the contents. It was ridiculous, but it felt as if the fifth member of the group was being abandoned. The four packed ten tins of meat each (small day rations), the second set of underwear scrounged at the first depot, ten field-dressings (Sparks took over the rest of the medical stuff), and the groundsheet. Washing bag and spare "foot rags" almost filled the assault pack. This was done in what was once a field barn, there was enough of it left to keep the snow out. The captain came along to check how thing were going. "For God's sake don't look so bloody miserable! I know how you feel, you're thinking you leave them," he made a vague gesture towards the west, "in the lurch and run away, don't you? All you could do for them now is join them and get blown to pieces. Mark my words, in a couple of days all hell is going to be let loose in the Hürtgen, I just heard the weather forecast and it's going to be clear for a few days and that can only mean one thing: carpet bombing. Anyway, we can still make plenty of trouble before we go underground and that will only be after 100 or 150 kilometers. So, snap out of it, will you? Concentrate on the job ahead of us, it's going to be dicey enough!"

For the first time in all those months, the groundsheets were buttoned together and turned into tents, previously it had always been a cellar, a dugout, or just a hole in the ground. "This is like going on a summer-camp," said Fischer, and Brink looked as if he would like to hit him. The tents were pitched next to the scout car, sheltered by old pines, which also provided branches for bedding. It was amazing how warm the inside became after a short while; after all, they had no blankets and outside it was below zero. "It's the stink we're emitting," said the No. 3. "You should be used to that from your cows."

"You cannot compare their stink with yours, Bert, it's much gentler." Brink had no answer to that.

In the morning Sparks suggested to Wagner that he would scout around for things to produce a hot meal with. "Excellent," answered the captain, "see if you can make enough for a couple of days." The rest of Berta came along as well, as it was better to do something than just sit around and brood. It would not be easy, the land was poor here, high up and exposed to the wind, the ground stony. The few scattered farms could have only just eked out a living. It did not take long to find one, small and stark looking. A copper stood in the washhouse and a pile of firewood was piled up next to it, that was a start. Spark asked Brink to bring some water to the boil ("Three buckets please."), a hand pump was conveniently next to the copper. He did not have to worry about the smoking chimney, it was not flying weather yet. Actually, it had turned out easier than it had looked at the beginning, a pile of potatoes had been left in the cellar, also carrots covered with sand and a sack of onions. A jar of salt stood on a kitchen shelf, also a box full of barley, but no meat. The No. 3 went round like a sniffer-dog but the place was bare. Chairs were carried from the kitchen to the wash-house and they sat in the warm room, peeling potatoes. When the copper was bubbling, Fischer went back to Wagner to tell him what was happening and to bring back a tin of meat from everyone to be emptied into the soup. He heard that the feldwebel had gone out on his motorbike "to do a bit of scouting."

The soup was taken to the kitchen where the range was lit before and it was sheer luxury eating from a table in a warm room. Afterward they returned to the tents with brimful mess tins for the next day, and Wagner and the rest walked to the farm for their portions.

Later in the afternoon the captain ordered them to sleep: "You have four hours, make the best of it."

Battlegroup Wagner left when it was almost dark. They had all found a place on top of the scout-car and, as long as they could stick to roads, nobody would fall off. The back half was even heated from the engine underneath and they swapped places from time to time. The only traffic in the next two hours were three ambulances at breakneck speed making use of the darkness as the red cross had ceased to be protection against an air attack a long time ago.

The general mood was still rather depressed, one would have thought the opposite would be the case with most of the danger being left behind, but it did not work that way. Most likely it was the thought of surrender overshadowing everything and it made them restless. The drone of many planes wakened them and indeed the sky was full of bombers. They came from the west and were just turning to go home. A cloudbank rose slowly where the Hürtgen was. Another wave arrived and the detonations came over loud and clear, the cloud increased in height. The captain looked at them and they looked at the captain, not a word was said. Later Brink whispered: "The old man was right again, how does he do it?" "You'd better hit the sack again; we won't move from here before evening," said Wagner, "but I want two sentries out from now on, well forward, two hour turn. Fischer, see to it!"

Late afternoon small-arms fire flared up in the distance, Wörner shouted: "Get ready, the No. 3's for ammo!" He was already passing out the boxes from the interior of the scout car. Within minutes they moved off towards the fighting, Wagner taking the lead, the feldwebel the tail end. Fischer noticed at once a startling transformation in the two men, both were exceptionally tall, well over six feet, but now, going into action, they had shrunk! They had drawn their heads in and were walking bent over, ready to drop. "See that? Like wild animals! They never taught us that!" said Brink.

Following the sound of the shooting, they finally looked down into a valley, 800 to 1,000 meters wide, flat, and without trees. Streaming through it from west to east were the remnants of the troops from the bombed sector. Streamed was not the right word, they stumbled along. Most of them without arms, many without their helmet, and even over the distance one could see they were confused and quite a few wounded. American infantry at a leisurely pace pursued them, taking a pot shot here and there. It was this fire that had alarmed the group. Now this was fair enough, but they had brought something else: two small flame-thrower-tanks were crawling in front of the Yanks picking off the fleeing men one by one and turning them into screaming torches. "Wörner!" shouted Wagner, "The red box!" The feldwebel ran back to the car. "The No. 1's!" When they gathered round they saw that Wagner's face had turned white with anger. "You're going to pay these bastards back! The Feldwebel is bringing four belts, they are a trial, penetrating light armor, one steel-core shot, one tracer. Berta goes for the right one, for the flame-oil tank at the back, see that hump? Bohlert, you go for the fighting compartment same tank which is open on top, you will kill the crew! Brand, you look for radio bearers, important! Emma and Dora the other tank, Emma the oil, Dora the crew. Don't bother about cover, they'll be too surprised for a while."

Wörner was back and threw a belt to each gunner. "Call out when you've locked on, I'll give the firing order!" The tanks were still too far away, not because of the range of the gun but with every meter nearer the impact-angle grew and the danger of the shots bouncing off decreased. All guns had locked on. "I think this will do, Wörner" "Few meters more, sir." "Say your prayers now you bastards!" said Brink. "Fire!" the captain shouted and within seconds the tanks were balls of flame and they ground to a halt. "Stop! Back to normal ammo, fire when you ready!" Wörner collected what was left of the steel belts and put them back into the box. Five guns were now devastating the troops, one would have been bad enough but five possessed frightening firepower, particularly on the coverless grassland. "Brink and Bohler! Stop! With me, we cover the left flank!" Wagner led them West and after 400 meters, there were no more Yanks. "Good, we've got them in the bag. Brink, you stay here, see that tall pine across the valley? Cover to that line. Bohler! Go back 100 the way we came and shoot from the same line to the right. Look for radios, but it's probably too late." Fischer had to change the barrel twice and the two ammunition boxes were empty but there was also nothing stirring in the valley anymore. They picked up Wörner and his men on the way back. "That was a job well done, men," said Wagner. "Are you feeling better now?" Which they did. "As soon as you have cleaned the guns and have eaten, we shall leave, it will be dark enough then. The No. 3's, I have some spare belts in the car, go and box them now."

The road they had come on was still deserted, but after a few miles they nearly rammed a car which had stopped on the verge. It had been shot up, the driver was dead, but, a blessing in disguise, it had a Jerry can of petrol strapped to the back, miraculously unexploded. The captain came up from the hatch: "If I got this right, we should cross a river after exactly ten kilometers, five kilometers further on are crossroads and there the two men from Karl should be waiting, keep your eyes peeled!" And they were there all right, a sorry sight. The radioman was unharmed, which could not be said about the No. 3. Wagner dragged him in front of the headlight-slot; "My God, man, have you not had a medic?" He hadn't because there had not been one available. Sparks took over: "Can I have twenty minutes, sir? This man can't wait." The captain nodded, not asking any questions.

The No. 3 had three fingers missing and a deep gash at the back of his neck which forced him to hold his head down permanently. "I shall have to clean you up first, here, have a swig, this is going to hurt," and he unhooked his water/Calvados bottle (medicinal purposes only). The neck was not too bad but the hand did not look good, inflamed and pussy, and Sparks smelled it for gangrene. After cleaning it meticulously he poured iodine over it, followed by his universal powder. No doctor could have done a better dressing. Wagner looked on in awe: "I'll be damned, I didn't know you were a medic? Did you know?" He had turned to Fischer. "We only found out when we needed attending to, sir," and he told him the fire brigade story.

Here was a stroke of luck: a horse cart in the ditch loaded with bread. No trace of the horses or the driver, dead or otherwise. "Make room for two loaves in your packs, but don't eat them! We load into the car what we need for everyday use." Minutes later they were joined by about twenty completely demoralized solders, tankers by the look of it. The lieutenant in charge had a sorry story to tell. Apparently they had belonged to a brand new Tiger unit who were just about to move into attack when they in turn were attacked by bombers. "There must have been two hundred or more, not one tank got through! Mine was turned over on its back and you know what a Tiger weighs? About fifty bloody tons! How can we fight back like that?" "Wörner," said Wagner out of earshot, "let's work out a more easterly route, we are getting too damn close for my liking. But I feel we will be out of the American sector soon."

A new route was easily found, running about ten kilometers to the east. The disadvantage was that it crossed open country, no cover on either side. Wagner gave his orders: "We'll have to drive quickly, lets hope the surface is reasonable, I don't want you to be shaken off, tie yourself to the aerial if necessary. One gun on top with the sights on so you can warn the driver!" The aerial was a strong frame of tubular steel rounding the top of the scout car, almost like a railing. "We shall have to do thirty kilometers, then we will be back in the woods again. Have something to eat now, ten minutes."

Things went well, only one roadblock came up but the heavily armed car and the feldwebel outrider looked too official to arouse suspicion. The second lieutenant in charge of the post had a warning: "Ten kilometers ahead," he pointed at the captain's map, "it must be here near Hershausen, the front has swung around ninety degrees, the Americans have broken through rolling east unchecked, be careful, sir." That was of course exactly what Wagner was waiting for. "Tell me, Lieutenant, this bunch of wounded there, what's going to happen to them?" "I'm expecting some form of transport to take them back." "I would like to leave this man with you, he is not fit to carry on." "You're welcome, sir!"

The distance to the danger zone was quickly covered, no mishaps occurred. The car was then driven into some dense bushes, "End of journey," said Wagner, "but we are almost out of petrol anyway." Wörner went off on foot to see what he could find out, taking two men with him. What he described on his return was what the captain had assumed, to the letter. They had been heading straight for a highway running west-east on which the American transport was rolling. "Plenty of gaps!" "We have about two hours of darkness left, time enough to make a dash for it, get your packs and the guns.

We'll not blow up the car, driver, disable the engine and the motorbike! One last cigarette, the next one only when I tell you!"

They were crouching in bushes near the highway on which the Americans thundered past. Wagner said: "I'll cross on my own, I'll signal with my torch from the other side so that you know where I am. I will then switch over to green, one green blink—one man to jump, don't cross unless signaled!" (The army torches had a red and a green slide which could be pushed over the bulb as needed.) A gap in the traffic came up and the captain disappeared like a cat, flashing immediately from the other side. On this side Wörner was "regulating the traffic" as he called it, giving each man a slap on the back when the green blip shone across. Berta were the last ones, but of course just at this moment a long line of Shermans appeared, filling the air with the stink of their exhausts and the awful screeching of tank tracks. "Put your face on your arms!" whispered Wörner, "and thank God for those uniforms!" After half an hour another gap came up and the green dot shone across immediately. With unsteady legs the last five jumped the road. "You all right, men?" asked Wagner. "That was a right shit, sir." "I know, Brink, but it's easy going from now on." "Famous last words!" Fischer muttered. They had not progressed all that far when the noise of another road came through the night, and it was the same procedure as before. By the time they were across, the sky turned grey in the East. A few men had formed a ring around the captain, shielding the light of his torch as he was consulting the map. "Very near to the left should be extensive woods, let's find cover for the day." It turned out just what they needed, the forest dense and wild, and they had to really tunnel into it. "You happy, Wörner?" "Perfect, sir." "We can smoke now, but don't light matches; I light mine and you pass the fag round." There was no end to the tricks that man had in store.

The captain was in the habit of wandering off on his own for a while and Fischer waited to catch him before he rejoined the group. "Permission to speak to the captain?" It was odd how easily this stilted language rolled off the tongue, even under these rough conditions, nobody thought anything of it.

"It looks as if this will be finished soon and the boys have asked me to tell the captain how much all the captain has done for us was appreciated. We would not be sitting here, in fact, we would probably be dead, if the captain would not have looked after us like he did. We wanted you to know that, sir." "It was only how I saw my position, but thank you all the same, Fischer, you and the others. And you can tell them you were a great bunch to lead!"

The following evening saw the crossing of the Canadian stream of traffic, which was becoming routine by now. Also they had occupied two roads, but there were no Poles, as the captain had expected. On the next evening they hit the British advance route, unmistakable by the Union Jack on the vehicles. They managed to break through between two groups of Shermans, although it was a close fit. Having found a hideout for the night, Wörner, taking Brand and Köhler with him, went off ""to do a bit of scouting," in fact, to find a place for the surrender. They did not stay away long. "An ideal spot," the feldwebel reported. Apparently it was a sandpit, accessible from the road by a short winding track and the worked-out part had turned into a lake, "where we can let things disappear." "Right," said Wagner, "this is what we are going to do: we'll approach the spot from the back, not the road and we do this at say 4:00 a.m.. We'll line the guns up in a row, dead accurate, take the bolts out, ammo-boxes next to them, empty, the rifles: pyramid next to the guns, bolts open. This goes into the lake: the one night sight we have left plus the battery, the machine pistols and field glasses because they like both as souvenirs, the pistols, the gun bolts, the remaining ammunition and the hand grenades. Take your watches off and put them in your boots or you'll lose them. I expect you to behave impeccably, we are going to do this with dignity and we are going to show them how we do things in this outfit!"

Everything worked out as planned and the preparations in the sandpit took only a few minutes. The traffic on the road had intensified and Wagner went from man to man shaking hands. "The crews fall in behind the guns now!" Then he took a piece of white material, like a pillow sheet, from his pack, Wörner tied that to a stick and walked along the track out of sight. "Christ," said Brink, "I don't know if would have that man's courage!"

It was not long before he appeared again, followed by a Jeep with four soldiers, one of them looked like an officer. The windscreen had been folded down and a machine gun was trained at Wörner's back. He walked calmly to the top of the line, where he fell in. The captain in front called out "Tenshun, eyes right!," it was amazing what a crack twenty odd pairs of boots can produce when brought together with a purpose, the officer actually jumped at the unexpected noise. Wagner walked up to the car, saluted, and said: "I am surrendering to you one officer, one NCO, twenty-two other ranks, five machine guns, and four rifles." The big surprise was that he said it in English! He then reached for his pistol (in the holster), which he had tucked under his left arm, but the English officer refused to accept it. The poor chap was clearly out of his depth, he was very young and obviously new, probably to make up for that he had grown an enormous handle-bar moustache, red at that, another strange thing was that he carried a short stick under his left arm. The difference between the two men was almost laughable, here Wagner in his dirty and worn uniform, his eye-patch (the glass-eye got lost) and his crippled left hand and the Englishman in a spotless uniform, shirt and tie. A tie! Also his men looked clean and smart, whereas that could not be said about Kampfgruppe Wagner. Their uniforms dirty and torn, boots and legs mud-caked, Berta with their vividly-colored pull-overs showing at the neck, they were a right sight!

"At ease!" Wagner called out, "you will be searched now." It was funny, the first places "searched" were the left wrists, but all the watches had disappeared. Trouble started when the troopers came across the rusty nails in the pocket flaps, probably thinking they were some sinister instruments of torture. Fortunately (and to their amazement) Wagner spoke fluent English but even he seemed to have difficulties making the connection between the nails and potato cakes. In any case, the nails had to be surrendered! "Our ways have to part now, men. I had an invitation from this officer to join him which, of course, I cannot refuse. Feldwebel Wörner will take care of you. God's speed and thank you for your loyalty. I shall find it difficult to forget you. Goodbye, men!" "Goodbye, captain!" He climbed into the jeep and Wörner barked "Tenshun!" which produced an even louder crash. Wagner waved and someone said in a carrying voice "Shit!" to which the captain saluted until the car had taken him round the bend. "I feel like a bloody orphan now" confessed Brand, by which he expressed everybody's sentiment.

"We'll go on to the road now and march east on the verge," said Wörner. "We are probably expected to go west but we don't know that, do we? Let's get into Germany as far as they let us. I shall bring up the tail with this flag." "Sir," asked Fischer, "were you not surprised when the captain surrendered in English?" "Why should I, he's an English teacher, didn't you know? They have probably nicked him for an interpreter, he'll be alright."

It took a bit of getting used to the British columns overtaking them continuously. From time to time they were thrown cigarettes from the lorries, which caused Wörner to say: "Now you can see what horseshit we've been smoking all those glorious years!" Twice they were turned around and pointed west but as soon as an opportunity came along direction was reversed again. After two days the march ended in a sports arena where thousands of prisoners were standing around already. A week passed and only a little bread and water was given out but, thanks to their own supplies, Berta did not suffer. Fortunately the weather had turned dry and warm.

CHAPTER 16
The Farm

One day the grapevine had it that all prisoners would be moved on, which was just as well because the first cases of illness appeared among the men who had not been exposed to outdoor life. Everybody lived and slept on the ground, which did not worry the line soldiers particularly and Berta had not discarded Spark's legwarmers yet. The next morning a platoon of British infantry marched into the compound, formed a line against the fence, and pushed the POWs back fifty meters. A German feldwebel had come with them and he explained: "We're going to divide you into batches of a hundred. See that gap in the line? Come through it one by one." When the number had passed through, they were told to form a single line, strip to the waist and raise their arms. Fischer stood next to a tanker sergeant and asked him if he knew what that was about. "Sure," he answered, "they are sorting these SS bastards out." When Fischer looked blank, he added: "They have their blood group tattooed under their arm, that's how bloody precious they were!" Five were found and they were herded into a corner of the compound; the others could get dressed again and they marched straight onto huge American lorries which could take the whole group on board, standing room only.

Before they moved off, the feldwebel walked from truck to truck, shouting up: "By the way, the war is over!" "Who won, feldwebel?" somebody shouted back.

The tent was pitched against a hedgerow, which sheltered it from the sea breeze, and then they collected armfuls of the coarse grass that covered the dunes, as it made very good bedding. "Do you think they're going to keep us here for a long time?" asked Sparks. The general opinion was they would not, what for? The war was over, feeding many useless men just hanging around just did not make sense. "What the hell are we going to do all day, we don't even have a deck of cards!" said Brink. "We could go fishing," Fischer suggested, "our stuff won't last forever and the rations are bound to be lousy!" "I have an idea," said the No. 3. "I'll have to do a bit of scouting around, though, as Wörner would have said." He would not let on what he had in mind and he disappeared.

He returned just before dark, looking mildly exited. "I went to that farm," pointing to rooftops just visible behind a bend in the dyke, and offered our help. It's middle sized and run by a woman on her own. Her husband is at least alive, POW in America. She handles the work with two Russians who have been there two years. She has a dairy herd and quite a few sheep. The three of them must work like blacks from morning until the day runs out, but they only just keep it ticking over. The substance of the farm is slowly but surely falling to bits. That's where we come in!" The others sat there open-mouthed, they knew the No. 3 as a quiet person, falling in with whatever had to be done, but now he bristled with authority! "I went over the place with the woman and made a plan of action, are you with me?" "Bloody hell!" said Brink. What a silly question, even Sparks was all smiles. "Now then, a lot of fences have to be renewed and some new ones put up. I would like Rolf and Bert to handle that part. Sparky, I would like you to help me with the automatic milker, that had broken down years ago. As it happens, we have the same model at home and it was my job to look after it. I know the thing inside out. The ditches of the draining system will have to be cleaned but we can't do that, it will take at least ten men, but I'll arrange something. Do we know who is in charge of us?" They did: next to them camped an assault engineer unit with their sergeant major who represented the authority for one hundred men, mostly for the upkeep of discipline and the distribution of rations, otherwise every man looked after himself. Hans would go and see him in the morning. "Do you think they'll feed us at this farm of yours?" Fischer asked. "Of course they will, we can't do this job on a slice of bread!" It was very comfortable in the tent after the week on the sports field.

"All sorted!" Hans had been to see the SM, all they had to do was to clock off and on with him. "One of the chaps will claim our rations and bring them over to us at night. Right, are you ready?" It was hard to come to terms with the new No. 3. He introduced them to Mrs. Moll, a woman of perhaps forty, pretty once, but now her face was careworn and her arms, shoulders, and hands were those of a man. She had pretty twin daughters, four years old. The Russians were Ivan (what else?) and Wassilij, huge men with friendly faces and colossal hands; they seemed to know quite a bit of German. "You're just in time for breakfast," said Mrs. Moll and all sat down round the kitchen table for the standard north German farm breakfast: milk soup and bread. The soup had the consistency of runny porridge and could be made with flour, oats, or noodles, whatever was available.

It must have been a well-organized farm a while ago, there was a large pile of fence posts; a good store of timber all sorts and sizes, a stock of bricks and a well-equipped workshop. The first fence, about 100 posts long, was a sorry sight: wire broken, posts down or about to break. "If you pull them all out, here's a tool for it, you can re-use the old holes. I have not found any new wire but I'll be able to nick it somewhere. I'll send one of the lvans along with the new posts." "I can't get over him, we had better take our finger out or we'll get ticked off!" said Brink. Soon Wassilij came along with the cart and dropped a post at each hole. "Going home to Mother Russia now, Wassilij?" Fischer asked him. "Nix go home Mother Russia, we go home, we puck puck." "Why would they shoot you?" "We work for Faschisti." "But that's nonsense, you had to." "You know, I know, but does Mother Russia know? Stalin not forgiving man. We hide here with good mother and give help." So that was that, the subject was never mentioned again. The work was pleasant, the sun shining, it was peaceful, and by lunchtime fifty new posts were in place. The girls came to fetch them for lunch. Hans had been able to repair the milker, it had been a matter of a few brittle hoses but he found the spares. He and Sparks had cleaned the system meticulously and it was working a dream. Mrs. Moll was beside herself, obviously it would save her and the Russians untold hours of work. "I'll come early to show you the ropes," he pointed to the Ivans. "We'll start at five!" "Da, da," said Ivan and Wassilij.

Somehow it had come out that Sparks was a tailor and Mrs. Moll asked him to run off a few new things for the girls, which he was delighted to do. "Listen, boys," Mrs. Moll said. "I'll heat the copper for the morning, bring your underwear and just drop them in, I'm sure they need it." That was very tactful, nobody would have handed her the disgusting things. On the way back to the tent, Fischer turned to Hans: "That horse doesn't look so good, is he on his last legs?" "He is, a second one is even worse. I have plans for a couple of new ones, haven't all the details yet."

Brink and Fischer were tackling another fence in the morning, when an agitated Ivan came running across the field: "Where Gospodin?" "What bloody Gospodin?" "Comrade with kaput arm." "He means Hans!" Fischer said incredulously, "Gospodin, I'll be damned!" This was a title from the pre-communist days when addressing superiors, meaning "Master." "Gospoding having a shit, why?" "Cow having calf, cow not happy cow!" Fischer ran across to the yard loo to bring Hans the good news. "I'm going over now, get a clean rope from the barn and ask the Missus for some soap, she'll know. And bring Bert!" "Take a bucket of water!" said Mrs. Moll. At the scene, the cow was on her side and, no, she did not look happy. Hans soaped his arm and "went in"; it looked awful. "Shit," he said, "it's the wrong way. Make a loop in the rope, wet it and give it to me!" He inserted it into the cow and fumbled about inside. "Pull now, gently, don't jerk!" Suddenly, a pair of hooves appeared, then a muzzle. "Keep pulling, the mother's too knackered!" What a proud moment!

Over lunch, as always, thick soup, Hans disclosed that he had all the dope on fresh horses. "The engineers told me. Ten kilometers from here is a center where they collect horses from the troops coming out of Denmark, hundreds of them, well, we'll see about that. The farm could also do with a couple of new carts, don't know how this one holds together! So I suggest the three of us take off very early, Mrs. Moll will give us two salamis in case we have to bribe somebody. You will probably be happier here, Sparky, you can get on with your sewing in peace. I can help with the fences now." He wanted to set two new short ones, "Be easier to control the sheep." All replacement posts were in the ground in a perfect line. "I didn't think you had it in you!" Brink and Fischer felt ridiculously proud. Beautifully clean underclothes were flapping on the line. The Russians were cleaning up the yard, no doubt by order of the Gospodin. "They'll be glad to get you off their backs!" said Fischer. "I don't think so, they don't mind the work, they don't see these things, so they don't tackle them." The girls were helping, obviously the Russians worshipped the children and they adored the Russians, calling them Uncle Ivan and Uncle Vassilij. Afterward they began to cut up the old fence posts for firewood, stacking it neatly in the barn. "Listen, Hans," said Brink, "why are you pushing so? Couldn't we make it last a bit longer?" "No, I heard farmers will be the first to be released and I want this place up and running by then, can't leave it to you, can I?" No one could argue about that. "I wonder if there are any carpenters amongst the engineers, should be!" He found three, who were of course delighted to come. The feldwebel had no objections, and they would report the day after tomorrow, because tomorrow was horse-buying day. They left at six. "This is a funny POW camp," said Fischer. "We roam around, nobody stopping us, no guards anywhere." Hans had the explanation (from the engineers). Since they were on the peninsular Eiderstedt, the guarding was done on three sides by the North Sea; the British had to watch the connection to the mainland only.

The horses were easily found, not hundreds but probably fifty. An elderly veterinary lieutenant was in charge. Hans started his story, but the officer interrupted: "You want to take over horses? You are welcome, take your pick, as many as you want." "We need only two, sir." "That's a pity, are there any more farms where you are billeted? Spread the word, I have to find places for the poor creatures, I have no fodder for them, you see?"

Hans went among them, looked into mouths, felt legs, and lifted up hooves. “Like an old horse-trader, isn't he amazing?” said Fischer. Hans picked two and brought them out into another small paddock. They went back to the lieutenant: “We would also need two harnesses, sir, and two carts, if possible?” “Help yourselves behind that copse.” “Get two harnesses from that pile,” said Hans. “They are all the same but get new-looking ones. I'll go and look at the wagons.”

“Got two beauties,” he came back, “and nosebags!” “What's a nosebag?” You feed oats from them when there's no trough.” “We haven't any oats to feed.” “Wrong, I brought some, thought they would be kept short.” He took off his backpack and halved the contents, the other two were lost for words. Having carried the gear back to the horses, Hans said: “Just stick their heads through the harnesses and I'll do the rest, I'll just give them their feed.” The horses, which had looked a bit hung-up before, perked up immediately. “You were hungry, poor sods, weren't you?” and he had a long whispered conversation with them. Then he sorted out the jumble of buckles, straps, and chains, and in no time the harnesses were properly in place. “Should I give a sausage to the lieutenant? I know we didn't have to haggle, but he was helpful. And two horses and two carts for one sausage is not bad.” “You're forgetting the nosebags!” said Fischer, “Yes, I think he should have it.” “Watch these two, there is something else I want to ask the vet.” “Got it, this is our day, I asked him for a place for barbed wire and you know what? There is a pioneer dump down the road! Let's get the horses hitched up.” Of course he had to do that.

“Will you drive one, Rolf? You can ride, can't you?” “Yes but not drive a cart.” “Makes no odds, just follow me, these horses are used to that.” They left past the Vet's tent, who looked at the horses. “Good choice, know something about nags, do you?” “Farmer, sir.” “Oh well, good luck and thanks for the you-know-what and please make it known that there are plenty more where yours came from.”

The feldwebel in charge of the dump was not co-operative, but the sausage changed his attitude at once. Plenty of wire was available and Hans asked them to load twenty rolls. “Da, Gospodin.” “I have to look for something else.” He came back with ten long-handled shovels over his shoulder: “For the men who will clean the ditches!” It was a triumphant return to the farm. Hans had managed to coax his horse into something like a trot up the drive, Fischer's simply followed. Mrs. Moll stood by the gate and tears were rolling down her cheeks, the girls were jumping up and down. They wanted the new horses to be called Ivan and Vassilij, “But they are...”

mares she wanted to say but decided against it. The carpenters were waiting, a Sergeant and two troopers. "Who is in charge?" the sergeant asked. "He is, the Gospodin..." "So, what's first?" "There is something wrong with all gates, six of them. I'll give you a Russian with a cart, you will want to take them to the workshop. The fence around the kitchen garden has had it; it's picket but all the new timber is here. The main drain to the sea has a flood gate that is in tatters and I thought you could vandalize the old cart for new doors. "What order?" asked the Sergeant, a man of few words. "Gates, fence, flood gate," and he and his men moved off. "And what have you in mind for us, Gospodin?" Hans did not take any notice of the joke any longer. "I'll come with you and show you how to wire the fences, that will probably take all day. Then I'll be down by the flood gate, taking the old one off, I hope. Vassilij will come with me, the culvert is full of sand, almost blocked. Mrs. Moll had produced a ball of string and rags to go round their hands, fortunately there was a bucket of staples left in the workshop. The string went along as the marker for the topmost wire. Hans had cut two sticks. "That's the distance for the other two strands, measure down from the top at each post, get it?"

"I've been thinking" said the sergeant after lunch, "you are going to clear the ditches? You must consider that our men are getting weaker by the day, not surprising on those lousy rations." They were down to one loaf for eight men per day, which equaled one thick slice, plus one tin of meat, also for eight. The lucky ones managed to catch fish or collect mussels. "I thought we could build something which will make it a lot easier for the men, I made a model." He put a bundle of sticks on the table which fitted together in an irregular square, the short one was to rest on the bottom of the ditch, the two middle-sized ones were bolted to it, pressing against the sides of the drain, and the longest one connected these two on top as a spacer. "I saw iron strips in the workshop which could act as blades, slicing off the surface of the sides and all the muck will drop down. A horse on either side of the ditch, and there you are." "Sarge," said Hans, "that is brilliant, that is really brilliant!" "We'll knock it up this afternoon then."

The wiring was finished earlier than they had planned and so there was time to dismantle the garden fence, pull the old posts, and sink new ones. The fence was left in sections for the carpenters to use as pattern and later on the Russians carried them over to the workshop. The frame for the ditches was finished, but it would be tested the next day. The new horses went into loose boxes for the night; Hans was worried they would eat too much grass, having been kept short for so long.

After a lot of adjusting to the towing gear, the ditch-cleaner worked as the sergeant had predicted; not only did it slice off the sides but it did so in a perfectly straight line. ("I was afraid the drains would look like a mad women's piss if it was done with shovels only," said Hans.) It took all day to do the entire network, Wassilij and Ivan were leading the horses, which fitted into their new job without trouble, in fact, they looked very happy.

"Tell me, Ivan," asked Fischer, "where do you get your Machorka? You don't seem to be short." "Nix Machorka," he looked around and pointed to a well-known weed, "This we smoke." "But it smells like Machorka." "May be smell like Machorka but taste like sheep shit, you try," and he held out a tin. Fischer, like Brink, had carried a pipe for a long time, found in a deserted house in France; the smoke was certainly an experience. Later on it became a habit. "We smell like Hiwis," said Brink.

The carpenters intended to finish the new fence before lunch, the trouble was the lack of paint. Mrs. Moll remembered that there should be some boat varnish around ("We had a boat once") and indeed there was, two large buckets. Sparks reserved the right to paint (I love it!) and by evening the new fence was up, looking very smart.

Next morning the engineers fell on their breakfast, a double quantity had been prepared. They split up in pairs so as not to get into each other's way and managed to clear the whole system in one day. Mrs. Moll told the sergeant who led them, to bring them back the next day "to eat with us" although the work was done. '"We can't do that, Missus, we'll not just come to eat off you! But I've been thinking: down by the water's edge is a patch of very coarse sand, how would it be if we brought a few loads up and spread it on the yard, that could do with a bit of levelling and it'll look nice." Not even the Gospodin had thought of that!

And so it was done, six loads went down and it looked great. Hans and Fischer had taken the old horses to drag two up-turned harrows along either side of the ditches to smooth out the debris thrown up from the drains, the horses could just about manage it. Well, that was about it, the place was beginning to look like a model farm. The carpenters had one day left and the floodgate was still to be built. The oaken sides of the old cart had a new purpose in life, and Ivan and Wassilij carried them down to the culvert like two pieces of cardboard. The three men then went over the farm to look for small repairs: a sagging door here, a sticking window there, it kept them busy for the rest of the day.

Berta went back the next morning to finish off little jobs. The farm felt very quiet after the activities of the last days, "My head was spinning most of the time," admitted Mrs. Moll, "this is going to be difficult for me now, I want to thank you, but how can I thank you for all you did? And it's not only for me, but the girls and my husband as well, when he comes back." She left the kitchen and came back with four small prints of the village. "We have a local artist here, I want you to remember us." She also had four small parcels "to keep you going."

The following morning the feldwebel came along to tell Hans that he would be released the next day. Sparks was due to leave in a week, due to his age. "That's going to be ducky, just the two of us," said Brink. "More room in the tent." Hans split his parcel from Mrs. Moll into three parts ("I don't have far to go.") and pushed them on to the others. Sparks wanted to do the same but they did not let him. "You've a long way and then there's your family." "I hope there is!" he answered glumly.

Saying farewell was not all that easy, having shared every minute of the day and night for nine months, exposed to the same dangers and fears, always there for the others, and now one just dropped out. "I'll be glad not to have to see your ugly face any longer." Brink said to Hans, "I shall miss you too, Bert," and these two brittle characters did something nobody expected, they hugged each other! "I hope you will come and see me, Rolf, it's not very far from you." Fischer promised and· "thanks for teaching us all the things at the farm." And then he was gone. "I have a bit of Calvados left, shall we have that now?" asked Sparks. After a week, he had also departed.

"What the hell are we going to do now, Rolf?" "Let's get some fresh bedding and burn this old stuff." Lighting a fire was not so easy anymore; they had kept five '"emergency matches" each and although Brink had a lighter, it was of course without fuel. But he had a revelation: "Do you remember reading about natives lighting fires by twirling a stick? I think we should try that, God knows how long we will be stuck in this bloody dump." It worked, in fact, it was quite easy. "God, haven't we come a long way?" said Fischer.

Then they had to move, why, nobody knew, it was toward the south side of the peninsula. They stuck with the Assault Engineers, at least a few familiar faces. They did not want to leave the fresh bedding behind and rolled it into the tent. "Bringing a body?" said the feldwebel and it was a good job they did, nothing was provided for at the other end. At least they had a well, originally for cattle, but the water was good and plentiful. The hope of better rations was shattered right from the start and the body reserves accumulated thanks to Mrs. Moll's cooking and generosity dwindled quickly. The general practice was now to eat half the bread-slice with the bit of meat and to toast the other half over a fire. When it was really hard, it was crushed between two stones and the men kept the crumbs in one trouser pocket. This way one could have the illusion of eating, and tasting, bread all afternoon. It sounded silly at first but after a week the body had got used to it and it certainly helped. Searching for bird eggs was another pastime, quail in particular. The harvest was good to begin with but too many hungry men caused it to peter out soon. 1946 would be a bad quail year!

And then dysentery struck, Fischer was hit first. It was not too severe to begin with and the loss of blood was tolerable, but all the same, it weakened the body so quickly that Brink had to escort him to the latrine to make sure he did not fall in. After all, it was only an open trench and a tree trunk running lengthwise across it and there had been cases where men, when trying to stand up, fell over backwards into the pit. The only treatment available was charcoal, homemade and crushed, mixed with water and forced down, but it helped to a certain extent. It did not cure the symptoms but reduced the constant loss of fluid and the blood was kept inside, perhaps it was being recycled? It took two weeks for Brink to catch it and fortunately Fischer had recovered a bit by then. His time was now divided between washing Brink down with cold water (he ran a high temperature) and dragging him to the bog. As so often with strong people, he had deteriorated very quickly and he was only skin and bones after one week. He would need something to eat, eggs, chicken, that sort of thing, laughable! But what about fish? Fischer remembered something he had learned as a little boy, it was called plaice-sticking. A certain type of plaice, smaller but thicker compared to the normal one, did not go out to the sea again with the tide but buried itself in the sand or mud. If one knew what to look for, it could be caught easily with a trident-like tool. Well, a fork would do the trick. The army cutlery was a fork and spoon combined, hinged in the middle and, when unfolded, it had a fork at one end and a spoon at the other. He tied that to a stick and asked one of the engineers who helped at the farm, to look after Brink, who could not be left alone yet. He would get a fish in return, if Fischer was lucky.

The beach was deserted, which was just as well, and in no time at all he had six fishes in his pack. Filleted, mixed with a few potatoes left over from the farm and some wild parsley, it turned into a, probably disgusting, stew over the fire; luckily, Sparks had left the rest of his salt behind. Brink had to be spoon fed but he took a good portion. "You know," he said, "I quite expected to die of this damned dysentery, but now I think I'll die of your cooking. Wouldn't it be ironic, we were so lucky all along and then to die of the shits, how heroic!"

In the neighboring sector there had been a few deaths, they spoke of twenty, all elderly men, quartermasters or something, who had come down from Denmark. "The guards were very coperative, they came and excavated the graves with a machine, the mass grave first and then ten single spare ones for later, now wasn't that nice of them?" A soldier from that area was telling the story. "Did they leave any drugs?" "Don't be silly, drugs! They never got out of the cab and when they had finished with the digging, they pissed off, you couldn't see them for dust!"

It was hard to understand why the men were not released more speedily, it was getting on to October and the war had finished five months ago. Surely it was a burden to keep these thousands of prisoners alive, albeit barely, and guard them. A standard Red Cross card to send home, saying they were alive, would have helped, but apparently nobody had thought of that. Rations had not improved and fish had become a vital supplement, although the periods when the tide was high during daylight hours, meant there was not even that available. One of the engineers had made a slingshot; he planned to bring down seagulls, "They are the size of a chicken!" Days of practice turned him into a marksman and the big day came, they sat round the fire where the bird was roasting on a spit. It did look like the real thing, but the meat was absolutely inedible. He concentrated on ducks afterward, only there were not so many of them.

The day came when railway support personnel (whatever that meant) were to be sent home, as train drivers and such had left long ago. Brink and Fischer decided to try and get out on a fiddle and hide in that particular group, the worst that could happen was that they would be sent back. Fischer faced the interrogation officer who spoke good German. "Your pay book says 'student.'" "It's railway student, sir." He looked exasperated, "Bullshit!" he said, but he stamped the release paper, "Get out before I change my mind!" Fischer learned the meaning of this word only years later; it was obviously not a term one was taught at school. The next morning saw them in a wired-off compound where they had to stop for the last time to be checked for the blood group. The air of elation which hung over the group was about to be shattered. The interrogation officer stepped out of his hut: "All men to be released to Bremen, over there to the left!" A few soldiers, guns at the ready, surrounded them. "I have orders to cancel your release, a gross act of sabotage has been committed against our American friends, their headquarters in Bremen has been blown up." There was only time to wave to Brink, what a miserable farewell! The group, about ten of them, were kept under guard for the rest of the day, and rumors were rife. To begin with, nobody believed the story, who in his right mind would, after five years of destruction, do something so utterly stupid, something that could only result in retaliation. Surely the Bremen people had other things to worry about. "We are going to be a penalty unit, you watch, lifting mines and that sort of shit!" "They will probably just shoot us!" There were many more suggestions, one grimmer than the last. They had to stay in the compound during the night, fortunately it was still quite warm as there were no provisions for sleeping, nor were any rations given out.

The next morning brought the anti-climax: the officer came over to them and announced that they could go now after all, the cause of the explosion had been a leaking gas pipe. His words were greeted with stony silence.

The truck took them on the road from Hamburg to the eastern boundary of Bremen, where there was a well-known landmark, a big hotel called, of all things, "City of London." While the lorry discharged its load, a second, smaller one pulled up next to them and a group of sailors got off, looking very smart and well-fed. Immediately the comments started to flow: "Look at the bloody Navy, sitting on their fat arses all the war!" Fischer got the shock of his life, one of them was Jakobsen! He did not recognize Fischer immediately, he wore a beard. Blink and he had shared the last razor blade until it gave out and that was probably two months ago, anyway, they had had no soap either. Jakobsen had been drafted into the U-boats and spent his entire war in the Channel. "It was hair-raising, I tell you, and our commander was an absolute lunatic!" When hostilities ceased, he was transferred to a mine-sweeping flotilla and that's what he did the last months.

In front of the hotel entrance sat a huge black American soldier in a rocking chair. He had his rifle between his legs and kept the rocking motion up with it. The men had to file past him and show their discharge, thereby being officially accepted into the American zone of occupation. This never interrupted his rocking! "He must be a brave man, look at all his medals," said Jacky. "Don't you believe it, they get medals for pissing against the same wall twice, I'm told. Don't you, fatso?" "Hitler kaput!" the Yank said by way of answer. "Obviously a man of considerable intellect!" It was good to hear Jacky still speaking his very precise German. He had always been the delight of the German master. "Why can you not, all of you, speak like Jakobsen instead of your rudimentary utterings?"

Twenty miles lay in front of them and they would be unable to cover that because of the curfew. As soon as they started off, Fischer noticed Jacky's pronounced limp, who said it was "that bloody shrapnel in Habichthorst. Do you remember the general asking why this man was wearing house slippers? Those were great days!" Halfway to Vegesack, Fischer began to feel quite weak and he had to sit down on a low garden wall. "What's the matter with you?" "Only hungry, Jacky." "When did you last eat?" That was two days ago and Jacky became very agitated. "Why on earth did you not say something? I have plenty!" "Not an easy thing to say, Jacky." "You idiot! How long have we known each other? I can't believe this!" While he was ranting on, he took things from his pack that made Fischer's eyes water but he had the sense to eat very little very slowly. "I should have joined the bloody Navy!" he said.

Having reached Vegesack (Jakobsen had cut a stick out of a hedge), they had run out of time, the curfew had started. Quite a few of their classmates used to live here but what they did of course not know, was what had happened to the boys, had they come back or not? They did not feel like knocking on any of the doors and be faced with tears. Consequently, they spent the night in the boiler room of the school, which a sympathetic caretaker had unlocked for them. The curfew ended at six and their ways parted now, Jakobsen branched off to Aumund having left a substantial breakfast. "See you in class!" "God willing," said Jacky. Fischer carried on toward Blumenthal, realizing more and more how Sparks must have felt approaching Frankfurt and not knowing what had happened to his family.

He need not have worried, the house was standing, even the windows were intact and the pear trees were laden with fruit. His father was, just this minute, coming out of the backdoor with a bucket, probably to feed the chicken. When he saw Fischer, he called out: "Are you bringing us news about Rolf?" "It's me, dad!" Father dropped the bucket and put his arms around him, they stood there, arms around each other, not saying anything. "I had better go and prepare your mother for this, wait here." Fischer thought, how odd he did not recognize me, but then it was only just getting light and Father did not wear his glasses. And it's about nine months since he saw me, I must have changed a bit in that time. It took a while before mother came out and she did what probably all mothers would do in a situation like that, at the end she said: "But you are wearing a beard!" with just a hint of criticism. Fischer nearly said: "Of course I'm wearing a bloody beard, I hate it myself but what else could I do without razor blades?" He shortened it to: "Yes, mother, it will come off as soon as dad finds a blade for me." The way back into civilian life was clearly mapped out, it seemed!

One morning, about four weeks later, Jacky rang and said he bumped into Horn who told him Drieling was back as well, minus one arm, the left one fortunately. "Is your bike in working order? I thought we might run over to Habichthorst and see what's become of the old place. Peter (that was Horn) will come with us. Let's meet at the school and see if anything is stirring there."

The school was undamaged, looking as it always had. The main door was unlocked but the inside was cold and deserted. They ended up at the headmaster's room, and there he was, looking even frailer than they remembered. He was doing paperwork in a thick overcoat, a single-bar electric fire trying in vain to warm the room. He could not remember their names but when told memory returned. "Gentlemen," he said, "I am very sorry to tell you that our school will not re-open for a long time yet, hopefully in spring. There is no coal for the heating and we are extremely short of masters. A number of them have not returned, if they ever will. Anyway, let me say I am extremely pleased you have lived through that madness, extremely pleased! But tell me, why are you still wearing your uniforms?" "We have nothing else that would fit us, sir," Jacky answered.

Since they would have to catch up with another year and a half at least, they would be over twenty by the time of the final exam. "I'll not bother anyway." Horn confided. They owned a large carpentry firm and his father had not come back. "Missing and we all know what that means!" Peter had four sisters and was head of the family now. "I shall have to take over the business, but first I'll do a shortened apprenticeship with my carpenter uncle."

They got the shock of their lives when they saw Habichthorst. Hardly a trace of the battery remained, no guns, no radar, well, that was to be expected, but no huts, no gun positions, no ammo bunkers. Everything had been flattened and cows had taken over again. Oddly enough, one of the latrines had been left in place, probably for the farmer's convenience. "Over here!" Jacky called from a hedgerow in an unsteady voice. He had stumbled onto two graves, one with a board "5 German soldiers" the other "4 Russian soldiers." Fischer said: "Let's see the farmer, he'll know more." He was in the yard leading a horse from the stable. "Morning, Mr. Merten," Jacky approached him. "We served in this battery and we were wondering if you knew anything about those graves over there?" "No," the farmer answered and walked away, pulling the horse after him. Jacky clapped a huge hand on his shoulder and spun him around: "Is that all the civility you can muster, you bloody clodhopper?" "Don't know anything." Jacky still held him in his grip and Jacky had grown into a big man! "Who buried them?" "My Russians." "Why not our Russians?" "Everybody had left." "Get your Russians then!" "They've gone back." "Merten," said Fischer, "you always were an arsehole. I remember when we were bombed and the captain asked for your help, I also remember the bad grace with which you brought your wagons across and you were not even asked to work, just wait by the horses. We all thought then what a piece of shit you were, and I bet anything you like that your farm is full of stuff you nicked from the battery!"

Horn, who was actually quite hot-tempered, had kept silent but now a change had come over him. He had come home with an ugly scar across his forehead that had turned blood red, quite frightening to look at. "Is there any reason why I should not hit this gentleman farmer?" he asked nobody in particular, but he thought better of it and just grabbed Merten by the jacket, shook him that his teeth actually rattled, and spat in his face. "I hope the Colorado beetle gets to your fields!" Fischer added: "When we come back and find that the cows have been shitting on the graves, we'll turn you inside out and that's a promise!" That had been Brink's favorite threat.

Horn was going to make some decent crosses in his workshop. "This orthodox one for the Ivans, do you remember if that second crossbar goes up on the right or the left?" Fischer hadn't a clue, but Jacky thought it was the right. They met a few days later to plant the crosses, on the German one Horn had added the battery number, 4/531, on the other one he had put "4 Russian Comrades." A cuckoo was calling while they hammered the crosses in; another one was answering in the distance.

Fischer wanted to know if winter had returned home yet. They had not come across each other in the POW camp, but that did not mean anything, the place was too huge. The church and the vicarage stood unharmed. Mrs. Winter opened the door and, yes, Gert was back, the Lord be praised! You had better praise captain Wagner, Fischer thought, he did all the protecting that could be done. The daughters were also there, as stunning as he remembered them. Not having seen any females for about nine months, they took his breath away and he felt quite helpless. But then Gert burst in and marched him off to his room. "Man, am I glad to see you!" he exclaimed. "My old man is driving me crazy. He is on to me about making my peace with God, he's on to me all the bloody time! I told him I was not in a state of war with God, but he drones on and on. I said to him if he didn't stop, I am going to join the Foreign Legion, that shut him up. What the hell could we do about the things we had to do? Tell me that!" He was really worked up, and Fischer had never seen him like this. He calmed down somewhat after he pulled a bottle out from under his mattress. "My old signaler comes from a farm in Meyenburg and they distil their own from plums. Here's to the old days when everything was so simple!" Gert made sure his father was not around when Fischer left, "or you'll catch a load of this drivel as well!"

A pathetically small group of the old class met at the school in spring of '46. Out of the original fifteen were only Jacky, Hauenschild (minus one foot), Gräpel, Jachens, and Fischer left. Köhler had of course been killed at his AA-gun, Horn and Drieling had dropped out, the latter to take over the farm, one arm or not, because his father had had a severe stroke. The rest had disappeared without trace during the last months of the war, the majority in the east. Missing in action was wishful thinking, they would not come back. All the same, the class was bigger than it had ever been, swelled by new arrivals, refugees from the east or boys who did not want to go back because the Russians were holding their hometown now.

"Aren't we the lucky five?" asked Gräpel, "What do you think of this 'Dolce at decorum est pro patria mori' now?" "Do you want to get flattened?" said Jachens.

CHAPTER 17
Berta's Last Mission

Many months later, it must have been early '47, Brink rang, he was so exited, he almost stammered. "I have located Wagner!" "How the hell did you do that?" "My dad has an old friend in Hamlin, he is a widower, and he visits us every year for a week with his son. We talked about school and it came out he has a new English master with no fingers on his left hand and a glass eye." Is his name Wagner?" "Yes, but how did you know?" "He was my commanding officer in the war." "Now what do you think of that?"

"I asked him to find out Wagner's number when he was home again. He did that and I rang. Wagner nearly fell off his chair, I tell you! We chatted for a while and then I said "With respect, sir, you sound depressed, are you alright?" "Far from it, Brink, far from it, it's my wife, she had pneumonia and they only just saved her but she can't get her strength back, just fading away. I'm very worried about her, but what else can you expect on these lousy rations?" (It was the winter when nearly a million town dwellers died of hunger or cold.) "I said, 'Don't worry, sir, we shall do something about that!' 'Who is we?' 'Berta of course, I will be in touch soon.' So there you have it, it's up to us now." "You did right, Bert, I shall ring Hans tonight, he is our best bet." The No. 3 was all for it, "I'll ring you back tomorrow." "Right," he said next morning, "can you come over today with a suitcase, no rucksack!" It meant a bicycle journey of three hours, twice, not a problem. Hans had got ready a whole side of bacon, smoked, ten assorted sausages, and a large tin of goose fat. The smell was tantalizing. "That's why I wanted you to bring a suitcase; in a rucksack the people on the ferry would have smelled it and you might have been asked some awkward questions."

"What can I contribute?" Fischer asked his mother, "we haven't got anything to give away on that scale?" "Wrong, I have cellar full of meat jars, the overflow of what Dad shot over the years, take as many as you want." They were the big two liter jars, the type where you pulled a rubber seal from under the lid to open them. So, if Fischer took five, that would mean about twelve kilos, probably all he could carry. He picked two wild boar, two deer, and one hare. Next on the plan was to inform Winter, who was absolutely floored by the news. "Of course I'm coming with you, it'll be just like the old days! But what can I bring? This is such a holy bloody household, you won't find anything illegal in it! I tell you what I can do, though: three bottles of that plum Korn, compliments of my old signaler, I'm sure I can twist his arm. And it's good stuff; Wagner can use it for bartering." "Can we do it next Sunday?" asked Fischer. "I'll check with Bert and let you know."

Bert was pleased. "My parents are still working out what to take, we need some fat urgently, but they will come up with something. Next Sunday will be fine. Catch a very early train from Bremen, it'll take you an hour and a half to us. I'll meet you at the station and we drive straight to Hamlin, another one and a half hours. I'll square it with Wagner and let me know your train."

On Monday, Fischer told his school master the story and asked permission to, perhaps, miss the Monday. He was very understanding, being an old soldier himself. "I planned a Latin paper for Monday, but I can easily move that to Wednesday, so you won't miss it." "How very bloody considerate of you!" Fischer thought.

All went according to plan. Brink was waiting in a small truck normally delivering bricks; in fact, there was a small stack in the back "in case somebody asks stupid questions." Also a cardboard box with three dozen eggs packed in straw, two neat little parcels in greaseproof paper, a chicken and a rabbit (oven ready), and a crock with butter. A bucket with a snap-on lid held the lunch. "When I told Wagner I'm bringing it he protested, probably his pride, but then I put mother on, she can be very persuasive."

Wagner opened the door and said, "Good morning, men." Like with one voice they came back, "Good morning, captain." And their posture was suspiciously close to "attention." After all that length of time, the old habits still persisted. He did not look very good, had lost a lot of weight. His wife, once definitely very pretty, looked ghastly, just skin and bones. The things went on to the kitchen table and she started to cry. The more was unpacked, the more she cried. She said something but nobody understood. "Pardon?'" asked Winter, it came out as "You are such wonderful comrades!" Brink and Winter answered together: "So was your husband!" Wagner had left the kitchen, probably he had to pull himself together, one could see it by his face when he came back. "Remember Feldwebel Wörner calling you a bunch of pirates? Haven't changed much, have you?"

Lunch was warmed and it was indeed a dream of a pea soup, thick and at least a quarter of it was meat. The Wagners polished off three plates and their color improved immediately. They must have been really starving. "I think it's time to break open one of these mystery bottles, don't you think?" "Don't, captain, we have a spare one for that occasion." "And is it not also time to stop calling me that, Winter?" "That'll be very hard, sir, you will always be the captain to us." "Then there is only one solution, we shall have to go on to Christian names, if that's alright with you, I'm Peter." "We'll be honored, Capt-," said Brink. "And my name is Irma," said Mrs. W., still in a tear-choked voice.

"How was your time as POWs?" "Hunger and dysentery," answered Fischer, "until our No. 3 organized work on a farm, where everything was in bad need of repair. The man was still away and his wife had only two Russians to help. But then the No. 3 kicked in." "He always struck me as a very unassuming chap?" said Wagner. "Not there," Brink continued the story, "he pushed everybody around: us, the Russians, and a group of assault engineers he had brought in for the heavy jobs. He taught us fencing, repaired the milking machine, and spirited two fresh horses and carts onto the farm. It was great fun and we learned a lot. And we had something to eat! By the way, he sends his best wishes but he could not leave the farm." "Thank you, what happened to that gentleman signaler of yours? A man of exquisite manners." "We lost track of him, he came from Frankfurt and that's of course one big ruin." "And what are you up to now?" "In a few months we shall sit our A-Levels at the ripe old age of twenty-one. I shall more or less take over the brick mill, my father is not too well."

"I would like to take heavy engineering," said Fischer, "but I don't hold out much hope, not enough university places reopened." Winter thought he might be luckier doing veterinary medicine, "but you never know!'" There followed two hours of reminiscing to which Mrs. W. listened in awe. Wagner liked the story about the SS roadblock best. "Now, before we say goodbye," Fischer said, "I must tell you that we have decided on the way here, to repeat this mission in a few months time, if things have not improved. Bert, being the nearest, will ring you and you must honestly tell him what the situation is." "You can't do this again, we cannot accept it!" Wagner protested. "You will have to, captain, we have accepted your care for about a year and the three of us would not be sitting here without your leadership. It was only a gesture anyway, because one cannot calculate one life equal to one liver sausage! And don't forget that our parents are immensely grateful to you as well. We would like it best if we did not have to discuss this subject anymore." Mrs. Wagner started to cry again. "Right, we shall only say thank you then and leave me your parent's addresses that we can thank them as well."

"Good hunting!" he called after them when they were on the way to the garden gate. Four months later it became necessary to put together another supply train, but from then on things took a slow turn to the better.

After a couple of years or so (Fischer was working in London by then) he received a letter from Wagner which went roughly like this:

"Dear Rolf, I am the bearer of happy and very tragic news. My wife has presented me with healthy twin boys, and we decided at once that we wanted you and Brink as godfathers. I rang Bert's number and, to my horror, his father told me that Bert had been killed in a car accident a couple of weeks before. Can you imagine their devastation and how helpless I felt? When I was trying to ring you, your mother told me that you live in London now, hence you will not be able to do us the honor either. How sad all this is!"

Afterword

After being demobbed from the Wehrmacht in 1945, at the age of eighteen, Rolf eventually found employment as a wool buyer for the recovering German economy. His employers sent him to London to learn to speak English, which he spoke with the fluency of a native speaker. This work saw him traveling regularly to Australia, which was then, as now, the leading producer of fine merino wool. On one of these trips, he met a Sydney woman, from a well-to-do family. They married, and returned to Germany, and lived in Bremen. Two children, a boy and a girl, resulted. Sadly, this marriage did not last. Still in Bremen, Rolf met Margaret, for whom this book was written. An Englishwoman living in Germany, and originally from Manchester, Margaret had lived through the same turbulent years as he had, albeit from the other side. Together they settled in England, breeding English Springer Spaniels. They lived in various parts of the UK, including Bath, Lime Regis in Dorset, Oxfordshire, and finally Lincolnshire.

Rolf's greatest regret was that the war denied him the education that he would have undoubtedly excelled at. Given that he was eighteen years old at the war's conclusion, he was too old to benefit from the long restructuring of German social infrastructure, and a university education was not available.

Rolf was comfortable living in the land of his former foes—soldiers follow orders and are rarely political zealots. Rolf certainly was not. Inculcated, then conscripted at the time of a man'slife when they are at their most indestructible—given terrible weapons, and a license to do whatever harm they might—this is the burden the boy soldier bears in manhood. This burden was not without effect on Rolf.

This book was his attempt to explain to Margaret where he came from, what he had been formed from—and then tormented by. An attempt to help explain the pain within. Rolf Fischer died in late March 2020, a couple of weeks before his ninety-third birthday. He was doted on by Margaret and her daughter and husband, deeply cared for by his own daughter and family in Germany, and his family in Australia.

This manuscript was left to Rolf's grandson, born and raised in Australia, his only descendant to bear the Fischer name. Despite the distance, Rolf was in constant contact, and it is due to his love and loyalty shown toward his grandson that this manuscript has been published.